CHOPSTIX

CHOPSTIX

Quick Cooking with Pacific Flavors

By
HUGH CARPENTER
and
TERI SANDISON

STEWART, TABORI & CHANG
NEW YORK

FRONTISPIECE: *Ingredients for Chili Shrimp with Basil
(recipe on page 25)*

Text copyright © 1990 Hugh Carpenter
Photographs copyright © 1990 Teri Sandison

Published in 1990 by
Stewart, Tabori & Chang, Inc.
740 Broadway, New York, New York 10003

Carpenter, Hugh.
    Chopstix: quick cooking with Pacific flavors / by Hugh Carpenter
and Teri Sandison.
      p.   cm.
    ISBN 1-55670-133-0: $29.95
    1. Cookery, Oriental.   2. Quick and easy cookery.   3. Chopstix Dim
Sum Café.   I. Sandison, Teri.   II. Title.
TX724.5.A1C35   1990   89-28334
641.595—dc20   CIP

Distributed in the U.S. by Workman Publishing,
708 Broadway, New York, New York 10003
Distributed in Canada by Canadian Manda Group,
P.O. Box 920 Station U, Toronto, Ontario M8Z 5P9
Distributed in all other territories by Little,
Brown and Company International Division, 34 Beacon Street,
Boston, Massachusetts 02108

Printed in Japan
10 9 8 7 6 5 4 3 2 1

This book is lovingly dedicated to our parents
Warwick and Peggy Carpenter and Robert and Barbara Sandison
who encouraged us to live life to the fullest.

CONTENTS

Chapter 5

. . . .

MU SHU FANTASIES AND
STIR-FRY TRIUMPHS 108

Chapter 6

. . . .

MAGICAL SIDE DISHES
FOR ANY ENTREE 128

Chapter 7

. . . .

SINFUL SWEETS 152

PREFACE

The aroma of Thai-High Barbecued Chicken sizzling on the grill drifts across the patio. Friends slather honey butter on California Cornbread speckled with currants, tangerine peel, and tender corn kernels. With informality and a sense of fun, each person picks up whole baby romaine lettuce leaves for a Crazy Caesar Salad speckled with lime zest, diced red pepper, and crushed roasted peanuts. From a nearby room comes the laughter of children as they sit around the VCR watching the latest movie and crunching Thai Chicken Tacos. Desserts of fresh strawberries tossed with luscious coconut cream (Strawberries Siam) and Orange Ginger Brownies quickly revive appetites. Corks pop off the Champagne bottles, and conversation turns to great food and the glorious memories associated with it. Already the next dinner is being planned.

Home entertaining is undergoing a revolution—a revolution based on easy recipes, simple menus, and casual dining. One night, a "signature dish" made at home serves as the entrée, augmented by side dishes purchased at gourmet stores, delicatessens, and pastry shops. Another night, friends contribute complementary dishes for an easy dinner gathering. Unexpected guests feast on broiled fish flavored simply with mint, chilies, and lime. Old college friends reminisce as they barbecue an Asian-flavored butterflied leg of lamb, while a neighborhood student acts as an assistant, washing dishes as they collect. Meals served at poolside or along the kitchen counter while friends observe the action, or those set out on a makeshift table in front of a blazing living-room fire, set the tone for casual home entertaining. Simple menus and innovative tastes accent the sharing of special times with family and friends.

Asian flavors will play an increasingly important role in home entertaining. Whether called "East-West," "Pan-Asian," or "Pacific Style" food, this type of cooking ranges from ideas as simple as swirling sweet butter into a classic Chinese black-bean sauce for a more velvet texture to drizzling an Asian sauce across the top of barbecued salmon to brushing butter infused with ginger, garlic, and cilantro on sourdough baguettes for a New Wave Garlic Bread.

Several trends have led to this merging of cuisines. During the late 1960s the environmental movement and the rising popularity of health foods caused many Americans to reevaluate their diet and move away from meals based heavily on fats, sugar, and starches. Within a few years, starting in the 1970s, the growing interest in a healthier diet resulted in a new type of French cooking, *nouvelle cuisine*, which included experimentation with Asian seasonings. At about the same time, Richard Nixon's 1972 trip to China caused an enormous surge in the popularity of Chinese food in America. Mandarin, Sichuan, and

Hunan restaurants began to open in large cities. Chinese and other Asian seasonings became commonplace in supermarkets.

While many of us were traveling through Asia, fascinated with these new flavors, a huge Asian emigration to America began. For example, in Los Angeles County, the Asian population grew from 250,000 in 1970 to 450,000 in 1980; presently it numbers 1 million. By the beginning of the next century, over 2 million Asians will live in Los Angeles County. Similar immigration from China, Vietnam, Thailand, Laos, Cambodia, Korea, the Philippines, and the South Pacific is changing the makeup of communities across the United States, with a projected U.S. population by the year 2000 of over 8 million Asian-Americans.

Thai, Vietnamese, Korean, Japanese, and Filipino restaurants now proliferate. The new dishes offered in these restaurants, the "exotic" condiments and fresh herbs available at local Asian markets, and a flood of Asian cookbooks reinforce this ongoing trend. Examples of Asian and Pacific-style food appear on the menus of many of America's top young chefs; newspaper food sections feature articles on Thai and Vietnamese cooking; supermarkets devote increasing space to Asian ingredients. The fresh tastes of the Pacific are becoming a common part of home cooking.

Our everyday foods will increasingly be modified by the blending of seasoning and cooking techniques from the diverse cuisines of the people who border the Pacific Basin. The menu at Chopstix restaurants reflects this growing trend. Customers eat charbroiled chicken rubbed with Thai seasonings, order steamed dumplings filled with fresh king salmon and Chinese black mushrooms, nibble on Tex-Mex won tons with Asian guacamole—and conclude their meals with three-peanut ice cream. The food is inexpensive and healthful and produces bursts of flavor with each bite. The open kitchen, the crowds waiting for seats on the patio, and the high-tech decor contribute a sense of fun and casual dining.

Chopstix: Quick Cooking with Pacific Flavors transfers the mood of the restaurants to your home. New menu ideas, easy recipes, vignettes of our eating adventures in Asia and Mexico, and a blaze of food images via the photographs bring the flavors of the Pacific to life. We hope these recipes and photographs, prepared with love and presented with enthusiasm, delight the senses and convey the same joy we feel when sharing this food with friends.

Hugh Carpenter and Teri Sandison
Los Angeles, 1990

INTRODUCTION

The easy-to-prepare dishes in this book have provided us with many hours of pleasurable eating, whether served simply for just the two of us, or more elaborately, when we have entertained family and friends. The fresh flavors, ease of preparation, and exciting combination of Asian and American ingredients may, as it has for us, forever change the way you think about cooking and eating. Begin this love affair by serving only *one* Chopstix dish as part of a meal. For example, try Hot and Sour Sichuan Tomato Soup with crusty sourdough bread, or Thai-High Barbecued Chicken accompanied by baked potatoes, or a beef stew served with Chopstix Noodle Magic.

As passions build and the urge for more intense Chopstix food rises to the surface, move on to a Chopstix dinner. Keep the menu simple by choosing just a few dishes and balancing them between do-ahead recipes and one or two requiring a little last-minute attention. By completing the salad dressing, marinades, sauces, and dessert a day ahead, you can offer a Chopstix dinner that avoids turning you into a kitchen slave or transforming the meal into a *kung fu* culinary sprint between stove and table.

ABOUT THE RECIPES A suggested menu is offered with nearly every recipe. Skim through the book to review the menus and you'll find many new party ideas for serving Chopstix food. In addition, keep in mind the following:

- Before beginning to prepare a dish, read the entire recipe for important menu advice and information about successfully completing the recipe.

- Review the ingredients list for special supplies. Essential Asian supplies are listed on pages 172–183. Purchase the best brands listed.

- When the word *minced* appears, chop the item so finely it resembles a purée. To speed the process, use a small electric minichopper. This is the most timesaving piece of equipment introduced since the food processor. Of the many brands, three excellent ones are Mouli's Electric Mincer, Seb's Minichop, and Cuisinart's Mini-Mate Chopper/ Grinder.

- When green onions are listed as an ingredient, use whole green onions—in other words, both green and white parts.

- When grated or minced citrus peel is called for, use just the outside colored skin, or zest. Grating the peel is an awful chore. Fortunately, the zest can be removed quickly with a little tool called a zester, available at all cookware shops. Once the peel has been zested, it takes little time to complete the mincing.

"Bungalow Teapot" by ceramic artist David Gurney.

- Every recipe states what can be prepared ahead of time and what needs to be done at the last moment, through headings such as Advance Preparation and Last-Minute Cooking. Use these as a guide for selecting recipes and planning your cooking.

- Some recipes have sauces thickened with a mixture of cornstarch and water. Add only a *small* amount of the mixture and bring the sauce to a low boil. Stir in a little more if the sauce does not lightly glaze your spoon. You will never need to add all the cornstarch mixture.

- At the end of cooking, the words *taste and adjust seasonings* mean that this is the time to make any adjustments in flavor rather than having your guests do it at the dining-room table.

- In terms of recipe serving quantities, we assume entrées will be accompanied with rice or noodles and a salad. Unless otherwise stated, all dishes can be doubled or tripled—except the stir-fry dishes. When doubling a stir-fry, have a friend simultaneously stir-fry the second portion in another wok, following your every move.

Not all the recipes give a specific recommendation as to what to drink. At the restaurants, we serve hot and iced teas, fruit smoothies, Chinese beer, hot sake, Champagne, Sauvignon Blanc, dry Gewürztraminer, dry Riesling, Beaujolais, and Cabernet Sauvignon wines. Because the Asian flavors in most of these recipes can obscure the subtlety of a fine wine, at home we offer guests Tsing Tao beer, a moderately priced dry white wine or red wine, or nonalcoholic choices of iced tea and mineral water. We often serve Champagne with appetizers, and always offer a fine tea and coffee with dessert.

ABOUT THE PHOTOGRAPHS I am happy to be part of a new generation of photographers that has been attracted to a career in food photography because of the possibility of artistic expression. Even ten years ago, the typical food shot was a technically correct representation of a kitchen or table scene, created as an assignment for a client. Today, food photographers can develop their own styles through projects in which they have more control and input.

My passion is to capture on film the meeting of food and art, and to do this with the same sense of creativity and fun, freedom, and excitement that fuels the art movement in Los Angeles. The photographs in this book are portraits of recipes that Hugh and I love. I listened to Hugh conceptualize the recipes, tasted in the test kitchen, listened to the reaction of customers to these new flavor combinations, and read the drafts for the book. From this personal, very intimate involvement, I created portraits to capture the essence of his food.

Many of the recipes include an introduction explaining what I am trying to achieve in the photo. For me, all the photos involve the same psychological process as for painting. I enter the studio in the morning and spend all day building a set from a blank white table, composing with color, light, and texture, and recording the "food art" on film rather than on canvas. The photos actually start weeks earlier as sketches in my notebook, beginning with the design of the food and then working outward until every inch of the page has been composed.

Next, I go to art galleries, artists' studios, tile shops, and marble showrooms looking for the right props to accent an aspect of the food, such as its texture, color, or key ingredient. Many of the tabletop artists, whose ceramic, glassware, flatware, and hand-painted tablecloths appear in this book, have a painting background. Their freehand drawings—and their use of bright, tropical colors—reflect sunny Southern California. They fit perfectly with the color combinations, textural contrasts, and flavor surprises of Hugh's Pacific-style food.

Often, to tie the food and contemporary tabletop art together, I paint backgrounds using watercolors, pastels, or oils. Next, a food stylist comes to my studio to prepare the recipes for the camera. Using the freshest ingredients available in Southern California markets and gardens, we endeavor to capture on film the tastes of each of Hugh's recipes. No matter how much advance planning has been done, however, there is always a magical moment when the photo begins to take on a life of its own under the lights and camera. The scene then demands the refinements in lighting, composition, or food styling that make the difference in an exciting photo. The tension builds as we try to have all the elements perfected at the same time while the food is fresh under the camera.

This creative tension and the anticipation of the result are the most compelling aspects of any artistic endeavor and the reasons I return to the studio every day.

Platter of Shiitake Yaki, Skewered Scallops with Red Pepper,
Yakitori, and Barbecued Salmon Ribbons

Chapter 1

WIN SUM AND DIM SUM

EVERY MEAL AT THE CHOPSTIX RESTAURANTS IS AN APPETIZER EVENT. CHEFS IN THE OPEN KITCHEN CUT BARBECUED THAI SHRIMP PIZZA INTO WEDGES, PLACE MOUNDS OF CHOPSTIX SHREDDED CHICKEN SALAD ONTO PLATES, AND CHOP GLAZED MAHOGANY-COLORED THAI-HIGH BARBECUED CHICKEN. ALONG THE COUNTER, CUSTOMERS EXCHANGE TIPS ON THE "HOTTEST" DISHES, SHARE APRICOT GUAVA DIP, AND ORDER MORE NEW AGE GUACAMOLE FOR THE TEX-MEX WON TONS.

BRING SOME CHOPSTIX FUN HOME WITH THESE APPETIZERS IDEAL FOR SMALL GATHERINGS OF FRIENDS. OR SERVE THEM AS QUICK, SPECTACULAR NIBBLES BEFORE GOING OUT TO DINNER OR THE BASIS FOR AN APPETIZER PARTY. OTHER RECIPES THAT MAKE GREAT APPETIZERS INCLUDE THE SALADS IN CHAPTER 2, THE CHILLED ASIAN AVOCADO SOUP IN CHAPTER 3, THE THAI-HIGH BARBECUED CHICKEN CHOPPED INTO PIECES OR SMOKED BABY BACK RIBS FROM CHAPTER 4, AND THE DANNY KAYE SHRIMP, THAI CHICKEN STIR-FRY WITH LETTUCE CUPS, AND MINIATURE MU SHU BEEF BONANZAS FROM CHAPTER 5.

BARBECUED SALMON RIBBONS

12 bamboo skewers, 4 inches long
¾ pound skinless salmon filet
2 tablespoons Oriental sesame oil
2 tablespoons dry sherry
1 tablespoon light soy sauce
1 tablespoon olive oil
½ teaspoon freshly ground black pepper
¼ cup chopped cilantro (fresh coriander)
2 tablespoons finely minced fresh ginger
Chopstix dipping sauces (pages 40–43) of your choice

AT THE SEAFOOD MARKET RESTAURANT IN BANGKOK, TOURISTS CHOOSE FROM 250 TYPES OF FRESH AND SALTWATER FOODS DISPLAYED AT ICED COUNTERS AND THEN, THROUGH WILD GESTURES AND PERHAPS A FEW IMPERFECTLY SPOKEN WORDS OF THAI, COMMUNICATE TO THE CHEFS THEIR CHOICE OF COOKING TECHNIQUE AND SUBTLETY OF SEASONING. CUSTOMERS SIT AT LONG TABLES AND EAT WHAT ONLY MOMENTS AGO TOUCHED THE SEARING SIDES OF THE WOK. THEY SEASON THE FOOD WITH MYSTERIOUS THAI CONDIMENTS. ICED SINGHA BEER AND CRISP GARLIC BREAD MOUNDED ON PLASTIC TRAYS LESSEN BUT NEVER ENTIRELY ELIMINATE THE ERUPTION OF FLAVOR FROM THAI CHILIES. THIS IS A TOURIST TRAP THAT IS TREMENDOUS FUN—AT LEAST FOR ONE EVENING.

ADVANCE PREPARATION Soak the bamboo skewers in water for 6 hours.

Cut the salmon into 12 rectangular pieces, each about 3 inches long, 1 inch wide, ¼ inch thick. Place 1 piece of salmon on a cutting board. Put the fingers of one hand on the salmon to stabilize it; with the other hand, push the skewer down the length of the salmon piece. The skewer should be visible only at either end. Repeat with remaining pieces.

Combine the sesame oil, sherry, soy sauce, olive oil, pepper, cilantro, and ginger. Rub the sauce over the salmon and marinate for 1 to 4 hours. Prepare optional dipping sauces.

LAST-MINUTE COOKING If broiling, place the broiling rack at the highest setting, then preheat the broiler to 550°F. Line a baking sheet with foil, set a wire rack on top, and coat the rack with nonstick spray. Lay the salmon pieces on the rack and cover the exposed ends of the skewers with pieces of foil.

Turn the oven setting to broil, and broil until the salmon loses its raw outside color, about 2 minutes. The skewers do not need to be turned while broiling. (If using an electric oven, leave the oven door slightly ajar during cooking.)

If using a gas barbecue, preheat to medium (350°F.). If using charcoal or wood, prepare a fire. When the coals or wood are ash covered, brush the barbecue rack with cooking oil, then grill the salmon about 1 minute on each side. Brush with the reserved marinade during cooking.

Serve at once, accompanied with one or more dipping sauces. Each person spoons a little of the sauce down the length of the salmon, and then nibbles the fish from around the skewer.

Serves: 4 to 8 as an appetizer.

YAKITORI

12 bamboo skewers, 4 inches
long
4 chicken thighs
¾ cup Chopstix Barbecue
Sauce (page 105)
Singapore Satay Sauce (page
41) or other dipping
sauces (pages 40–43)

SMALL FISHING VILLAGES AS WELL AS THE LARGE CITIES OF JAPAN OFFER A WEALTH OF EXCITING FOOD EXPERIENCES FOR THE TRAVELER. CASUAL RESTAURANTS AND FOOD BARS CAN BE DISCERNED BY THE RED LANTERNS AT THE DOORS OR BY PLASTIC REPLICAS OF THEIR STANDARD MENU ITEMS DISPLAYED IN FRONT OF THE RESTAURANTS. WE FIND IT SO MUCH FUN TO EAT *RUBATA-YAKI* STYLE. SEATED AT LONG COUNTERS AND WITH RUDIMENTARY LANGUAGE SKILLS, WE POINT AT OUR NEXT COURSE TO BE GRILLED BY A SMILING CHEF. *YAKITORI*, LITERALLY "GRILLED CHICKEN," IS A STANDARD, SUCCULENT CHOICE AT THESE SMALL RESTAURANTS. OTHER TYPES OF MEAT THAT ARE GOOD TO BARBECUE ON SKEWERS ARE BEEF TENDERLOIN, TOP SIRLOIN, AND MEAT FROM A LEG OF LAMB.

ADVANCE PREPARATION Soak the bamboo skewers in water for at least 6 hours.

Bone the thighs if the butcher has not already done so, then pull away and discard the skin. (To bone the thighs, cut around the bone at one end of each thigh. Pinch the end of the bone with your thumb and index finger, and pull your fingers down the bone, stripping off the meat.) Cut each thigh into 4 strips. Place 1 piece of chicken on a cutting board. Put the fingers of one hand on the chicken strip to stabilize it; with the other hand, push the skewer down the length of the strip. The skewer should be visible only at either end of the chicken strip. Repeat with remaining strips.

Rub the Barbecue Sauce on the chicken strips. Marinate for 30 minutes or longer.

Have the dipping sauces ready to serve with the chicken.

LAST-MINUTE COOKING If broiling, place the broiling rack at the highest setting, then preheat broiler to 550°F. Line a baking sheet with foil, set a wire rack on top, and coat the rack with nonstick spray. Lay the chicken strips on the rack and cover the exposed ends of the skewers with pieces of foil.

Turn the oven setting to broil and broil until the chicken is firm, about 4 minutes. The skewers do not need to be turned while broiling.

If using a gas barbecue, preheat to medium (350°F.) If using charcoal or wood, prepare a fire. When the coals or wood are ash covered, brush the barbecue rack with cooking oil. Then place the chicken strips over medium heat and grill for about 2 minutes on each side, basting with the marinade.

Serve the chicken strips at once, accompanied with one or more dipping sauces. Each person spoons a little of the sauce down the length of the meat and then nibbles the meat from around the skewer.

Serves: 4 to 8 as an appetizer.

SKEWERED SCALLOPS
WITH RED PEPPER

12 bamboo skewers, 4 inches
    long
1 sweet red pepper
¼ pound bay scallops
2 tablespoons plum sauce
2 tablespoons dry sherry
2 tablespoons minced green
    onions
½ teaspoon Chinese chili
    sauce
Chopstix dipping sauces
    (pages 40–43)

At Chopstix restaurants, ribbons of meat and seafood, threaded on bamboo skewers and glistening with a Chinese or Thai seasoning blend, sizzle on the open grill. Flames leap around the food and quick fingers twist the skewers as customers watch the action. While the following recipe uses bay scallops, medium-size sea scallops are great cooked this way as long as the tough little muscle attached to one edge of each scallop is removed.

ADVANCE PREPARATION Soak the bamboo skewers in water for at least 6 hours.

Stem, seed, and remove ribs from the red pepper. Cut the pepper into ½-inch strips, then cut the strips into triangles the same size as the scallops. Combine the plum sauce, sherry, green onions, and chili sauce. Thread the scallops and pepper pieces alternately onto each skewer, then brush with the marinade. Marinate for 30 minutes.

LAST-MINUTE COOKING If broiling, place the broiling rack at the highest setting, then preheat the broiler to 550°F. Line a baking sheet with foil, set a wire rack on top, and coat the rack with nonstick spray. Lay the skewers on the rack and cover the exposed ends with pieces of foil.

Turn the setting to broil, and broil until the scallops just become firm to the touch, about 1 minute. The skewers do not need to be turned while broiling. (If using an electric oven, leave the oven door slightly ajar during cooking.)

If using a gas barbecue, preheat to medium (350°F). If using charcoal or wood, prepare a fire. When coals or wood are ash covered, brush the barbecue rack with cooking oil. Then place the skewers over medium heat and grill for about 1 minute on each side. Brush with the marinade during cooking.

Serve at once, accompanied with one or more dipping sauces.

Serves: 4 to 8 as an appetizer.

Menu Ideas: Informal dinner for 4—Skewered Scallops with Red Pepper, served with Coconut Curry Explosion and a spinach salad tossed with an oil and vinegar dressing.

SHIITAKE YAKI

12 bamboo skewers, 4 inches
   long
½ cup unsalted butter
5 cloves garlic, finely minced
1 tablespoon finely minced
   fresh ginger
1 bunch chives, minced
Juice of 1 lemon
¼ teaspoon freshly ground
   black pepper
24 medium shiitake
   mushrooms

IN KURASHIKI, THE WONDERFUL FOLK-ART CAPITAL OF JAPAN, IS A SMALL RESTAURANT OFF THE HISTORIC SHOGUN GRAINERY DISTRICT, NEAR THE WILLOW-LINED RIVER. IT IS HERE THAT TERI FIRST TASTED THESE GRILLED SHIITAKE MUSHROOMS WITH JUST A SQUEEZE OF LIME. IT WAS A TASTE NOT TO BE FORGOTTEN.

ADVANCE PREPARATION Soak the bamboo skewers in water for at least 6 hours.

In a small saucepan, place the butter, garlic, and ginger. Heat until the butter melts and the garlic sizzles (but does not turn brown), about 2 minutes. Remove from the heat and add the chives, lemon juice, and pepper; then transfer to a small container and set aside.

Cut off and discard the mushroom stems or use when making soup stock. Place 2 mushrooms on each skewer, running the skewer through the flat surface of each mushroom.

LAST-MINUTE COOKING If broiling, place the broiling rack at the highest setting, then preheat the broiler to 550°F. Line a baking sheet with foil, set a wire rack on top, and coat the rack with nonstick spray. Brush the mushrooms lightly with the seasoned butter. Place on the rack and cover the exposed ends of the skewers with foil.

Turn the oven setting to broil, and broil the mushrooms until heated through, 2 to 4 minutes. The skewers do not need to be turned while broiling. (If using an electric oven, leave the oven door slightly ajar during cooking).

If using a gas barbecue, preheat to medium (350°F). If using charcoal or wood, prepare a fire. When the coals or wood are ash covered, brush the mushrooms with melted butter. Place the mushrooms over medium heat and grill, turning until heated through, about 2 minutes.

Serves: 4 to 8 as an appetizer.

Menu Ideas: Barbecuing Shiitake Yaki alongside hamburgers and then placing both inside perfectly toasted buns with crisp lettuce and thousand island dressing, creates a hamburger taste sensation!

FLAME-ROASTED GREEN BEANS

12 bamboo skewers, 4 inches
    long
14 green beans
2 tablespoons finely minced
    garlic
1 tablespoon crushed Sichuan
    peppercorns
4 strips thinly sliced bacon
Chinese Pepper Blend (page
    43)

NANBAN-KAN RESTAURANT IN SANTA MONICA IS WELL KNOWN IN THE JAPANESE COMMUNITY FOR SERVING THE BEST *ROBATA-YAKI* FOOD. EVERY NIGHT JAPANESE BUSINESS MEN AND TOURISTS WATCH THE CHEFS JUST A FEW FEET AWAY BARBECUE GIANT CLAMS, CHICKEN LIVERS WRAPPED WITH *SHISO* LEAVES, BUTTERFLIED SHRIMP BRUSHED WITH TERIYAKI SAUCE, AND FLAME-ROASTED GREEN BEANS. FLAVORED FROM THE WOOD FIRE, THE CRISP BACON, AND SEASONINGS, THE GREEN BEANS ARE A PERFECT APPETITE TEASER.

A GOOD VARIATION ON THIS RECIPE IS TO SUBSTITUTE FRESH WATER CHESTNUTS FOR THE GREEN BEANS. TRIM OFF THE BLACK SKIN, ROLL THE WATER CHESTNUTS IN SEASONINGS, AND WRAP IN BACON; THEN BROIL OR BARBECUE UNTIL THE BACON IS CRISP. OR TRANSFORM THIS RECIPE INTO A NEW CREATION BY REPLACING THE GREEN BEANS WITH CHICKEN LIVERS. TRIM OFF ALL THE FAT FROM ½ POUND OF CHICKEN LIVERS. CUT LARGE CHICKEN LIVERS IN HALF, THEN SEASON WITH THE GARLIC AND SICHUAN PEPPERCORNS. WRAP WITH THE BACON AND COOK UNTIL THE BACON IS CRISP AND THE LIVERS ARE FIRM, ABOUT 5 MINUTES. SERVE THE CHICKEN LIVERS WITH ONE OR MORE OF THE CHOPSTIX DIPPING SAUCES.

ADVANCE PREPARATION Soak the bamboo skewers in water for at least 6 hours.

Trim the stems from the beans, then cut each bean into 3 pieces; season the beans with the garlic and pepper. Cut the bacon into 1½-inch lengths, then wrap each piece around a bean, using only enough so that the bacon just overlaps. Secure the bacon by pushing a skewer crosswise through the bean at its center. Place 4 wrapped beans on each skewer, then refrigerate.

LAST-MINUTE COOKING If broiling, place the broiling rack at the highest setting, then preheat the broiler to 550°F. Line a baking sheet with foil, set a wire rack on top, and coat the rack with nonstick spray. Lay the skewers on the rack and cover the exposed ends with pieces of foil.

Turn the setting to broil, and broil until the beans turn bright green and the bacon is crisp, about 2 minutes on each side. (If using an electric oven, leave the oven door slightly ajar during cooking.)

If using a gas barbecue, preheat to medium (350°F). If using charcoal or wood, prepare a fire. When coals or wood are ash covered, brush the barbecue rack with cooking oil. Place the skewers over medium heat and grill for about 2 minutes on each side.

Serve at once, accompanied with Chinese Pepper Blend.

Serves: 4 to 8 as an appetizer.

GRILLED EGGPLANT COINS

12 bamboo skewers, 4 inches
    long
5 small Oriental eggplants
3 cloves garlic, finely minced
1 tablespoon grated or finely
    minced lemon peel
⅓ cup lemon juice
¼ cup dry sherry
3 tablespoons safflower oil
2 tablespoons light soy sauce
2 tablespoons Dijon-style
    mustard
½ teaspoon freshly ground
    black pepper
Salt to taste
Chopstix dipping sauces
    (pages 40–43)

THE "GREAT EGGPLANT WAR" RAGES ON AS MORE AND MORE SUPERMARKETS DISPLAY BOTH THE SLENDER PURPLE OR WHITE ORIENTAL EGGPLANTS AND THE TRADITIONAL GLOBE VARIETY. IN THIS BATTLE FOR THE TASTE BUDS OF AMERICA, ORIENTAL EGGPLANTS WILL TRIUMPH. THEIR ADVANTAGES ARE MANY, INCLUDING NEVER NEEDING TO BE PEELED, HAVING NO BITTER TASTE AND VERY FEW SEEDS, AND ABSORBING VERY LITTLE OIL WHEN SAUTÉED. FROM NOW ON, STRIKE A BLOW IN FAVOR OF BETTER TASTE: BYPASS THE GLOBE EGGPLANT AND USE ORIENTAL EGGPLANT FOR ALL RECIPES—CHINESE, EUROPEAN, AND AMERICAN.

ADVANCE PREPARATION Soak the bamboo skewers in water for at least 6 hours.

Cut the eggplants on a slight diagonal into ⅓-inch-thick oval pieces, or cut the eggplant lengthwise into long ⅓-inch-thick slices. Thread enough eggplant onto each skewer so that the skewer is only visible at either end. Combine the remaining ingredients except the dipping sauces and marinate the eggplant in the mixture for 1 hour.

LAST-MINUTE COOKING If broiling, place the broiling rack at the highest setting, then preheat broiler to 550°F. Line a baking sheet with foil, set a wire rack on top, and coat the rack with nonstick spray. Lay the skewers on the rack and cover the exposed ends with foil.

Turn the oven to broil, and broil the eggplant until golden, about 4 minutes, brushing with marinade midway through the cooking. Skewers do not need to be turned while broiling. (If using an electric oven, leave the oven door slightly ajar during cooking).

If using a gas barbecue, preheat to medium (350°F.). If using charcoal or wood, prepare a fire. When the coals or wood are ash covered, brush the barbecue rack with cooking oil. Then place the eggplant over medium heat and grill, brushing with marinade, until the eggplant is golden, 4 to 6 minutes on each side. Serve at once. Accompany with one or more dipping sauces. Each person spoons a little sauce across the eggplant slices for added flavor.

Serves: 4 to 8 as an appetizer.

Menu Ideas: Dinner cooked on the barbecue—Thai-High Barbecued Chicken, Grilled Eggplant Coins, New Wave Garlic Bread, Orange Ginger Brownies served with Raspberry Cabernet Sauvignon Sauce.

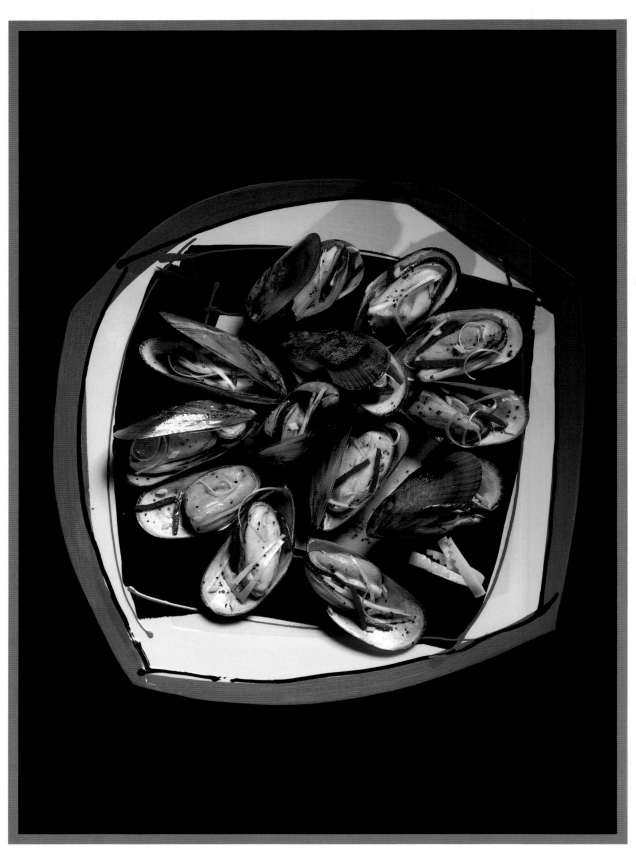

Spicy Marinated Mussels

SPICY MARINATED MUSSELS

TO STEAM MUSSELS
18 small mussels
salt

MARINADE
**¼ cup slivered sweet red
    pepper**
**2 tablespoons chopped
    cilantro (fresh coriander)**
**2 tablespoons minced green
    onions**
1 clove garlic, finely minced
**1 tablespoon finely minced
    fresh ginger**
**3 tablespoons white wine
    vinegar**
**2 tablespoons Oriental
    sesame oil**
1 tablespoon safflower oil
**½ teaspoon Chinese chili
    sauce**
¼ teaspoon salt

TO FINISH
3 tablespoons olive oil

WE DISCOVERED THE WORK OF LOS ANGELES CERAMIC ARTIST HELAINE MELVIN AT THE MUSEUM OF CONTEMPORARY ART, WHILE WORKING ON OUR *PACIFIC FLAVORS* BOOK. HELAINE'S TECHNIQUES ENABLE HER TO ACHIEVE THE RICH, SATURATED COLORS IN THE GLAZES. SHE USES A LOW-FIRE UNDER GLAZE WITH A CLEAR, HIGH-GLOSS GLAZE ON TOP AND THICKLY APPLIED BRUSH STROKES TO MAKE HER CALLIGRAPHIC MARKS.

FOR FOOD PHOTOGRAPHY, I LOOK FOR DISHES OR ACCESSORIES THAT WILL ACCENT A PARTICULAR ASPECT OF A RECIPE, SUCH AS ITS TEXTURE OR THE COLORFUL VARIETY OF ITS INGREDIENTS. TABLETOP WARE SUCH AS HELAINE MELVIN'S, WHICH HAS BOLD AND SIMPLE DECORATION AT THE OUTER EDGE OF THE PIECE, IS ESPECIALLY SUITABLE.

ADVANCE PREPARATION AND COOKING Scrub the mussels vigorously, and pull away the beards and any seaweed from between the shells. In a 4-quart pot, bring 1 inch of water to a vigorous boil. Lightly salt the water, then add the mussels and cover the pot. Cook until the mussels open, about 3 minutes. Transfer the mussels to a colander, let cool, then refrigerate for 1 hour. Discard any mussels that do not open.

Combine the ingredients for the marinade and mix well. Carefully remove the mussel meat and toss with the marinade.

Open the mussel shells wide but do not detach the halves. Place the shells in a bowl, add the olive oil, and toss until evenly coated. Transfer the shells to a plate and place a marinated mussel in each shell. Chill thoroughly, up to 8 hours in advance of serving.

To serve, place the mussels on a decorative plate.

Serves: 4 to 8 as an appetizer or 4 as a first course.

Menu Ideas: Dinner for 4—Spicy Marinated Mussels, Smoked Baby Back Ribs with Chopstix Barbecue Sauce, California Cornbread, a tossed green salad, and homemade ice cream.

GINGER GRAVLOX

SALMON
½ pound skinless salmon filet, very fresh
¼ cup minced fresh ginger
¼ cup chopped fresh dill
2 tablespoons vodka
2 tablespoons light soy sauce
1 tablespoon sugar
1 tablespoon salt
1 tablespoon crushed Sichuan peppercorns
1 teaspoon freshly ground white pepper

TO SERVE
Champagne Mustard Sauce (page 42) or another sauce from pages 40–43
Dill or cilantro (fresh coriander) sprigs
¼ cup red sweet ginger
Thin slices of pumpernickel bread

SALMON MARINATED IN GINGER, DILL, SICHUAN PEPPERCORNS, AND VODKA RESULTS IN A BLOSSOMING OF FLAVORS. THESE LITTLE PYRAMIDS OF ALTERNATING COLORS AND TASTES CAN BE ASSEMBLED IN ADVANCE, STARTING WITH THE WHIMSICALLY SHAPED, THINLY SLICED PUMPERNICKEL BREAD, SLICES OF GRAVLOX, A DRIZZLE OF CHAMPAGNE MUSTARD SAUCE, AND SPRIGS OF CILANTRO OR DILL AS CROWNS. FOR A FUN ALTERNATIVE, LET GUESTS ASSEMBLE THEIR OWN GRAVLOX APPETIZERS, CHOOSING FROM VARIOUS CRACKERS AND THINLY SLICED BREADS, THEN TOPPING THE PAPER-THIN SALMON SLICES WITH ONE OF SEVERAL CHOPSTIX DIPPING SAUCES AND FRESH HERB SPRIGS. LEFTOVER GRAVLOX MAKES AN EXCELLENT LUNCH OR DINNER ENTRÉE, JUST DOTTED WITH BUTTER AND PLACED IN A VERY HOT BROILER FOR A FEW SECONDS.

ADVANCE PREPARATION (3 DAYS BEFORE SERVING) Check salmon for bones and remove any strays. Combine the ginger, dill, vodka, soy sauce, sugar, salt, peppercorns, and white pepper. Place salmon and marinade in small plastic food bag. Seal and put on a tray, then place a 5-pound weight on the salmon. Refrigerate for 3 days, turning salmon twice a day.

LAST-MINUTE PREPARATION The day of serving, have the Champagne Mustard Sauce or another sauce ready. Set aside the herb sprigs. Very finely sliver the red sweet ginger. Cut the bread into 24 appetizer-size pieces.
　　Scrape most of the marinade off the salmon. Very thinly slice the salmon, keeping the blade wet so the fish does not tear. Refrigerate the pieces until ready to serve. You should have about 24 pieces.
　　Place a slice of salmon on each piece of bread, then add a little drizzle of sauce, a dill or cilantro sprig, and a sliver of red ginger. Serve at once.

Serves: 6 to 10 as an appetizer.

CHILI SHRIMP WITH BASIL

SHRIMP
1 pound raw medium shrimp
salt
½ sweet red pepper
8 chives
2 tablespoons unsalted roasted
    peanuts

SAUCE
2 tablespoons fish sauce
2 tablespoons lime juice
2 tablespoons water
2 teaspoons sugar
1 teaspoon Chinese chili sauce
2 cloves garlic, finely minced
2 tablespoons chopped
    fresh basil

ONE OF THE MANY JOYS OF LIVING IN A COASTAL TOWN SUCH AS SANTA BARBARA IS HAVING SPECIAL RELATIONSHIPS WITH LOCAL FISHERMAN AND SEAFOOD VENDORS. HUGH'S FAVORITE HOME-TOWN SOURCE FOR THE FAMOUS SANTA BARBARA SPOT PRAWNS, SHOWN HERE WITH THE HEADS ON, IS THE SEAFOOD SPECIALITIES PROCESSING WAREHOUSE RIGHT NEAR THE WATER. KNOWN FOR THEIR INTENSE SWEETNESS, AND FOUND FROM SANTA BARBARA NORTH TO THE ALEUTIAN ISLANDS, SPOT PRAWNS ARE NOT WIDELY FISHED, GIVING THEM A MYSTIQUE AMONG THE INITIATED. THIS IS ONE OF SEVERAL RECIPES IN THE BOOK THAT WE FELT HAD SUCH BEAUTIFUL INGREDIENTS THAT A STILL-LIFE PRESENTATION WAS CALLED FOR. I CHOSE THE TILES FOR THE BACKGROUND TO ADD TO THE MEDITERRANEAN FEELING OF THE PHOTO.

ADVANCE PREPARATION Shell the shrimp, then devein by cutting along the top of the curve, starting at the tail and making a progressively deeper cut so the knife nearly cuts through the shrimp at the thick end. Rinse out the vein. Bring a large amount of lightly salted water to a rapid boil and add the shrimp. Cook until shrimp are done, between 1 and 2 minutes. To test, cut a shrimp in half; it should be white in the center. Transfer the shrimp immediately to a bowl of ice water to cool. When chilled, drain and refrigerate until ready to use.

Mince and place in separate containers the red pepper and chives. Finely chop the peanuts in a food processor and set aside. Combine the sauce ingredients and mix well.

LAST-MINUTE PREPARATION Toss the shrimp with the sauce. Put in a decorative bowl and place the bowl in crushed ice. Sprinkle the shrimp with the red pepper, chives, and peanuts. Serve at once.

Serves: 4 to 8 as an appetizer or 4 as a first course.

Variations: This is also excellent made with squid. Use 1½ pounds small squid, and clean and cut as described for Flower Blossom Squid. Then drop the squid into 4 quarts of rapidly boiling water. As soon as the squid turns white, in about 15 seconds, immediately plunge it into ice water. Chill, drain, and refrigerate. When ready to serve, proceed with the instructions.

Firecracker Dumplings and Melrose Avenue Spring Rolls (recipe on page 28)

FIRECRACKER DUMPLINGS

THIS IS ONE OF THE MOST POPULAR DIM SUM ITEMS AT CHOPSTIX. THE FILLING CAN BE MADE QUICKLY IN A FOOD PROCESSOR, AND THE DUMPLINGS FOLDED AND THEN REFRIGERATED OR FROZEN. THE COOKING PROCESS IS JUST AS EASY, FOR THE DUMPLINGS ARE COOKED IN BOILING WATER BEFORE BEING TOSSED IN A RICH CHINESE "PESTO" SAUCE. FIRECRACKER DUMPLINGS ARE EXCELLENT AS AN HORS D'OEUVRE OR ENTRÉE ACCOMPANIED BY THE SAME DISHES YOU MIGHT HAVE WHEN SERVING HOMEMADE RAVIOLI.

DUMPLINGS
1 cup chopped carrots
2 green onions
1 pound ground raw chicken
1 tablespoon light soy sauce
2 teaspoons dry sherry
1 teaspoon Oriental sesame oil
1 teaspoon Chinese chili sauce
¼ teaspoon salt
1 tablespoon white sesame seeds
30 won ton skins
4 tablespoons cooking oil

DRESSING
12 ounces spinach leaves,
   washed and dried
2 cloves garlic, minced

2 teaspoons minced fresh ginger
1 teaspoon grated or minced
   orange peel
¼ cup chopped cilantro (fresh
   coriander)
8 basil leaves
1 green onion
1 tablespoon light soy sauce
2 tablespoons dry sherry
2 tablespoons distilled white
   vinegar
2 tablespoons Oriental
   sesame oil
2 teaspoons hoisin sauce
2 teaspoons sugar
½ teaspoon Chinese chili sauce

ADVANCE PREPARATION Prepare the filling. Place the carrots and green onions in a food processor and mince coarsely. Transfer to a bowl and add the chicken, soy sauce, sherry, sesame oil, chili sauce, and salt. Thoroughly mix and set aside. Toast the sesame seeds until golden in an ungreased skillet, then set aside.

Within 5 hours of cooking, assemble the dumplings. Trim the won tons into round circles, then place 2 teaspoons of filling in the center of each won ton. Moisten the edges with water and fold the dumpling in half over the filling, being careful not to flatten the filling.

Press the edges of each won ton together; the dumplings will be a half-moon shape. Moisten each end of the dumpling, then touch the moistened ends together; the dumpling should now look like a little cap. Place the dumplings on a baking sheet coated generously with cooking oil. Refrigerate, uncovered, or freeze the dumplings.

Prepare the dressing. Place the spinach in a food processor and finely mince. Add the garlic, ginger, orange peel, cilantro, basil, and green onion. Finely mince, then add the remaining ingredients. Blend for 1 minute. Pour into a blender and purée the mixture (about 20 seconds). Transfer the dressing to a small bowl.

recipe continues on next page

- **LAST-MINUTE COOKING** Bring 5 quarts of water to a vigorous boil. Add the
- dumplings (fresh or frozen), and give them a gentle stir. When all the
- dumplings float to the surface (in about 3 minutes), gently tip the
- dumplings into a colander and drain thoroughly.

    Transfer the dumplings to a mixing bowl. Add the dressing and toss.
Transfer the dumplings to a heated serving platter, sprinkle on the
sesame seeds, and serve at once.

Serves: 6 to 8 as an appetizer, or 4 as an entrée.

Menu Ideas: A menu with a vegetarian emphasis—Firecracker Dumplings, Peking Chive Pancakes (made a week ahead and frozen), served
with Stir-Fried Garden Vegetables and South Seas Salsa, Crazy Caesar
Salad, Asian Avocado Adventure (made a day ahead), Champagne Rice
Pilaf, and fresh fruit with Orange Ginger Brownies.

MELROSE AVENUE SPRING ROLLS

½ pound *chorizo* or other
    spicy sausage
1 ounce rice sticks
6 dried Chinese black
    mushrooms
2 cups shredded green
    cabbage
2 cups bean sprouts
1 cup julienned carrots
2 green onions, minced
2 tablespoons dry sherry
1 tablespoon oyster sauce
1 tablespoon Oriental
    sesame oil
1 teaspoon Chinese chili sauce
½ teaspoon sugar
3 cloves garlic, finely minced
2 tablespoons cornstarch
3 cups plus 2 tablespoons
    cooking oil
12 to 14 spring roll skins (see
    Note)
2 eggs, well beaten
Chopstix dipping sauces
    (pages 40–43)
20 bibb lettuce leaves

THE UNUSUAL SPICY FLAVOR OF THESE MELROSE AVENUE SPRING ROLLS IS DERIVED FROM THE MEXICAN SAUSAGE CALLED *CHORIZO*, BUT A SPICY AMERICAN OR ITALIAN SAUSAGE WORKS WELL TOO. WHILE EVERYTHING, INCLUDING THE STUFFING OF THE SPRING ROLLS, CAN BE COMPLETED A DAY IN ADVANCE, IT IS THE LAST-MINUTE DOUBLE-FRYING OF THE SPRING ROLLS THAT GIVES THESE THEIR INCREDIBLY CRISP EXTERIOR.

ASIAN MARKETS SELL 6-INCH SQUARE OR ROUND SHEETS CALLED SPRING ROLL SKINS, SHANGHAI WRAPPERS, OR LUMPIA SKINS. AVOID AT ALL COST THE VASTLY INFERIOR EGG ROLL SKINS SOLD IN AMERICAN SUPERMARKETS; THESE ARE CUT AT CHINESE NOODLE FACTORIES FROM THE SAME GIANT SHEETS OF THICK EGG NOODLE DOUGH USED FOR WON TON SKINS. SINCE SPRING ROLL SKINS ARE SOLD FROZEN, AND THEIR QUALITY IS NOT AFFECTED BY FREQUENT THAWING AND REFREEZING, BUY A GENEROUS AMOUNT.

ADVANCE PREPARATION If the sausage is in links, slit the casing and squeeze the meat out. Place the sausage meat in a small frying pan or wok. Cook over low heat until thoroughly cooked and the fat is ren-
dered, about 15 minutes. Stir occasionally. Transfer to a sieve and press the meat with the back of a spoon to eliminate all fat. If the sausage meat is still in lumps, chop finely.

Soak the rice sticks in hot water for 20 minutes. Drain and cut into 2-
inch lengths. Soak the mushrooms in hot water until soft, about 20 minutes. Discard the stems and shred the caps.

Combine the sausage, mushrooms, rice sticks, cabbage, bean sprouts, carrots, and green onions. Separately combine the sherry, oyster sauce, sesame oil, chili sauce, sugar, and garlic. Combine the cornstarch with an equal amount of cold water and set aside.

Place a 12-inch skillet or wok over high heat. When hot, add 2 tablespoons cooking oil; when the oil becomes hot, add the sausage mixture. Stir-fry until the vegetables are brightly colored, about 2 minutes, then add the sauce. Stir-fry until the vegetables just begin to wilt, about 1 minute more. Add a little of the cornstarch mixture to thicken the sauce, then transfer to a bowl. Cool to room temperature, and then place in the freezer until thoroughly chilled, about 1 hour.

Separate the spring roll skins. Position each spring roll so one of the corners is pointing at you. Place about ½ cup of the filling in the bottom third of the skin and then form the filling into a cylinder, stretching between the side corners. Bring the corner nearest you over the center of the filling and then tuck the tip under the filling. Roll the spring roll a turn. Brush all the edges and along the top of the cylinder with beaten egg. Bring the two side corners one-third over the top of the cylinder. Now finish rolling the spring roll into a cylinder. Place on a small tray as you complete the rest of the spring rolls. Store, unstacked and uncovered, in the refrigerator. (These can be done a day ahead.)

LAST-MINUTE COOKING Place 3 cups of cooking oil in a 12-inch skillet and heat over high heat. When the oil reaches 370°F. (bubbles will escape from the end of a wooden spoon when placed into the oil for 10 seconds), fry the spring rolls in 3 batches, cooking them on both sides until light golden, about 3 minutes. Drain on a wire rack.

Heat the oil again, this time until it reaches 400°F. Fry the spring rolls a second time in 2 batches until they are dark golden, about 1 minute. Drain. The second frying makes the spring rolls crispier.

Serve spring rolls whole or cut in half, with one or more dipping sauces. Guests should wrap a spring roll in a lettuce leaf, dip it in sauce, and enjoy.

Serves: 8 to 12 as an appetizer.

Menu Ideas: Melrose Avenue Spring Rolls, Asian Barbecued Salmon, an avocado salad, and chocolate chip cheesecake.

Variations: Any stir-fry dish that has been cooked and then thoroughly chilled can be used as a spring roll filling. We have often done this by using a dish ordered from a nearby Chinese restaurant. Drain, then chill the stir-fry. Add 1 ounce rice sticks, softened in hot water for 20 minutes and cut into 2-inch lengths. The rice sticks help to absorb additional moisture. Be the first in your neighborhood to try mu shu spring rolls, Kung Pao spring rolls, and tangerine beef spring rolls.

SCALLOP RAVIOLI IN SAFFRON-CAVIAR SAUCE

RAVIOLI

12 ounces spinach leaves
¼ cup chopped jicama
1 green onion
1 tablespoon finely minced
    fresh ginger
½ pound bay scallops
¼ pound ground raw chicken
2 tablespoons light soy sauce
2 teaspoons dry sherry
¼ teaspoon freshly ground
    white pepper
20 won ton skins
4 tablespoons cooking oil

GARNISH

2 ounces top-quality black
    caviar
¼ cup Chinese chili sauce
1 bunch chives

SAUCE

2 cups heavy (whipping) cream
½ cup dry sherry
2 teaspoons Oriental
    sesame oil
½ teaspoon salt
Pinch of saffron
1½ tablespoons finely minced
    fresh ginger

A DISH WE TASTED AT MICHEL RICHARD'S QUINTESSENTIAL CALIFORNIA RESTAURANT, CITRUS, INSPIRED THESE DUMPLINGS. THE TENDER SCALLOP DUMPLINGS, GLAZED WITH A RICH GINGER-CREAM SAUCE ARE ACCENTED BY CHINESE CHILI SAUCE AND CAVIAR. A NEW YEAR'S EVE APPETIZER PARTY FOR 10 MIGHT INCLUDE THIS RECIPE PLUS GINGER GRAVLOX, PACIFIC STYLE QUESADILLAS, YAKITORI WITH SATAY SAUCE, AND CHILLED VEGETABLES WITH TWO CHOPSTIX DIPPING SAUCES. ACCOMPANIED BY DOM PERIGNON CHAMPAGNE, THIS WOULD BE A GLORIOUS WAY TO ANTICIPATE THE NEW YEAR!

ADVANCE PREPARATION Prepare the filling. Drop the spinach leaves into 1 quart of boiling water. When the spinach wilts, transfer to a colander and rinse under cold water. Using your hands, press all the moisture from the leaves. Mince together the spinach, jicama, green onion, and ginger by hand or in a food processor. Transfer to a mixing bowl. Chop the scallops by hand or in a food processor; scallop pieces should still be fairly large. Transfer to the mixing bowl. Add the chicken, soy sauce, sherry, and pepper. Mix thoroughly, then refrigerate.

Within 5 hours of cooking, assemble the ravioli. Trim the won tons into circles. Place about 2 teaspoons of filling in the center of each won ton. Moisten the edges with water and fold the won tons in half over the filling, being careful not to flatten the filling. Press the edges together; they will be a half-moon shape. Moisten each end of the won tons, then touch the moistened ends together; they should look like little caps. Place on a baking sheet coated generously with cooking oil. Refrigerate, uncovered, until ready to cook.

Set aside the caviar. Place the chili sauce in a blender and purée, then set aside. Mince the chives and set aside. In a small bowl, combine the sauce ingredients.

LAST-MINUTE COOKING Pour the sauce into a 12-inch skillet. Bring to a vigorous boil over high heat and cook until the sauce thickens enough so the spoon leaves a "path" as the sauce is stirred, about 8 minutes. Turn the heat to very low and keep warm.

Bring 5 quarts of water to a vigorous boil. Add the ravioli and give them a gentle stir. When the ravioli float to the surface (in about 3 minutes) gently tip them into a colander to drain.

Transfer the ravioli to serving plates. Spoon the sauce over the top. Sprinkle on the chopped chives, then decorate each plate with a little caviar and a dot of the chili sauce. Serve at once.

Serves: 4 to 8 as an hors d'oeuvre or first course, or 2 as an entrée.

TEX-MEX WON TONS WITH NEW AGE GUACAMOLE

FILLING

2 green onions
½ cup chopped carrots
1 ear corn
2 cloves garlic, finely minced
½ pound ground pork or lamb
1 tablespoon oyster sauce
1 tablespoon light soy sauce
½ egg, well beaten
1 teaspoon Chinese chili sauce
¼ teaspoon salt

TO ASSEMBLE

24 won ton skins
Cooking oil for shallow frying
New Age Guacamole (page 42)

ARTIST JEFF STILLWELL, WHO CREATED THIS SET, IS VERY INTERESTED IN THE COLLABORATIVE PROCESS BETWEEN ILLUSTRATORS AND PHOTOGRAPHERS. JEFF PROCESSES A RECIPE IDEA THROUGH HIS FERTILE IMAGINATION, AND OUT COMES A MAGICAL WORLD POPULATED BY SUCH CREATURES AS THIS "XENA," A HALF-DOG, HALF-CAT WHO HAS A REAL PASSION FOR HUGH'S MEXICAN-ASIAN TASTES! JEFF'S WORK, WHICH IS EXHIBITED WIDELY IN SOUTHERN CALIFORNIA, IS PERFECT FOR CHOPSTIX FOOD PHOTOS BECAUSE IT EPITOMIZES THE FUN AND CREATIVE FREEDOM THAT THE RESTAURANTS ARE KNOWN FOR.

ADVANCE PREPARATION Mince together the green onions and carrots with a knife or in a food processor. Transfer to a mixing bowl. Stand the ear of corn on one end and cut off all the kernels. Add the raw kernels to the bowl along with the garlic, meat, oyster and soy sauces, beaten egg, chili sauce, and salt. Mix thoroughly.

Assemble the dumplings: With one point of a won ton skin facing you, place 1½ teaspoons of filling in the center of the skin. Fold the skin in half by bringing the opposite tip forward over the filling; the won ton tips should not quite meet each other. Roll the won ton once into a cylinder with the side tips still open. Turn the cylinder 180° and lightly moisten each end of the cylinder with water. Touch the moistened tips together, forming a cap. Place the won tons on a tray liberally rubbed with cooking oil. Refrigerate, uncovered, for up to 5 hours prior to cooking.

LAST-MINUTE COOKING In a 12-inch skillet, pour in enough cooking oil to come up ½ inch, then heat to 365°F. To test the oil, drop in a little piece of won ton skin; if the oil is hot enough, the skin will bounce across the surface. Add about 10 won tons to the oil and fry until golden on one side, then turn and fry on the other side—about 1½ minutes total. Drain the won tons on a wire rack, while you fry the remainder. Serve with New Age Guacamole.

Serves: 6 to 12 as an appetizer.

Menu Ideas: A New Age dinner for 8—Tex-Mex Won Tons with New Age Guacamole, Melrose Mushroom Salad, Thai Sautéed Shrimp, Champagne Rice Pilaf, and Lemon Ice Cream with Chocolate Grand Marnier Sauce. Accompany with imported beers and iced herb teas.

Tex-Mex Won Tons shown with New Age Guacamole

BARBECUED THAI SHRIMP PIZZA

CRUST

1½ teaspoons active dry yeast
2 teaspoons sugar
¾ cup warm water
  (105°–115°F.)
2 tablespoons olive oil
1½ teaspoons salt
¼ cup minced fresh basil
2 cups bread flour

TOPPING

3 tablespoons olive oil
2 teaspoons Chinese chili
  sauce
½ pound raw medium shrimp
2 tablespoons lime juice
2 tablespoons fish sauce
1 tablespoon honey
4 ounces part-skim mozzarella
  cheese
1 large vine-ripened tomato
⅓ cup chopped fresh mint
2 tablespoons grated or
  minced lime peel
¼ cup finely chopped unsalted
  roasted peanuts

PIZZA DOUGH, BRUSHED WITH EXTRA-VIRGIN OLIVE OIL, THEN GENTLY LAID OVER THE GRILL OF A HOT BARBECUE FOR A FEW MINUTES OF COOKING ON BOTH SIDES, PICKS UP A WONDERFUL FLAVOR. THIS IS A TECHNIQUE THAT CHEF AND COOKING FRIEND GRANT SHOWLEY USES AT HIS NEWPORT BEACH RESTAURANT, SHOWLEY'S. ONCE THE PIZZA DOUGH IS BARBECUED, IT CAN BE LAYERED WITH VARIOUS TOPPINGS AND THEN BAKED IN THE OVEN HOURS LATER. IN THIS RECIPE THE PIZZA TOPPINGS COVER SIX 5-INCH PIZZAS. CUT INTO QUARTERS, THEY MAKE A SPICY, FUN APPETIZER. YOU WILL HAVE EXTRA PIZZA DOUGH, SO BARBECUE AND FREEZE THIS FOR ANOTHER TIME, WHEN A PIZZA CRAVING SUDDENLY ATTACKS.

ADVANCE PREPARATION Prepare the dough. Sprinkle the yeast and sugar over the warm water. When bubbles appear on top (about 5 minutes), the yeast has been activated. Stir in the olive oil, salt, and basil. Then add the yeast mixture to the flour and stir until a soft dough forms. Lightly flour your hands and knead the dough until smooth and no longer sticky, about 5 minutes. Lightly oil a small bowl. Rotate the dough in the bowl to coat with oil, cover with a towel, and let rise for about 30 minutes. Knead briefly again, cover, and let rise for another 30 minutes.

Meanwhile, light the charcoal, or prepare a wood fire. The coals are ready when they are covered with white ash. Or, if using a gas barbecue, set on medium heat.

Cut the dough in half and freeze one of the halves. Roll out the remaining dough on a lightly floured surface until less than ¼ inch thick. Cut into 6-inch circles. Brush one side of dough rounds with olive oil. Place a round of dough, oiled side down, on the barbecue and grill for 15 to 20 seconds; give the dough a one-quarter turn and grill for another 20 seconds. The dough should be lightly golden and have grill marks. Do not be concerned if the barbecued dough has large air bubbles. Brush oil on top of the dough, flip the dough over, and repeat the grilling procedure; then continue with the remaining dough pieces. The grilled dough can now be refrigerated for a day, or frozen.

Prepare the topping. Combine the olive oil and 1 teaspoon of chili sauce, and set aside. Shell the shrimp, split in half lengthwise, and rinse out the vein; marinate the shrimp for 30 minutes in the lime juice, fish sauce, honey, and remaining teaspoon of chili sauce. Shred the cheese. Cut the tomato into paper-thin slices. Set aside the mint, lime peel, and peanuts.

LAST-MINUTE COOKING Preheat the oven to 425°F. Brush the top of each pizza with the olive oil–chili sauce blend. Sprinkle on a thin layer of cheese. Add a thin layer of tomato, followed by shrimp, then sprinkle on some mint, a little more cheese, and then a bit of grated lime and chopped peanuts.

Bake on 1 or 2 baking sheets until the cheese bubbles and the edges of the pizza are golden, about 8 minutes. Cut each pizza into 4 wedges. Serve at once.

Serves: 6 to 12 as an appetizer or 6 as a first course.

Menu Ideas: Chopstix appetizer party for 12 around the pool—Barbecue Thai Shrimp Pizza, Thai Fried Dumplings, Yakitori, Flame-roasted Green Beans, Barbecued Salmon Ribbons, and Sprouting Noodle Salad.

Variations: There are many exciting variations on this recipe. In place of the shrimp, substitute the meat from Thai-High Barbecued Chicken. Or use as a topping the Lamb Fajitas: after stir-frying the dish, let it cool completely in a colander; spread a little hoisin sauce over each barbecued pizza dough; add the meat topping and then a sprinkling of shredded mozzarella.

If you don't want to barbecue the pizza dough, lay the dough on a baking sheet sprinkled with cornmeal, brush the top of the dough with the olive oil and chili sauce mixture, and then add the pizza toppings. Cook in a 425°F. oven for about 12 minutes, until the edge of the dough is golden and the cheese bubbles.

THAI FRIED DUMPLINGS

12 ounces spinach leaves
½ cup chopped carrots
2 small green onions
1 tablespoon finely minced
    fresh ginger
2 cloves garlic, minced
¾ pound raw shrimp
1 tablespoon light soy sauce
¼ teaspoon Chinese chili
    sauce
24 won ton skins
Cooking oil

SAUCE

1 tablespoon minced fresh basil
1 tablespoon minced fresh mint
1 tablespoon minced green
    onion
¼ cup coconut milk
¼ cup chicken broth
2 tablespoons dry sherry
1 tablespoon oyster sauce
½ tablespoon curry powder
½ teaspoon sugar

TO FRY

3 tablespoons cooking oil

DUMPLINGS FILLED WITH SEAFOOD OR MEAT AND BROWNED IN A FRYING PAN UNTIL THE BOTTOMS TURN A DEEP GOLDEN ALWAYS APPEAR AS AN APPETIZER AT OUR PARTIES. AS GUESTS CRUNCH THROUGH THE CRISP SKINS, EACH BITE REVEALS A SAVORY FILLING ACCENTED BY THE RICH SAUCE. IT WILL TAKE VERY LITTLE PRODDING TO GET GUESTS TO COMPLETE THE FOLDING OF THE DUMPLINGS WHILE YOU HEAT THE PAN AND HAVE A GLASS OF WINE.

ADVANCE PREPARATION Drop the spinach leaves into 1 quart of boiling water. When the spinach wilts, transfer to a colander and rinse under cold water. Using your hands, press all the moisture from the leaves. Mince together the spinach, carrots, green onions, ginger, and garlic by hand or in a food processor, then transfer to a mixing bowl. Shell and devein the shrimp. Chop the shrimp by hand or in processor and then transfer to the bowl with the vegetables. Add the soy and chili sauces and mix thoroughly.

Within 5 hours of cooking, assemble the dumplings. Trim the won tons into circles. Place 1 tablespoon of the filling on the center of each won ton skin. Bring the edges of the skin up around the filling. Place each dumpling in the soft hollow of one hand, between your thumb and index finger, and squeeze the "waist" gently with that same index finger while also pressing the top and bottom of the dumpling with your other index finger and thumb. The dumplings should look like round, thin cylinders with a flat top and bottom. Place the dumplings on a plate rubbed with cooking oil. Refrigerate, uncovered.

Combine the sauce ingredients and mix well. Set aside.

LAST-MINUTE COOKING Place a 12-inch nonstick skillet over high heat. Add the cooking oil and immediately add dumplings. Fry the dumplings until the bottoms are dark golden, about 2 minutes. Pour in the sauce and immediately cover the pan. Reduce the heat to medium and steam the dumplings until they are firm to the touch, about 2 minutes.

Remove the cover. Over high heat, continue frying the dumplings until the sauce reduces completely, about 1 minute. While cooking, shake the pan so that the dumplings turn over and are glazed all over with the sauce. Tip out onto a heated serving platter and serve at once.

Serves: 4 to 8 as an hors d'oeuvre or first course, or 2 as an entrée.

Menu Ideas: Chopstix dinner for 4—Asian Avocado Adventure, Thai Fried Dumplings, Melrose Mushroom Salad, and Coconut Flan Supreme.

Variations: The taste of this dish can be changed dramatically by substituting an orange-garlic sauce, made with ½ cup orange juice, 1 tablespoon oyster sauce, ½ teaspoon Chinese chili sauce, 1 teaspoon minced orange peel, and 2 minced garlic cloves.

CHINESE SANDWICH SURPRISES

MEAT FILLING

⅔ cup Chopstix Barbecue
    Sauce (page 105)
1½ cups shredded barbecued
    meat
1½ cups shredded iceberg
    lettuce
3 ounces enoki mushrooms
½ cup cilantro (fresh
    coriander) sprigs

SHRIMP FILLING

½ cup Chopstix Barbecue
    Sauce (page 105)
⅓ pound cooked, shelled
    shrimp, split
½ cup chopped fresh mint
1 tablespoon dried red chili
    flakes
2 tablespoons chopped roasted
    unsalted peanuts

CHICKEN FILLING

New Age Guacamole (page 42)
1½ cups meat from Thai-High
    Barbecued Chicken (page
    103)
daikon sprouts

TO ASSEMBLE

5 Peking Chive Pancakes (page
    150) or 4 (10-inch) flour
    tortillas
South Seas Salsa (page 39) or
    a dipping sauce (pages
    40–43)

THIS IS AN EASY AND FUN DISH TO SERVE AS A SNACK FOOD OR ON INFORMAL OCCASIONS SUCH AS A ROSE BOWL GAME GATHERING. EACH FLOUR TORTILLA OR PEKING CHIVE PANCAKE IS HEATED OVER AN OPEN FLAME, THEN LAYERED WITH FRESH HERBS, BARBECUED MEAT OR SHRIMP, AND AN ORIENTAL BARBECUE SAUCE BEFORE BEING ROLLED INTO A CYLINDER AND SECURED WITH A TOOTHPICK. SERVED WITH SOUTH SEAS SALSA OR ONE OF THE CHOPSTIX DIPPING SAUCES, THESE "SANDWICHES" DISAPPEAR FAST.

ADVANCE PREPARATION Set aside the ingredients for one of the fillings.

If using an electric stove, heat a 12-inch skillet until hot. Add a pancake or tortilla and cook until well heated, about 30 seconds (the tortillas will begin to puff). Repeat with the remaining pancakes or tortillas. If using a gas stove, hold the pancake or tortilla by tongs and heat directly over the flame.

If you want a free-form look, cut the pancakes into twelve 2½-inch strips. Place a very thin layer of the filling along the surface of the pancake strip, adding in the order listed. Then roll the pancake or tortilla into a cylinder and secure with a toothpick. Repeat with the remaining pancake strips.

If you want a neat, compact look, leave the pancake whole, layer the ingredients evenly across the surface, roll the pancake tightly into a long cylinder, and then cut crosswise into 2-inch lengths. Secure with toothpicks. Repeat with the remaining pancakes.

Serve at room temperature with South Seas Salsa or one of the dips to give the "sandwiches" an additional zing.

Serves: 6 to 8 as an appetizer.

PACIFIC-STYLE QUESADILLAS

⅓ pound barbecued beef
    or lamb
⅓ cup Chopstix Barbecue
    Sauce (page 105)
½ papaya, not overly ripe
¼ pound brie cheese
2 green onions
8 (10-inch) flour tortillas
3 tablespoons unsalted butter

EVERY MORNING AT THE BEAUTIFUL RESORT IN IXTAPAN DE LA SAL, THE WAITERS SERVE APPETIZERS THAT HERALD ANOTHER DAY OF EATING. ONE SUCH DISH IS A TINY FLOUR TORTILLA FOLDED IN HALF TO HIDE AVOCADO, CHEESE, AND HIGHLY SEASONED BARBECUED MEAT. THIS GREAT TASTE SENSATION INSPIRED THESE CHINESE-MEXICAN QUESADILLAS. PACIFIC-STYLE QUESADILLAS CAN BE FILLED AND COOKED AN HOUR BEFORE YOUR GUESTS ARRIVE AND THEN REHEATED IN THE OVEN FOR A FEW MINUTES. THE TASTE OF PAPAYA, BARBECUED MEAT, BRIE, AND CHINESE BARBECUE SAUCE IS AN INTRIGUING COMBINATION OF FLAVORS. IF PAPAYA IS UNAVAILABLE, SUBSTITUTE FRESH MANGOES, PEACHES, OR NECTARINES.

ADVANCE PREPARATION Cut the meat into 1-inch slivers. Set aside the barbecue sauce. Peel, seed, and mince the papaya. Trim the brie of all rind, then cut the cheese into 1½-inch slivers. Mince the green onions.

Using a 4-inch round cookie cutter, make 16 small tortillas (a 12-ounce can of Planters peanuts works perfectly).

Assemble the quesadillas. On one half of a tortilla round, place in this order: 2 strips of brie, ½ teaspoon minced papaya, 3 or 4 shreds of meat, ½ teaspoon barbecue sauce, and ½ teaspoon green onion. Gently fold the tortilla round in half to create a small crescent. If necessary, secure with a toothpick. Repeat with the remaining tortillas.

Heat a 12-inch sauté pan over medium-high heat. When hot, add 1 tablespoon of butter. When the butter bubbles, add about a third of the quesadillas. Sauté on each side until very light golden, about 3 minutes. Set aside and continue with the remaining ones, adding more butter if the pan becomes too dry. The quesadillas can be sautéed up to 4 hours ahead of serving and refrigerated.

LAST-MINUTE COOKING Preheat the oven to 300°F. Place the quesadillas on a baking sheet and reheat for 5 minutes in the oven. Serve at once.

Serves: 4 to 8 as an appetizer, or 4 as a first course.

Menu Ideas: A Chopstix Tex-Mex dinner for 8—Pacific-style Quesadillas; Crunchy Baja Salad; Mesquite Barbecued Lamb, Chopstix Style and Mango Ice Cream with Tequila Sauce.

SOUTH SEAS SALSA

1 pound vine-ripened tomatoes
1 cup chopped green onions
⅓ cup chopped fresh basil
⅓ cup chopped fresh mint
⅓ cup chopped cilantro (fresh coriander)
3 cloves garlic, minced
3 tablespoons lime juice
2 tablespoons safflower oil
2 tablespoons fish sauce or soy sauce
1½ tablespoons light brown sugar
1½ teaspoons Chinese chili sauce

SOUTH SEAS SALSA TAKES JUST MINUTES TO MAKE, WHETHER YOU DO THE CHOPPING BY HAND OR IN THE FOOD PROCESSOR, AND IT HAS MANY USES. THE FRESH TASTE OF VINE-RIPENED TOMATOES ACCENTED BY BASIL, MINT, LIME, AND CHILIES PRODUCES A SALSA PERFECT FOR CHILLED SHRIMP. IT'S ALSO AN INTRIGUING ADDITION INSIDE PEKING PANCAKES WITH A MU SHU FILLING, OR AS A SIDE DISH ACCENT TO BARBECUED SEAFOOD OR MEAT. OFTEN FOR A QUICK LUNCH I ADD CHICKEN BROTH TO LEFTOVER SALSA AND CREATE A THAI-MEXICAN GAZPACHO SOUP, OR I TOSS THE SALSA WITH FRESHLY COOKED *SOBA* NOODLES.

ADVANCE PREPARATION Cut the tomatoes in half and squeeze out the seeds; chop with a knife or in food processor. Chop together the green onions, basil, mint, and cilantro using a knife or food processor. Combine with the remaining ingredients. Do not refrigerate the salsa if serving that day; if prepared a day in advance, bring the salsa to room temperature before serving.

Serves: 6 to 10 as a seasoning, dip, or sauce.

Chopstix Dipping Sauces

THE APPEALING ASPECT OF DIPPING SAUCES IS THAT THEY ADD A SPECIAL TASTE TO MANY DISHES, PARTICULARLY APPETIZERS. USE THESE SAUCES FOR CHILLED COOKED SHRIMP AND OTHER SEAFOOD, AS DIPS FOR VEGETABLES, TO GLAZE CRISP DEEP-FRIED WON TONS AND SPRING ROLLS, FOR DRIZZLING OVER RIBBONS OF BARBECUED MEAT AND SEAFOOD PLACED ON SKEWERS, AND FOR RUBBING ACROSS THE SURFACE OF PEKING CHIVE PANCAKES OR TORTILLAS BEFORE ADDING A FILLING OF STIR-FRIED BARBECUED MEAT AND LETTUCE. CHOPSTIX DIPPING SAUCES ARE GREAT WITH CRISP TORTILLA CHIPS, AND GINGER GRAVLOX, OR TO PLUNGE SHRIMP INTO AS THEY ARRIVE SIZZLING-HOT, STRAIGHT FROM THE WOK. USE THESE RECIPES AS A STARTING POINT FOR CREATING YOUR OWN VARIATIONS.

CHOPSTIX PLUM LEMON DIP

- 1 tablespoon white sesame seeds
- ¼ teaspoon finely minced garlic
- ½ teaspoon grated or finely minced lemon peel
- 2 tablespoons lemon juice
- 5 tablespoons plum sauce
- ¼ teaspoon Chinese chili sauce
- ⅛ teaspoon cinnamon

ADVANCE PREPARATION Toast the sesame seeds in a small skillet until golden, about 4 minutes. Combine with the remaining ingredients; then refrigerate. Use within 3 weeks. Makes ½ cup.

APRICOT GUAVA DIP

- 12 dried apricots
- 12 ounces apricot nectar
- ½ cup guava nectar
- ½ cup sugar
- ¼ cup plum sauce
- ⅔ cup distilled white vinegar
- 1 teaspoon Chinese chili sauce
- 1 tablespoon minced fresh ginger

ADVANCE PREPARATION Place all the ingredients in a non-corrosive saucepan. Bring to a low boil, reduce the heat to low, cover, and simmer for 25 minutes. Transfer to a food processor and blend thoroughly, about 30 seconds. Cool and refrigerate. Use within 3 weeks. Makes 3 cups.

SINGAPORE SATAY SAUCE

- 2 tablespoons unsalted roasted peanuts
- 1 small shallot
- 1 clove garlic
- 6 tablespoons coconut milk
- ¼ cup top-quality peanut butter
- 2 tablespoons peanut oil
- 1 teaspoon sugar
- ½ teaspoon Chinese chili sauce
- ¼ teaspoon ground cumin
- ¼ teaspoon ground coriander
- ⅛ teaspoon turmeric (optional)

ADVANCE PREPARATION Mince the peanuts in a food processor and set aside. In a food processor, mince the shallot and garlic. Add all the remaining ingredients except the peanuts and process until completely smooth, about 20 seconds. If you want a little deeper color, add the turmeric and blend again. The sauce should be as thick as very rich cream. Transfer to a small container to store. Use within 3 days.

Sprinkle nuts over the sauce just before serving. Satay sauce should always be served at room temperature. If it has been refrigerated, bring to room temperature and stir vigorously. You may have to add a little peanut oil or water to thin the sauce. Makes ¾ cup.

CHAMPAGNE MUSTARD SAUCE

- ¼ cup dry mustard
- ¼ cup Champagne or beer
- ¼ cup honey

2 tablespoons Dijon-style
  mustard
2 tablespoons rice vinegar
¼ teaspoon salt

ADVANCE PREPARATION Combine all the ingredients in a small saucepan. Beat with a whisk until completely smooth, then bring to a low boil over medium heat. Reduce the heat to low and cook for 2 minutes, stirring continuously. (Cook a little longer if you want it thicker.) Transfer to a storage container and refrigerate. Use within 2 weeks. Good warm or chilled. Makes 1 cup.

NEW AGE GUACAMOLE

- ¾ cup mashed ripe avocado
- ½ cup chopped water
  chestnuts
- 1 ear white corn, husked
- 2 tablespoons minced green
  onions
- 1 tablespoon minced cilantro
  (fresh coriander)

½ teaspoon finely minced
  garlic
Approximately 1 tablespoon
  lemon juice
1 teaspoon Chinese chili sauce
¼ teaspoon salt

ADVANCE PREPARATION In a mixing bowl, combine the avocado and water chestnuts. Standing the corn on one end, cut off all the kernels. Add the raw kernels to the avocado along with the remaining ingredients. Mix thoroughly. If doing this in advance, sprinkle the top with a little extra lemon juice. Cover with plastic wrap and refrigerate. Best used the day it is made. Makes 1½ cups.

CHINESE PEPPER BLEND

- 1 tangerine or small orange
- ¼ cup Sichuan peppercorns

¼ cup white sesame seeds
2 teaspoons dried red chili
flakes

ADVANCE PREPARATION With a zester, remove the outside of the tangerine or orange peel in thin threads. Spread out the threads on a dish and let dry for 1 to 2 days. Use the remaining fruit for another purpose.

Place the Sichuan peppercorns in a small ungreased skillet and toast over high heat until they begin to smoke. Transfer to a plate. When cool, place the pepper in small Ziploc bag and crush with a rolling pin.

Place the sesame seeds in an ungreased skillet and toast until light golden, about 3 minutes. Finely mince the dried tangerine or orange zest, then combine with the peppercorns, sesame seeds, and chili flakes. Store in a spice jar. The mixture will keep its flavor for up to 3 months. Makes ⅓ cup.

THAI DIPPING SAUCE

- 2½ tablespoons water
- 2 tablespoons fish sauce
- 2 tablespoons lime juice
- 2 teaspoons honey
- ½ teaspoon Chinese chili
  sauce

1 clove garlic, finely minced
1 tablespoon shredded fresh
  basil or mint
2 teaspoons shredded fresh
  ginger

ADVANCE PREPARATION Combine all the ingredients. Store in the refrigerator and use within 1 week. Serve at room temperature. Makes ½ cup.

Rainbow Salad with Raspberry Vinegar

Chapter 2

CRUNCHY, CRISPY, CRACKLING SALADS

ONE AUTUMN DAY, IN THE ANCIENT NORTHERN THAI CITY OF CHIANG MAI, WITH THE AIR CLEAR AND CRISP, WE SPENT SEVERAL HOURS AT AN IDYLLIC ORCHID FARM SURROUNDED BY RICE PADDIES. AROUND THE CORNER OF ONE OF THE OLD BUILDINGS, WE DISCOVERED A TYPICAL THAI OPEN-AIR KITCHEN AND EATING AREA. THE SMELL OF HONEY-COATED CHICKEN GRILLED OVER WOOD DRIFTED TO US, AS SEVERAL GENERATIONS OF WOMEN WORKED SIDE BY SIDE PREPARING OTHER REGIONAL SPECIALITIES. OUR THOUGHTS TURNED IMMEDIATELY TO LUNCH, IN THIS SPOT OF TRANQUILITY WHERE, STIMULATED BY A SUCCESSION OF SMALL SALADS, WE RECALLED RECENT ADVENTURES RIDING ELEPHANTS THROUGH TROPICAL RAIN FORESTS, TAKING EARLY MORNING PILGRIMAGES TO GOLD-ENCRUSTED TEMPLES, AND TREASURE-SHOPPING AT THE NIGHT BAZAAR.

WHETHER SERVED IN SIMPLE SURROUNDINGS LIKE THOSE WE ENCOUNTERED IN CHIANG MAI, OR AMID THE FRENETIC ACTIVITY OF FOOD VENDORS IN SINGAPORE—OR EVEN HIGH IN THE MOUNTAINS OF BALI—THE SALADS OF THE SOUTH SEAS BLEND GREENS ENLIVENED WITH TANGY, SPICY DRESSINGS. TRY THESE SALADS AS APPETIZERS, AS FIRST COURSES, OR AS PALATE CLEANSERS FOLLOWING THE ENTRÉE. OR MAKE ONE OF THESE SALADS A MAIN COURSE AND ACCOMPANY IT WITH A NEW WAVE SOUP AND CRUSTY BREAD, FOLLOWED BY A SINFUL SWEET.

RAINBOW SALAD WITH RASPBERRY VINEGAR

SALAD

12 ounces spinach leaves
1 small head radicchio
4 ounces shiitake mushrooms
1 sweet red pepper
2 ounces rice sticks
4 cups cooking oil

DRESSING

1 tablespoon finely minced
    fresh ginger
1 teaspoon grated orange peel
3 tablespoons raspberry
    vinegar
2 tablespoons safflower oil
2 tablespoons juice from a jar
    of red sweet ginger
½ teaspoon Chinese chili
    sauce
½ teaspoon salt

To go through life recipe-bound, tantalizingly close to the fertile soil of culinary imagination, must be a fate as limiting as that felt by a struggling, root-bound plant. What joyful triumphs of the creative process are foretold when you throw away the measuring spoons, disregard the recipes, and cook with passion!

For this recipe, you might substitute another herb vinegar, or toss in meat from a barbecued chicken to transform the dish into an entrée. Or deep-fry thin strips of won tons rather than using the crisp rice sticks. Serve this salad as a light appetizer to stimulate the palate, or after the entrée as a palate-cleansing prelude for a rich dessert; or have it as an after-theater nibble, washed down with Champagne to sustain an evening of romance.

ADVANCE PREPARATION Wash and thoroughly dry the spinach, then bunch together and cut into very thin slivers. Shred the radicchio. Discard the stems from the mushrooms, then shred the caps. Stem, seed, and shred the red pepper.

Cook the rice sticks in the cooking oil as described on page 52.

Mince together the ginger and orange peel in a food processor. Add the remaining dressing ingredients and blend thoroughly. Set aside.

LAST-MINUTE ASSEMBLING Place all the salad ingredients except the rice sticks in a very large salad bowl. Shake the dressing, add to the salad and toss. Then gently fold in the rice sticks, being careful not to crush them. Serve at once.

Serves: 6 to 8 as the salad course.

Menu Ideas: Pacific-style salads served as appetizers for a group of 12—Rainbow Salad with Raspberry Vinegar, Melrose Mushroom Salad, and Sprouting Noodle Salad. We like to follow these appetizers with easy American entrées to accent the wonderful and distinct Asian flavors that begin the meal.

CRUNCHY BAJA SALAD

SALAD

3 ears sweet corn, husked

1 avocado

⅓ pound jicama

2 vine-ripened tomatoes

1 sweet red pepper

4 cups bite-size pieces mixed
salad greens

2 tablespoons extra-virgin
olive oil

2 cups blue corn tortilla strips

DRESSING

2 tablespoons finely minced
ginger

3 tablespoons chopped
cilantro (fresh coriander)

1 bunch chives

⅓ cup extra-virgin olive oil

¼ cup balsamic vinegar

2 teaspoons light soy sauce

1 teaspoon dry mustard

½ teaspoon salt

½ teaspoon Chinese chili
sauce

½ teaspoon grated or finely
minced orange peel

¼ teaspoon freshly ground
black pepper

DURING THE SUMMER, WHEN CORN IS AT ITS PEAK OF TENDERNESS, CUT THE KERNELS OFF THE COB AND TOSS THEM RAW INTO YOUR SALAD. WITH EACH BITE, THE SWEET JUICE BURSTS FROM THE TENDER, CRUNCHY KERNELS. WE CALL THIS OUR BAJA SALAD, BECAUSE ITS CORN, JICAMA, AVOCADO, TOMATO AND RED PEPPER ARE FAMILIAR INGREDIENTS IN BAJA CALIFORNIA. YOU CAN QUICKLY TURN THE SALAD INTO AN ENTRÉE BY ADDING COOKED SHRIMP OR BARBECUED CHICKEN. OR DRIZZLE THE SALAD DRESSING ACROSS PIECES OF ROAST CHICKEN THAT HAVE BEEN CHILLED AND SLICED.

ADVANCE PREPARATION AND SERVING Stand the ears of corn on their ends and cut off the kernels. Seed, peel, and thinly slice the avocados. Peel the jicama and cut into thin bite-size rectangles. Seed the tomatoes, then cut just the outside section into ½-inch chunks. Seed and stem the pepper, then cut into ½-inch cubes. Toss salad greens with the olive oil. Set aside the tortilla strips.

Mince the ginger in a food processor. Add the cilantro and chives and mince again. Add the remaining dressing ingredients, then process for 20 seconds.

Arrange the greens on 4 salad plates. Sprinkle the tortilla strips over greens. In a bowl, place the corn, avocado, jicama, tomatoes, and peppers; add the dressing and toss. Spoon onto center of the lettuce. Serve at once.

Serves: 2 as an entrée, or 4 to 6 as the salad course.

Menu Ideas: A Saturday night dinner for 6—Barbecued Veal Chops with Macadamia Nuts, Wild Chinese Rice, Crunchy Baja Salad, and Ginger Chocolate Petit Pots.

GOAT CHEESE SALAD WITH GINGER AND MACADAMIA NUTS

SALAD

5 ounces soft-style goat cheese, chilled (chèvre)

3 ounces roasted macadamia nuts

4 cups lettuce greens, preferably baby leaves

DRESSING

1 tablespoon finely minced fresh ginger

½ clove garlic

¼ cup chopped cilantro (fresh coriander)

7 tablespoons extra-virgin olive oil

3 tablespoons rice vinegar

¼ teaspoon salt

⅛ teaspoon freshly ground black pepper

TO SERVE

1 tablespoon extra-virgin olive oil

WHEN WE ARE AT OUR HOME IN NAPA VALLEY, EVEN THE SLIGHTEST MENTION OF THE FAMED MUSTARD'S RESTAURANT IS ENOUGH TO PROVOKE A SHORT DRIVE TO SAMPLE THEIR SMOKED BARBECUED RIBS, GRILLED FISH, AND SALADS MADE FROM BABY GREENS PULLED FROM THE RICH NAPA SOIL THAT DAY. THE FOLLOWING RECIPE IS BASED ON ONE OF THEIR MOST POPULAR DISHES. THE SOFT GOAT CHEESE IS CUT INTO THIN SLICES, ROLLED IN CHOPPED NUTS, AND PAN-FRIED IN A LITTLE OLIVE OIL BEFORE BEING PLACED ON A BED OF TINY LETTUCE GREENS. YOU CAN VARY THE CHOICE OF NUTS, SUBSTITUTING RAW CRUSHED ALMONDS OR PECANS, BUT BE SURE TO PURCHASE SOFT GOAT CHEESE SO THE NUTS WILL ADHERE TO ITS SURFACE.

PREPARATION AND SERVING Gently cut the goat cheese into 4 thin slices. If the nuts are salted, rinse briefly and pat dry. Place the nuts in a food processor and chop coarsely, then transfer to a plate. Coat each cheese slice with the nuts and refrigerate.

Wash and dry the lettuce greens. If using more mature lettuce, tear into bite-size pieces.

Prepare the dressing. Mince the ginger and garlic in a food processor. Add the cilantro and mince again. Add the remaining ingredients and process for 2 minutes. Set aside.

To serve, arrange the greens on 4 plates. Place a 12-inch skillet over medium-high heat. When hot, add the tablespoon of olive oil. Heat the oil, then gently add the goat cheese slices. Sauté on both sides until the cheese is just heated through and the nuts are golden brown, about 2 minutes. Gently transfer to the center of the greens. Stir the dressing and spoon over the greens. Serve at once.

Serves: 4 as the salad course.

Menu Ideas: A Chopstix variation of a lunch at Mustard's Restaurant, Napa Valley, serving 4—Goat Cheese Salad with Ginger and Macadamia Nuts, Smoked Baby Back Ribs with Chopstix Barbecue Sauce, New Wave Garlic Bread, Chopstix Tart with Raspberry Cabernet Sauvignon Sauce.

Goat Cheese Salad with Ginger and Macadamia Nuts and Ginger Summer Salad (recipe on page 65)

ASIAN RED PEPPER SALAD

LAYERS OF ROASTED RED PEPPER, FETA CHEESE, AND BASIL GLISTEN IN AN EXTRA-VIRGIN OLIVE OIL DRESSING ACCENTED WITH FRESH GINGER. VIVID COLORS CONTRASTING WITH THE WHITE PLATES; THERE ARE RICH TEXTURAL INTERPLAYS AND TASTE EXPLOSIONS WITH EACH BITE. ASIAN RED PEPPER SALAD IS A GREAT BEGINNING TO A PARTY, WHETHER SERVED AS AN APPETIZER OR AS A FIRST COURSE.

SALAD
1 large sweet red pepper
16 basil leaves
2 ounces feta cheese
1 lime

DRESSING
2 cloves garlic, finely minced
1 tablespoon finely minced
    fresh ginger
¼ cup extra-virgin olive oil
1 teaspoon Oriental sesame oil
½ teaspoon freshly ground
    black pepper

ADVANCE PREPARATION Preheat the oven to broil. Stem, core, and seed the pepper, then cut into quarters. Place the peppers on a broiling pan skin side up and put the pan 3 inches under the broiler. Broil until the pepper skin begins to blacken, about 5 minutes. Place the pepper pieces in a plastic food bag and let sit for 15 minutes. Peel off the blackened skin, and cut each quarter into 2 pieces. Set aside the basil. Slice the feta into 8 slices. Cut the lime into wedges.

Place a strip of pepper on a small salad plate. Add a slice of feta, then 2 basil leaves, then another layer of pepper, feta, and basil. Repeat for remaining 3 servings (or divide the ingredients between 2 plates for an entrée). Refrigerate.

Place the garlic, ginger, olive oil, and sesame oil in a small skillet over medium heat and cook until the oil bubbles and the garlic turns white, about 1 minute. (If the garlic browns, discard and start over). Transfer the mixture to a bowl and let cool. (This can be completed several hours prior to serving.)

SERVING To serve, bring the salad to room temperature. Drizzle the dressing over the pepper salad and sprinkle the pepper on top. Serve with wedges of lime to squeeze over the salad.

Serves: 4 as a first course, or 2 as a light dinner salad.

Menu Ideas: Dinner for 6 with a Mediterranean-Thai flavor—Asian Red Pepper Salad (double the recipe); Thai Bouillabaisse and New Wave Garlic Bread (double the soup recipe); steamed asparagus drizzled with the peanut dressing from Yummy Yam Gai (serve the dressing at room temperature); and Strawberries Siam.

Asian Red Pepper Salad

SPICY SHREDDED DUCK SALAD

SALAD

1 Chinese roast duck
12 ounces spinach leaves
1 cup shredded carrots
1 cup shredded red cabbage
½ cup slivered almonds
4 cups cooking oil
2 ounces rice sticks

DRESSING

¼ cup red wine vinegar
2 tablespoons light soy sauce
2 tablespoons Oriental
   sesame oil
1 tablespoon plus 1 teaspoon
   sugar
1 tablespoon hoisin sauce
1 teaspoon Chinese chili sauce
1 teaspoon dry mustard
½ teaspoon salt
2 tablespoons finely minced
   fresh ginger
2 cloves garlic, finely minced

PERHAPS BECAUSE CHINESE MARKETS FILL THE CAVITY OF DUCKS WITH STAR ANISE, HONEY, AND HOISIN SAUCE, THE TASTE OF A CHINATOWN ROAST DUCK HAS NO RIVAL. IF YOU LIVE NEAR A CHINESE MARKET, PURCHASE SEVERAL ROAST DUCKS AND ASK THAT THEY BE LEFT WHOLE.

AT HOME, REMOVE THE MEAT IN LARGE PIECES, DISCARD THE SKIN, THEN TIGHTLY WRAP THE MEAT IN SMALL AMOUNTS AND FREEZE. EVEN AFTER A MONTH, WHEN THAWED AND SLIVERED FOR DUCK SALADS OR AS A TOPPING FOR PIZZA, THE TASTE IS OUTSTANDING. SPICY SHREDDED DUCK SALAD, A CRUNCHY COMBINATION OF TEXTURES, MAKES A GOOD FIRST COURSE OR ENTRÉE. SINCE THE SALAD DRESSING LASTS FOR WEEKS WHEN REFRIGERATED, MAKE A GENEROUS AMOUNT IN CASE YOU WANT TO GIVE THE SALAD MORE FLAVOR, OR TO USE FOR A DRESSING ON OTHER SALADS.

ADVANCE PREPARATION Remove all the meat from the duck and discard the skin. Shred the duck meat. Wash and thoroughly dry the spinach, then bunch together and cut into very thin slivers. Set out the carrots and cabbage. Toast the almonds in a 325°F. oven until golden, about 15 minutes.

Heat the oil in a 10-inch skillet set over medium-high heat to 375°F. Test with a strand of rice stick; it will puff up immediately when ready. Add a small number of rice sticks at a time. As soon as they expand, in about 5 seconds, turn the rice sticks over with chopsticks or tongs and push them back into the hot oil to cook for 5 more seconds. Drain on paper towels while you fry the remaining rice sticks.

Combine all the ingredients for the dressing and mix well.

LAST-MINUTE ASSEMBLING Place all the salad ingredients except the rice sticks in a very large salad bowl. Shake the dressing and add half to the salad. Toss immediately. Gently fold in the rice sticks, being careful not to crush them. Taste the salad, and add more dressing for a more pronounced flavor, but be careful that the rice sticks do not become soggy. Serve at once.

Serves: 4 as an entrée, or 6 to 8 as the salad course.

Menu Ideas: This salad makes an impressive entrée accompanied by other Chopstix-style dishes. Try the following menu for a group of 6: Hot and Sour Sichuan Tomato Soup (double the recipe and serve in a large bowl), accompanied by California Cornbread; Spicy Shredded Duck Salad; and fresh fruit with Orange Ginger Brownies.

MELROSE MUSHROOM SALAD

SALAD

1 pound mixed mushrooms
  (button, shiitake, enoki,
  oyster)
½ pound jicama
1 sweet red pepper
3 cups bean sprouts
6 tablespoons chopped fresh
  parsley

DRESSING

2 tablespoons thinly sliced
  fresh ginger
1 clove garlic
¼ cup chopped green onions
5 tablespoons white wine
  vinegar
¼ cup mild olive oil
3 tablespoons Oriental
  sesame oil
2 tablespoons oyster sauce
2 teaspoons sugar
¼ teaspoon freshly ground
  black pepper

WILD MUSHROOMS, ONCE HIDDEN DEEP UNDER COMPOSTS OF OAK LEAVES, OR THRUSTING UP THROUGH SOIL IN SHADY PINE FORESTS, OR CLINGING TO ROTTING STUMPS, ARE NOW CONVENIENTLY PACKAGED AND SOLD IN THE PRODUCE SECTION OF MOST SUPERMARKETS. THIS BEAUTIFUL PHOTOGRAPH OF SHIITAKE, ENOKI, HONEY, BUTTON, CLOUD EARS, AND OYSTER MUSHROOMS SHOWS SOME OF THE CHOICES TO CONSIDER WHEN MAKING THE SALAD. AN EASY-TO-PREPARE DRESSING OF SESAME OIL, OYSTER SAUCE, AND GARLIC PERFECTLY ACCENTS THE VARYING TEXTURES OF THE MUSHROOMS.

ADVANCE PREPARATION Cut the button mushrooms into thin slices. Discard the stems from the shiitake mushrooms and cut the caps into eighths. Cut the dirty ends off the enoki mushrooms and separate the long stems. Cut the oyster mushrooms into quarters or eighths.

Peel the jicama. Cut into bite-size rectangles about ¼ inch thick. Cut the pepper into the same size pieces. Set aside the jicama, pepper, sprouts, and parsley.

Place the ginger and garlic in a food processor and mince fine. Add the remaining dressing ingredients and blend for 30 seconds.

LAST-MINUTE ASSEMBLING About 30 minutes before serving, toss the mushrooms in the dressing. Just before serving, stir in the jicama, pepper, sprouts, and parsley. Serve at once.

Serves: 4 to 6 as the salad course.

Menu Ideas: A quick dinner for 4—salmon filet marinated in soy sauce, lemon, and ginger, then steamed or broiled; Melrose Mushroom Salad; noodles tossed with olive oil and Parmesan cheese; fresh fruit.

OVERLEAF: *Ingredients for Melrose Mushroom Salad*

SPROUTING NOODLE SALAD

SALAD

½ pound dried spaghetti-style
    noodles, preferably
    Chinese
2 cups bean sprouts
2 ounces daikon sprouts
3 ounces alfalfa sprouts
3 tablespoons white sesame
    seeds

DRESSING

¼ cup red wine vinegar
2 tablespoons dark soy sauce
2 tablespoons Oriental
    sesame oil
1½ tablespoons sugar
1 teaspoon Chinese chili sauce
⅓ cup minced green onions
2 tablespoons finely minced
    fresh ginger

SALADS MAKE GREAT APPETIZERS. THEN, IF FRIENDS ARE DELAYED OR UN-FORESEEN EVENTS OCCUR IN THE KITCHEN, YOU'VE GOT READY A FAIRLY SUBSTANTIAL DISH TO ACCOMPANY BEFORE-DINNER DRINKS. SPROUTING NOODLE SALAD, WITH ITS ASSORTMENT OF CRUNCHY SPROUTS AND A SWEET-PUNGENT DRESSING FEATURING GINGER, CHILI, AND SESAME OIL, TICKLES THE PALATE IN ANTICIPATION OF LATER CULINARY SURPRISES. TO VARY THE TASTE, USE A DIFFERENT COMBINATION OF VEGETABLES, OR IN PLACE OF THIS DRESS-ING TOSS THE SALAD WITH SOUTH SEAS SALSA (PAGE 39), OR USE A DOUBLE PORTION OF THE PEANUT DRESSING FROM YUMMY YAM GAI (PAGE 61).

ADVANCE PREPARATION Bring 6 quarts of water to a rapid boil and add the noodles. When the noodles are still firm but no longer raw tasting in the center, tip into a colander. Rinse under cold water and drain thoroughly.

Set aside the bean and daikon sprouts. Pull the alfalfa sprouts apart. In a small ungreased skillet placed over high heat, toast the sesame seeds until golden, about 4 minutes. Immediately tip out and set aside. Combine the dressing ingredients and mix well. Toss the noodles with the dressing and then refrigerate. (The salad can be made up to this point hours ahead of serving.)

SERVING Just prior to serving, toss the noodles with the sprouts. Turn out onto a serving plate, sprinkle with the sesame seeds, and serve at once.

Serves: 3 as an entrée, or 4 to 6 as the salad course.

CHOPSTIX GLASS NOODLE SALAD

SALAD

8 ounces bean threads or
    rice sticks
1 cup shredded red cabbage
⅓ pound snow peas
1 sweet red pepper
3 ounces enoki mushrooms
3 ounces daikon sprouts, or
    other sprouts

DRESSING

2 tablespoons finely minced
    fresh ginger
2 cloves garlic
1 tablespoon grated or minced
    orange peel
¼ cup minced cilantro (fresh
    coriander)
¼ cup minced green onions
9 tablespoons red wine vinegar
¼ cup Oriental sesame oil
2 tablespoons safflower oil
1 tablespoon sugar
1 teaspoon Chinese chili sauce
1 teaspoon salt

I N BANGKOK, AFTER A DAY OF FRANTIC SILK SHOPPING, TEMPLE EXCURSIONS, AND THREE-WHEEL *TUK TUK* RIDES IN MASSIVE TRAFFIC JAMS, WE RETREATED TO THE TRANQUILITY OF LEMON GRASS RESTAURANT. THE ATMOSPHERE OF THE CHARMING OLD HOUSE, WITH ITS SOFT SHAPES OF POLISHED TEAK AND ECLECTIC BLEND OF EUROPEAN ANTIQUES AND ORIGINAL THAI ARTWORK SOOTHED OUR NERVES. AT A LONG TEAK TABLE, WE ENJOYED COURSE AFTER COURSE, EACH ACCENTED WITH THE BEAUTIFULLY BALANCED THAI SAUCES FOR WHICH THE RESTAURANT IS FAMOUS. THE LEMONGRASS CHICKEN, DUCK WITH GREEN CURRY SAUCE, CRISP THAI FRIED DUMPLINGS, AND THIS GLASS NOODLE SALAD, WHICH WE ADAPTED FOR THE CHOPSTIX MENU, FIRED OUR IMAGINATIONS FOR LATE-NIGHT ADVENTURES.

PREPARATION AND SERVING Soak the bean threads in hot water until soft, about 30 minutes. Drain thoroughly and then cut into 4-inch lengths. There should be 4 cups.

Shred the red cabbage into 2-inch lengths. Stem the snow peas, then drop into 2 quarts of boiling water. After 5 seconds, transfer the snow peas to a bowl with ice water. Chill, drain, pat dry, and then shred. Stem, seed, and sliver the pepper into 2-inch lengths. Discard the dirty ends of the mushrooms and separate the long stems. Set aside the daikon sprouts.

Mince the ginger and garlic in a food processor. Add the orange peel, cilantro, and green onions. Mince again, then add the remaining dressing ingredients and blend well.

To serve, combine the bean threads with the rest of the vegetables. Add the salad dressing and toss to mix evenly. (The salad can be marinated for up to 2 hours, after which the vegetables lose their crisp texture.)

Serves: 6 to 8 as the salad course.

Menu Ideas: An Asian picnic for 6—Chili Shrimp with Basil (cook the shrimp and make the dressing a day in advance); Smoked Baby Back Ribs with Chopstix Barbecue Sauce (make the barbecue sauce a week in advance); Chinese Sandwich Surprises (make the day of the picnic); Chopstix Glass Noodle Salad (soak the bean threads and make the dressing the day before the picnic). Accompany the picnic with iced tea and beer, and end by churning homemade ice cream in one of the portable ice cream machines available at most department stores and cookware shops.

TROPICAL PARADISE SALAD

SALAD

2 ripe avocados
Juice of 1 lemon or lime
(optional)
2 vine-ripened tomatoes or 1½
cups thinly sliced jicama
2 ripe mangoes, peaches,
nectarines, or papaya
2 tablespoons unsalted roasted
peanuts

DRESSING

2 tablespoons slivered basil
leaves
3 tablespoons lime juice
2 tablespoons fish sauce
1 tablespoon honey
½ teaspoon Chinese chili
sauce

FOR THIS AVOCADO, TOMATO, AND MANGO SALAD, ARTIST JEFF STILLWELL CREATED A SCENE THAT CAPTURES THE FEELING OF A THAI TROPICAL PARADISE. JEFF'S FREE-STANDING PAINTED PIECES OF FOAM-CORE BOARD CREATE A CURIOUS DISCREPANCY IN THE PERCEPTION OF DEPTH. IN THIS WORK, FLAT, PAINTED PIECES ARE CUT OUT AND STOOD UP TO CREATE A THREE-DIMENSIONAL ILLUSION. THE USE OF PAINTED SCENES IN A PHOTOGRAPH, CALLED MIXED MEDIA, IS A LIVELY PART OF THE LOS ANGELES ART SCENE TODAY.

PREPARATION AND SERVING Seed, peel, and thinly slice the avocados. If done ahead, squeeze a little lemon or lime juice over the avocado. Thinly slice the tomatoes. Peel the mangoes, then cut the flesh from the pit in large sections and slice thinly. Place the peanuts in a food processor and chop finely. Combine the dressing ingredients, stirring well.

On each salad plate, fan sections of avocado, tomato (or jicama), and mango. Spoon the dressing over the salad, sprinkle on the peanuts, and serve at once.

Serves: 4 to 6 as the salad course.

Menu Ideas: A tropical dinner for 6—South Seas Salsa with cooked chilled shrimp, Thai-High Barbecued Chicken, Champagne Rice Pilaf, Tropical Paradise Salad, and Lemon Ice Cream with Chocolate Grand Marnier Sauce.

Tropical Paradise Salad

ORIENTAL SHRIMP LOUIS SALAD

SALAD

½ pound raw medium shrimp
1 avocado
Juice of ½ lemon (optional)
4 cups bite-size pieces mixed salad greens
1 to 2 cups assorted vegetables (optional), such as mushrooms, red pepper, zucchini, cucumber, asparagus

DRESSING

½ cup mayonnaise
¼ cup heavy (whipping) cream
3 tablespoons lemon juice
1 tablespoon catsup
1 tablespoon small (nonpareil) capers
1½ teaspoons Chinese chili sauce
1 teaspoon Worcestershire sauce
¼ teaspoon freshly ground black pepper
¼ cup chopped green onions
1 tablespoon finely minced fresh ginger

AT A RESTAURANT NEAR KUTA BEACH, BALI, GRAY SMOKE FROM THE OPEN-AIR GRILLING SWIRLS AROUND MEMBERS OF A LOCAL DANCE TROUP AND OBSCURS THE IMAGE OF THE GIANT WINGED GARUDA (MYTHICAL BIRD) POISED IN THE BACKGROUND, THEN FINALLY DRIFTS HIGH INTO THE WOODEN RAFTERS. AT THE LONG BUFFET TABLE, WE HELPED OURSELVES TO GRILLED FISH WRAPPED IN BANANA LEAVES, STIR-FRIED RICE FLAVORED WITH TAMARIND AND PEANUTS, AND A "HILL AVOCADO SALAD" INCLUDING SHRIMP AND CHUNKS OF FIRM WHITE FISH TOSSED IN A DELICIOUS LOUIS-TYPE DRESSING. A LINE OF RIPE PAPAYA SLICES RAN DOWN ONE SIDE OF THE SALAD AND A COOKED LOBSTER CURLED AT THE EDGE OF THE PLATTER. THIS SALAD GOES WONDERFULLY WITH ANY BARBECUED MEAT OR SEAFOOD AND ONE OF THE SIDE DISHES FROM CHAPTER 6.

PREPARATION AND SERVING Shell the shrimp; cut in half lengthwise and rinse out the vein. Bring 2 quarts of water to a vigorous boil and add the shrimp. Shrimp are done when they turn white and curl, in about 2 minutes, but check by cutting a shrimp in half; it should be white in the center. Immediately tip into a colander and then transfer to a bowl of ice water. Chill, pat dry, and set aside.

Seed, peel, and thinly slice the avocado. If done more than 30 minutes prior to serving, squeeze a little lemon juice over the avocado. Set the salad greens aside. If adding other vegetables, cut them into bite-size pieces. Combine the dressing ingredients and mix well.

Place the salad ingredients in a large bowl. Add the dressing and toss. Serve at once.

Serves: 2 as a main course, or 4 to 6 as the salad course.

Menu Ideas: A quick dinner for 2—Oriental Shrimp Louis Salad, New Wave Garlic Bread, and a summer melon served with lime wedges.

YUMMY YAM GAI

SALAD

1 chicken, about 3 pounds, split in half
4 cups bite-size pieces mixed salad greens
1 cup slivered jicama
1 cup slivered hothouse cucumber
1 cup slivered carrots
½ cup chopped mint or basil leaves
1 lime, cut into wedges

DRESSING

4 small shallots, minced
4 cloves garlic, minced
½ cup peanut oil
5 tablespoons lime juice
¼ cup top quality peanut butter
¼ cup fish sauce
2 tablespoons honey
1 teaspoon Chinese chili sauce

TO SERVE

2 tablespoons olive oil

PYRAMIDS OF TENDER CHICKEN, CRISP JICAMA, JADE CUCUMBER, JULIENNE CARROTS, AND BABY LETTUCE GREENS FORM A DRAMATIC CONTRAST AGAINST BLACK OR ROSE-COLORED SALAD PLATES. GUESTS SPOON A LITTLE OF THE RICH PEANUT DRESSING OVER THE SALAD, SPRINKLE ON CHOPPED MINT OR BASIL, AND FINISH WITH A SQUEEZE OF LIME JUICE. YUMMY YAM GAI (LITERALLY, "SALAD CHICKEN"), IS A FUN WAY TO BEGIN A DINNER, FOLLOWED BY A SOUP OF SCALLOP BLOSSOM SURPRISE, CALIFORNIA CORNBREAD, AND CONCLUDING WITH ICE CREAM AND SLICED STRAWBERRIES. IF YOU WANT TO LESSEN LAST-MINUTE PREPARATION, THE DAY PRIOR TO THE DINNER MAKE THE SALAD DRESSING, SIMMER THE SCALLOPS IN CHICKEN BROTH, AND MAKE THE ICE CREAM.

ADVANCE PREPARATION Preheat the oven to 425°F. Place the chicken on a baking sheet lined with aluminium foil. The chicken does not need to be seasoned or rubbed with oil. Roast the chicken until the internal temperature is 165°F., about 30 minutes. The juices from the chicken should be clear when the meat is deeply pierced with a fork. Let the chicken cool, then discard the skin and bones and pull the meat into bite-size pieces. Set aside.

Set aside the salad greens, jicama, cucumber, carrots, mint and lime wedges.

Place the shallots, garlic, and peanut oil in a small skillet over medium heat. Cook until the oil sizzles and the garlic turns white (if garlic browns, discard and begin again). Immediately tip out of pan and let cool. Transfer to a food processor along with the remaining dressing ingredients and blend thoroughly. Keep the dressing at room temperature up to 1 day in advance; refrigerate if keeping longer.

SERVING To serve, toss the salad greens with 2 tablespoons olive oil, then arrange the greens on 4 salad plates. Top with the vegetables and chicken. Serve the dressing and herbs in little bowls. Each person spoons the dressing over the salad ingredients, sprinkles on basil or mint, and squeezes lime juice over the salad.

Serves: 4 as the salad course, or 2 as an entrée.

Crazy Caesar Salad

CRAZY CAESAR SALAD

SALAD

2 heads romaine lettuce

2 strips thin bacon

4 tablespoons unsalted butter

1 clove garlic, finely minced

1 cup stale bread cubes, in ½-inch cubes

1 sweet red pepper

¼ cup crushed unsalted roasted peanuts

2 teaspoons grated or finely minced lime peel

½ cup best-quality grated Parmesan cheese

DRESSING

½ cup extra-virgin olive oil

3 to 4 tablespoons lemon juice

Dash of Worcestershire sauce

Salt and freshly ground black pepper to taste

1 egg

THE GLASS PLATTER IN THE PHOTO, BY ARTIST KERRY FELDMAN, IS SO DRAMATIC AND PAINTERLY THAT IT INSPIRED THE COMPOSITION OF THE ENTIRE PHOTO.

KERRY USED A HAND-BLOWN GLASS TECHNIQUE FOR THIS PLATTER. THE UNUSUAL COLORS ARE ACHIEVED BY THE APPLICATION OF POWDERED GLASSES IN LAYERS AND SMALL PIECES OF HAND-BLOWN SHEET GLASS, WHICH HE MAKES. THE IMAGERY IS DERIVED FROM A SERIES HE HAS DONE ON DREAMS. THE ARTIST HAS A LOVE OF FUNCTIONAL OBJECTS, OF HAVING HIS BEAUTIFUL PIECES USED IN PEOPLE'S DAILY LIVES.

ADVANCE PREPARATION Pull off the large outer leaves of the romaine and set aside for another salad. Separate the tender interior leaves, then wash, dry, and set aside. Sauté the bacon until crisp or cook in the microwave; pat dry and chop finely. Melt the butter in a 12-inch skillet over medium-high heat, then add the garlic and sauté for a few seconds until the garlic sizzles; add the bread cubes and sauté until well browned, about 8 minutes. Remove the croutons from the pan, leaving the garlic in the pan.

Stem, core, and seed the pepper, then mince fine. Set aside the peanuts, lime peel, and Parmesan cheese.

LAST-MINUTE ASSEMBLING In a very large mixing bowl, position all the romaine leaves in the same direction. Gently toss the leaves with about half of the olive oil; add 3 tablespoons of the lemon juice and toss again. Add a dash of Worchestershire sauce and a little sprinkling of salt and pepper; toss again.

Add the remaining olive oil. Place the egg in rapidly boiling water to coddle and cook exactly 30 seconds. Momentarily chill the egg under cold water, then crack into a bowl, beat for a second with a fork, and pour onto the lettuce leaves. Gently toss the leaves again.

Sprinkle the bacon, croutons, pepper, peanuts, lime zest, and half of the cheese on top. Gently toss the lettuce leaves to evenly mix. Taste and adjust the seasonings, adding more oil and lemon juice if necessary.

Place the lettuce on 4 to 6 salad plates and sprinkle with the remaining Parmesan cheese. Serve at once.

Serves: 4 to 6 as the salad course.

Menu Ideas: Holiday dinner for 12—Crazy Caesar Salad (double the recipe); Scallop Ravioli in Saffron-Caviar Sauce (triple the recipe); steamed asparagus served with South Seas Salsa; Crystal Soup (triple the recipe); and Lemon Ice Cream with Chocolate Grand Marnier Sauce (double the recipe). Accompany the dinner with a fine Chardonnay.

SOUTH SEAS BEEF SALAD

SALAD
½ pound beef filet
2 teaspoons dark soy sauce
2 teaspoons hoisin sauce
2 teaspoons Oriental
    sesame oil
5 cups bite-size pieces mixed
    salad greens

DRESSING
1 clove garlic
2 tablespoons chopped basil
½ teaspoon grated or finely
    minced orange peel
3 tablespoons extra-virgin
    olive oil
2 tablespoons lime juice
1½ tablespoons light soy sauce
1 tablespoon honey
½ teaspoon Chinese chili
    sauce
½ teaspoon freshly grated
    nutmeg

TO SERVE
1 tablespoon extra-virgin
    olive oil

THE FLAVORS OF THIS SALAD EVOKE MEMORIES OF A DISH SERVED AT THE WATER GARDEN RESTAURANT, AT THE ROYAL TEMPLE IN MENGWI, BALI. WE SAT ON A VERANDAH OVERLOOKING THE ANCIENT CANAL AND WATCHED TWO OLD BOATMEN PULLING A SMALL PASSENGER FERRY ACROSS BY ROPES. THE ETHEREAL SOUNDS OF BALINESE INSTRUMENTAL MUSIC FILLED THE BACKGROUND AS WE GAZED ACROSS THE WATER AT THE LICHEN-COVERED STONE WALLS SURROUNDING THE HINDU TEMPLE. BITES OF SIZZLING BEEF PLACED ON A BED OF GREENS, AND MORE ORDERS OF *BIR SINGH*, INTENSIFIED OUR ANTICIPATION OF AN AFTERNOON VISIT TO THE MONKEY FOREST.

PREPARATION AND SERVING Trim all the fat from the beef. Cut the meat against the grain into ⅛-inch-thin slices, then cut the slices in half. Combine the soy sauce, hoisin sauce, and sesame oil, add the meat and marinate for at least 20 minutes. Refrigerate if marinating longer.

Set aside the salad greens.

Mince the garlic in a food processor. Add the basil and mince again. Add the remaining dressing ingredients and process until well blended, about 2 minutes.

If the meat has been refrigerated, return to room temperature. Arrange the salad greens on serving plates. Place a 10-inch skillet over high heat. When hot, add the remaining 1 tablespoon olive oil. When the oil just begins to smoke, add the beef and toss over high heat until the meat just loses its raw color on the outside, about 20 seconds. Immediately place the meat in the center of the salad greens. Stir the dressing and spoon a little on top of each plate of greens. Serve at once.

Serves: 2 as an entrée, or 4 to 6 as the salad course.

Menu Ideas: A casual dinner for 4: South Seas Beef Salad, Asian Avocado Adventure, Crazy Coconut Noodle Toss, and Ginger Chocolate Petit Pots. For this dinner, serve each dish as a separate course. The last-minute kitchen duties are so minimal that the menu is nearly as easy when done for 10 people.

GINGER SUMMER SALAD

SALAD
½ hothouse cucumber
1 avocado
Lemon juice
1 papaya, not overly ripe
1 small sweet red pepper

DRESSING
1 tablespoon finely minced
    fresh ginger
1 tablespoon minced cilantro
    (fresh coriander)
1 green onion, minced
3 tablespoons lime juice
2 tablespoons light brown
    sugar
1 tablespoon fish sauce
½ teaspoon Chinese chili
    sauce

THIS REFRESHING SUMMER SALAD IS A GOOD CHOICE ON A HOT SUMMER NIGHT, WHEN SERVED WITH AN ENTRÉE SUCH AS THAI-HIGH BARBECUED CHICKEN OR ASIAN BARBECUED SALMON. BECAUSE OF THE SOFT TEXTURE OF AVOCADO, FIRST COMBINE THE CUCUMBER, PAPAYA, AND RED PEPPER, TOSS WITH THE SALAD DRESSING, AND THEN GENTLY ADD THE AVOCADO.

AS AN APPETIZER, SERVE THIS SALAD IN INDIVIDUAL BOWLS. FOR A DINNER SALAD, MAKE A LITTLE ADDITIONAL DRESSING AND TOSS WITH MIXED SALAD GREENS; THEN ARRANGE THE GINGER SUMMER SALAD ON THE GREENS.

PREPARATION AND SERVING Peel, seed, and cut the cucumber into ½-inch cubes. Pit and scoop out the avocado, then cut into ½-inch cubes. Sprinkle with a little lemon juice and set aside. Peel, seed, and cut the papaya into ½-inch cubes. Stem, seed, and cut the red pepper into ½-inch cubes.

Combine the dressing ingredients and mix well.

In a large bowl, toss the cucumber, papaya, and pepper, then stir in the dressing. Add the avocado, toss gently, then transfer to 4 salad plates and serve at once.

Serves: 4 as a small dinner salad.

Thai Bouillabaisse

Chapter 3

NEW WAVE SOUPS

IT'S PARTY TIME! FRIENDS COMING OVER TONIGHT . . . GOT TO GET UP EARLY TO WASH ALL THE VEGETABLES . . . COMBINE THE SAUCES . . . HOURS OF SHELLING AND DEVEINING THE SHRIMP . . . FALLING BEHIND SCHEDULE . . . HAVEN'T EVEN STARTED TO MAKE THE CHOCOLATE MOUSSE . . . NO TIME FOR A SHOWER . . . TOO TIRED TO EAT . . . MOUNTAINOUS STACKS OF DIRTY PLATES . . . I HATE SERVING CHINESE FOOD! MONTHS PASS WITHOUT AN ASIAN INGREDIENT COMING OUT OF THE PANTRY.

INSTEAD, FOLLOW THE CHOPSTIX PHILOSOPHY: KEEP THE MENU SIMPLE, CHOOSE EASY RECIPES, AND DO MOST OF THE PREPARATION A DAY IN ADVANCE. FOR EXAMPLE, ANY OF THESE NEW WAVE SOUPS IS PERFECT AS THE MAIN DISH FOR A DINNER. BEGIN WITH AN EASY APPETIZER, THEN, AS THE ENTRÉE, SERVE GENEROUS PORTIONS OF SOUP ACCOMPANIED BY NEW WAVE GARLIC BREAD OR CALIFORNIA CORNBREAD; HAVE A SIMPLE GREEN SALAD AND CONCLUDE THE MEAL WITH A SINFUL SWEET. EASY COOKING, GREAT FOOD, AND PLENTY OF TIME FOR FRIENDS— THIS IS THE NEW WAVE OF ENTERTAINING.

THAI BOUILLABAISSE

2 tablespoons olive oil
4 cloves garlic, minced
2 shallots, minced
1 tablespoon finely minced
    fresh ginger
1 stalk lemongrass, cut into
    1–inch lengths (no leaves)
4 cups chicken broth
3 cups coconut milk
½ cup dry white wine
2 tablespoons fish sauce
1 teaspoon Chinese chili sauce
Large pinch of saffron
20 small mussels
½ pound medium shrimp
½ pound skinless salmon filet
½ pound vine-ripened
    tomatoes
2 tablespoons cornstarch
⅓ cup shredded fresh basil
Freshly grated nutmeg
Salt to taste

I N THE CHAPTER OPENING TRIPTYCHS, I TRIED TO CAPTURE THE SENSE OF MYSTERY THAT COMES FROM NOT BEING ABLE TO SEE THE WHOLE SCENE AT ONCE, AS WHEN VIEWING A JAPANESE FOLDING SCREEN. I WANTED TO DESIGN A SUCCESSFUL COMPOSITION IN WHICH EACH OF THE THREE PANELS WORKS SEPARATELY AS WELL AS TOGETHER. THESE TRIPTYCHS, WITH THEIR RATHER LIGHT AND AIRY PROPS AND BACKGROUNDS, GIVE ME THE SAME SENSE AS LOOKING AT SCENES IN SHOP WINDOWS, WHERE THE GLASS REFLECTS AND DISTORTS AN IMAGE IN INTERESTING WAYS.

ADVANCE PREPARATION Place a 4-quart saucepan over medium heat. Add the olive oil, garlic, shallots, ginger, and lemongrass. Sauté until the garlic sizzles and turns white, about 1 minute, then add the broth, coconut milk, wine, fish sauce, chili sauce, and saffron. Bring to a low boil, reduce the heat to low, and simmer for 30 minutes. Cool to room temperature and, if completed hours in advance, refrigerate the soup (up to 8 hours) in its saucepan.

Scrub the mussels, pulling away the beards from between the shells. Shell, devein, and split the shrimp in half. Cut the salmon into bite-size pieces. Set the seafood aside in separate containers.

Cut the tomatoes in half and squeeze out the seeds. Cut the flesh into slivers. Set aside.

LAST-MINUTE COOKING Bring the soup to a simmer. Transfer 2 cups of the soup liquid in a 3-quart saucepan and bring to a rapid boil. Add the mussels, cover, and cook until they open, about 5 minutes. Discard any mussels that do not open, then through a fine-meshed sieve, strain the liquid back into the soup. Reserve the mussels.

Bring the soup back to a low boil. Mix the cornstarch with an equal amount of cold water, then stir into the soup to thicken slightly. Add the shrimp, salmon, tomatoes, basil, and nutmeg. Simmer until salmon just begins to flake, about 1 minute. Taste and adjust the seasonings, particularly the nutmeg, chili sauce, and salt. Add the mussels still in their shells. Turn into a soup tureen or individual bowls. Serve at once.

Serves: 4 as an entrée, or 6 to 8 as the soup course.

HOMEMADE CHICKEN BROTH

3 pounds chicken wings
2 to 3 thin slices fresh ginger
   (optional)
Garlic skins from a few cloves
1 green onion (optional)

WHY BROIL TRAYS OF BEEF BONES, SEARCH THROUGHOUT THE CITY FOR PERFECTLY FRESH VEAL KNUCKLE BONES, OR LUG HOME POUNDS OF FISH HEADS FOR STOCK? MOST PEOPLE WILL NOT BE ABLE TO TELL THE SLIGHTEST DIFFERENCE WHEN A RECIPE CALLS FOR BEEF, VEAL, OR FISH STOCK, AND YOU SUBSTITUTE HOMEMADE CHICKEN BROTH. EVERYONE WILL APPLAUD JUST AS VIGOROUSLY.

A COUPLE OF TIMES A YEAR WE MAKE A BIG BATCH OF CHICKEN BROTH. AFTER A FEW HOURS OF GENTLE SIMMERING, WE PACKAGE THE BROTH IN SMALL PLASTIC BAGS AND TOSS THESE INTO THE FREEZER, WHERE THEY STAY UNTIL NEEDED. START WITH CHICKEN WINGS, PERHAPS AUGMENTED BY OTHER POULTRY AND PORK SCRAPS, AND SIMMER THEM IN A BIG POT SO THAT GRADUALLY THE BONE, MARROW, AND MEAT ESSENCES CREEP INTO THE LIQUID—NOW THAT'S A BROTH TO CURE THE COMMON COLD!

ADVANCE PREPARATION Rinse the chicken wings in cold water and drain. Place in a large stockpot. Add enough cold water to cover by 2 inches. Place over high heat and bring to a very low boil. Reduce the heat to low and skim off the foam that rises to the surface. Add the ginger, garlic skins, and green onion. Simmer the stock, partially covered, for 5 hours, periodically adding more water if necessary to keep up the level.

Pour the broth through a colander lined with a kitchen towel or dampened cheesecloth and discard the solids. The chicken meat will have no use because all the flavor will have escaped into the broth. Set the bowl aside and let the broth cool to room temperature before refrigerating.

After refrigerating the broth overnight, scrape off and discard the hard layer of fat on the surface. Because the broth is highly perishable, place 1-cup amounts of the jellied broth in plastic food bags and freeze. The broth can be thawed and refrozen repeatedly.

Makes: 3 quarts (12 cups) rich chicken broth.

ASIAN AVOCADO ADVENTURE

1½ cups seeded and chopped tomatoes, about 1 pound

1 cup chopped hothouse cucumber

1 ripe avocado

½ papaya, not overly ripe

1 green onion, minced

¼ cup chopped fresh mint

3 tablespoons chopped fresh basil

3 cloves garlic, minced

3 tablespoons lime juice

1 tablespoon fish sauce

1 teaspoon Chinese chili sauce

½ teaspoon salt

4 cups chicken broth

TO SERVE

¼ cup sour cream

WE LOVE SILLY, BIZARRE RECIPE TITLES AS A MEANS OF DISPELLING FOOD PRETENSION. BUT STRANGE MENU TITLES ARE NOT LIMITED TO TRENDY RESTAURANTS IN HOLLYWOOD. TRAVELING THROUGH SOUTHEAST ASIA YOU MIGHT CHOOSE SUCH MYSTERIOUS DISHES AS "BALI GRANNY", "KING CO-CONUT," "RUMBLE JUNGLE," "BEACH BEAUTY," OR, IF THERE IS A FLIGHT DELAY AT THE BANGKOK AIRPORT BUFFETERIA, WEARY PASSENGERS SOOTHED BY MARIACHI MUSIC CAN ORDER "JUNGLE CURRY" AND "MACARONI MIRACLE." AT YOUR OWN LUMBA-LUMBA GRILL TRY THIS "CHILLED ASIAN AVOCADO AD-VENTURE" WITH CRAZY CAESAR SALAD, THAI-HIGH BARBECUED CHICKEN, NEW WAVE GARLIC BREAD, AND STRAWBERRIES SIAM.

ADVANCE PREPARATION In a 6-cup bowl, add the tomatoes and cucumber. Pit the avocado, scoop out the flesh, and cut into bite-size pieces. Peel and seed the papaya, then cut into bite-size pieces. Add the avocado, papaya, green onion, mint, basil, garlic, lime juice, fish sauce, chili sauce, and salt to the bowl. If you are using homemade broth that becomes jellied when chilled, dilute the broth with a little water in which you have soaked a few dried black Chinese mushrooms. Stir in the broth, then refrigerate until thoroughly chilled. (This can be made a day in advance of serving.)

SERVING To serve, taste the soup and adjust the flavors of chili, lime, and salt. Ladle the soup into bowls and top each bowl with sour cream. Serve at once.

Serves: 2 as an entrée, or 4 as the soup course.

SCALLOP BLOSSOM SURPRISE

⅓ pound sea scallops
6 thin slices fresh ginger
6 cups chicken broth
2 green onions
1 sweet red pepper
12 sprigs cilantro (fresh
    coriander)
2 eggs
1 tablespoon dry sherry
Juice from ½ lemon
2 teaspoons Oriental
    sesame oil
¼ teaspoon freshly ground
    white pepper
About 1 teaspoon salt

YEARS AGO A SMALL BAND OF US TRAVELING THROUGH CHINA FOUND OUR WAY TO A FAMOUS SUZHOU ESTABLISHMENT, THE MOON IN VIEW RESTAURANT. ABOUT TO CLOSE FOR THE EVENING, THE MANAGEMENT CROWDED US AROUND A BIG CIRCULAR TABLE PUSHED UP AGAINST TALL WINDOWS FACING A BUSY STREET. OUR PRESENCE CREATED A SENSATION. FOR TWO HOURS THE GATHERING AUDIENCE OUTSIDE WATCHED OUR CHOPSTICKS FLASH. FRESH QUAIL ON WATER SPINACH, CRISP EEL IN CARAMELIZED SAUCE . . . THE PRESS OF BLUE CLOTHED BODIES CLOSE TO OUR CHAIRS . . . SUZHOU CARP ROLLS, STEWED TURTLE . . . FACES PRESSED FLAT AGAINST THE RESTAURANT WINDOWS . . . SWEET-AND-SOUR WHOLE FISH . . . TINY BABIES HELD HIGH BY MOTHERS TO VIEW THE "BARBARIANS" . . . SCALLOP BLOSSOM SOUP, SWEET BEAN PASTRIES, AND GIANT PEACHES . . . WAITERS PUSHING THROUGH THE CROWD TO DELIVER TALL CELADON-COLORED BOTTLES OF BEER . . . LATER, A WALK DOWN DARKENED SYCAMORE-LINED LANES TOWARD OUR BEDS, ENDED ANOTHER DAY OF CHINA SURPRISES.

THIS WAS THE SCALLOP SOUP WE FEASTED ON. THE SEA SCALLOPS ARE SIMMERED IN CHICKEN BROTH FOR 1 HOUR, WHICH CAUSES THEM TO BREAK APART INTO LITTLE TENDER THREADS—THAT'S THE SURPRISE!

ADVANCE PREPARATION Pull off and discard the muscle from each scallop. Combine the scallops, ginger, and broth. Bring to a low simmer, cover, and cook for 1 hour. Discard the ginger and press the scallops with the back of a fork in the soup so they break apart into little threads. Set aside.

Shred the green onions. Stem, seed, and chop the red pepper. Set both aside with the cilantro.

LAST-MINUTE ASSEMBLING Bring the broth to a low boil. Beat the eggs well, then stir 2 tablespoons of hot soup into the eggs to warm them. Pour the eggs in a thin stream into the soup stock, stirring where the eggs hit the hot liquid. Stir in the sherry, lemon juice, sesame oil, and white pepper. Add salt to taste.

Turn the soup into a tureen or individual bowls. Stir in the green onions, red pepper, and cilantro. Serve at once.

Serves: 2 as an entrée, or 4 to 6 as the soup course.

Menu Ideas: As a dinner for 4, serve Scallop Blossom Surprise with California Cornbread, a large dinner salad, and Calorie Cheesecake Counterattack.

MAGICAL SALMON SOUP

3 ounces skinless salmon filet
2 green onions
1 ounce shiitake mushrooms
2 teaspoons finely minced
    fresh ginger
2 tablespoons chopped fresh
    herbs, such as basil,
    thyme, or oregano
1 cup cooked brown rice
1 cup chicken broth
1 tablespoon extra-virgin
    olive oil
1½ teaspoons light soy sauce
1 teaspoon Oriental sesame oil
Salt and freshly ground black
    pepper to taste

FOR EXECUTIVES ON THE RUN, HARRIED HOMEMAKERS, OR ANYONE CHRON-
ICALLY BEHIND SCHEDULE, HERE'S A WAY TO CREATE A LITTLE MAGIC. THIS
QUICK ONE-DISH MEAL TAKES APPROXIMATELY 12 MINUTES FROM START TO
FINISH, YET THE DELICATE FLAVORS LEAVE A WONDERFUL LINGERING TASTE.
SOME OF THE VARIATIONS WE HAVE TRIED INCLUDE USING DIFFERENT TYPES
OF FISH OR SUBSTITUTING COOKED CHICKEN, REPLACING THE BROWN RICE
WITH COOKED NOODLES, AND EXPERIMENTING WITH DIFFERENT MIXES OF
CHOPPED FRESH HERBS.

PREPARATION AND SERVING Cut the salmon into bite-size pieces. Cut the
green onions on a diagonal into ½-inch pieces. Discard the mushroom
stems and thinly slice the caps. Place all the ingredients in a saucepan
and bring to a low simmer. Simmer for about 6 minutes. Or place the
soup ingredients in a 3-cup soup bowl and heat on HIGH in full-wattage
microwave oven until soup is piping hot, about 3 minutes. Serve at
once.

Serves: 1 for lunch or dinner.

Hot and Sour Sichuan Tomato Soup and New Wave Garlic Bread (recipe on page 147)

HOT AND SOUR
SICHUAN TOMATO SOUP

SOUP

1 large vine-ripened tomato
½ block bean curd
8 small button mushrooms
1 skinless, boneless chicken
    breast
1 cup slivered carrots
½ cup slivered green onions
6 cups chicken broth
2 eggs

SEASONING MIX

6 tablespoons red wine vinegar
1 tablespoon dark soy sauce
1 tablespoon Oriental
    sesame oil
1 teaspoon finely ground white
    pepper
1 teaspoon salt
½ teaspoon Chinese chili
    sauce

TO THICKEN

2 tablespoons cornstarch

HOT AND SOUR SOUP, WITH ITS THICK BLEND OF TOFU, STRIPS OF TENDER MEAT, AND RIBBONS OF EGG FLOWERS, ALL ACCENTED WITH PEPPER AND VINEGAR, IS ONE OF THE WORLD'S GREAT SOUPS. EXCEPT FOR STIRRING IN THE EGG AND CORNSTARCH THICKENER, THE SOUP CAN BE MADE A DAY IN ADVANCE AND SIMPLY BE REHEATED FOR SERVING.

BECAUSE EVERYONE'S TASTES DIFFER, GO LIGHTLY ON THE SEASONINGS, AND INSTEAD ACCOMPANY THE SOUP WITH A WHITE PEPPER GRINDER OR A LITTLE BOWL OF CHINESE CHILI SAUCE, AS WELL AS A PITCHER OF RICE VINEGAR SO EACH PERSON CAN ADJUST THE SPICY AND SOUR TASTE. AS FOREHEADS REDDEN AND PERSPIRE, SERVE A MILD DISH SUCH AS CHOPSTIX NOODLE MAGIC AND LOTS OF TSING TAO BEER.

ADVANCE PREPARATION Cut the tomato in half and squeeze out the seeds. Sliver the flesh. Cut the bean curd into bite-size pieces. Very thinly slice the mushrooms. Cut the chicken breast into very thin bite-size pieces. Set aside the carrots and the green onions. Separately set aside the broth and the eggs. In a small bowl, combine the seasoning mix.

COOKING Bring the broth to a low boil. Add the chicken and give the soup a vigorous stir to separate the meat. Add the vegetables, bean curd, and seasoning mix. Combine the cornstarch with an equal amount of cold water. Bring the soup back to a low boil and stir in the cornstarch mixture. Beat the eggs well and add 2 tablespoons of hot soup to the eggs to warm them, then slowly pour the eggs into the soup while beating with a fork as they hit the hot broth. Remove from the heat and adjust for salt, spice, and tartness. Except for adding the eggs and cornstarch thickener, the soup can be made several hours in advance and reheated. Turn into a soup tureen or individual bowls and serve.

Serves: 4 as an entrée, or 6 to 8 as the soup course.

Menu Ideas: An easy dinner for 4—Asian Barbecued Salmon, Hot and Sour Sichuan Tomato Soup, Chopstix Noodle Magic, and a fruit tart for dessert.

CHOPSTIX CRAB MISO SOUP

1 (2-pound) Dungeness crab,
    cooked, cracked, and
    cleaned
3 cloves garlic
2 shallots
2 tablespoons olive oil
5 cups chicken broth
5 thin slices fresh ginger
1 block bean curd
2 cups broccoli florets
1 tablespoon cornstarch
¼ teaspoon freshly ground
    white pepper
½ cup white miso
Salt to taste

MANY OF THE SOUPS IN THIS CHAPTER MAKE A PERFECT ENTRÉE, AND THIS ONE IS NO EXCEPTION. BY SIMPLY REHEATING THE SOUP AND STIRRING IN THE CRABMEAT, BROCCOLI, AND MISO, THE DISH IS READY TO COME TO THE TABLE IN INDIVIDUAL SOUP BOWLS OR A SOUP TUREEN. A GREAT DINNER WITH A MINIMUM AMOUNT OF LAST-MINUTE FUSS WOULD BE CRAZY COCONUT NOODLE TOSS TO BEGIN, THEN ON TO A GENEROUS SERVING OF CHOPSTIX CRAB MISO SOUP, FOLLOWED BY CRUNCHY BAJA SALAD AND, AS A GREAT CONCLUSION, ORANGE GINGER BROWNIES WITH COCONUT CREAM.

ADVANCE PREPARATION Remove the meat from the crab in large pieces and set aside. Save the shell.

Mince the garlic and shallots. Place a 3-quart saucepan over medium heat, then add the olive oil, garlic, and shallots. Sauté until the garlic turns white, about 1 minute, then add the broth, ginger, and crab shells. Simmer, uncovered, for 30 minutes.

Strain the broth through a dampened cheesecloth or kitchen towel. Discard the shells and ginger slices. Let the broth cool to room temperature, then refrigerate (up to 1 day).

Drain the bean curd and cut into bite-size pieces. Set aside broccoli.

LAST-MINUTE ASSEMBLING Combine the cornstarch with an equal amount of cold water and set aside.

Bring the broth to a simmer, then add the broccoli, bean curd, and pepper. Bring the soup to a low boil and stir in the cornstarch mixture to thicken slightly. Combine the miso with 1 cup of the hot broth and mix with a fork until blended. Remove the soup from the heat and stir in the miso. Let the soup rest for 2 minutes, then add the crab meat. Taste the soup and adjust for salt and pepper. Turn into a soup tureen or individual bowls, and serve at once.

Serves: 2 to 4 as an entrée, or 6 to 8 as the soup course.

PACIFIC STOCK EXCHANGE

DUMPLINGS

1 tablespoon finely minced
fresh ginger
½ cup minced carrots
2 green onions, minced
½ pound raw shrimp, shelled
and deveined
1 egg white
1 tablespoon light soy sauce
2 teaspoons cornstarch
24 won ton skins

SOUP MIX

1 cup thinly sliced fresh
mushrooms
½ cup shredded carrots
Shredded green onions or
sprigs of cilantro (fresh
coriander), as garnish
½ block bean curd
6 cups chicken broth
1 tablespoon light soy sauce
1 tablespoon Oriental sesame
oil
2 tablespoons cornstarch
Salt and freshly ground white
pepper to taste

THE TRADITIONAL CANTONESE FLAVOR OF THIS SOUP CAN BE QUICKLY MODIFIED BY REPLACING 2 CUPS OF THE BROTH WITH COCONUT MILK, A SQUEEZE OF LIME JUICE, A STALK OF LEMONGRASS CUT INTO 1-INCH LENGTHS, AND CHILI SAUCE OR SHREDDED FRESH RED CHILIES. WHETHER YOU MAKE THIS MODIFICATION OR NOT, WON TON SOUP IS EXCELLENT WITH THE ADDITION OF ¼ POUND DRIED NOODLES, COOKED, DRAINED, RINSED, AND THEN STIRRED INTO THE SOUP. OR, IF YOU ADD CHINESE ROAST DUCK, BARBECUED MEAT, OR SMOKED CHICKEN THE SOUP GAINS ANOTHER COMPLEX ENRICHMENT. A WON TON SOUP COMBINING ALL THESE MODIFICATIONS MIGHT BE CALLED SPICY THAI COCONUT WON TON SOUP WITH LIME, LEMONGRASS, CHILIES, NOODLES, AND ROAST DUCK!

ADVANCE PREPARATION Combine the ginger, carrots, and green onions in a mixing bowl. Place the shrimp and egg white in a food processor and mince. Add to the bowl along with the soy sauce and cornstarch. Mix thoroughly. Fill the won ton skins and fold the dumplings as described on page 27.

Prepare the soup mix. Set aside the mushrooms, carrots and green onions or cilantro. Cut the bean curd into bite-size pieces. In a bowl, combine the broth, soy sauce, and sesame oil.

LAST-MINUTE ASSEMBLING Bring the broth to a simmer and add the bean curd. Bring 6 quarts of water to a rolling boil, and add the won tons; stir gently. As soon as the won tons float to the surface, in about 2 minutes, transfer to the broth. Bring the broth to a low boil and add the mushrooms and carrots. Mix the cornstarch with an equal amount of cold water, then stir into the soup.

Remove the soup from the stove. Add the salt and pepper to taste. Turn into a soup tureen or individual bowls, and garnish with the green onions or cilantro. Serve at once.

Serves: 4 as an entrée, or 6 to 8 as the soup course.

Menu Ideas: A dumpling festival dinner for 8—Thai Fried Dumplings, Pacific Stock Exchange, and as a light entrée Scallop Ravioli in Saffron Caviar Sauce with a simple green salad.

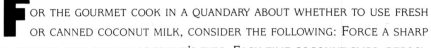

COCONUT CURRY SOUP EXPLOSION

¼ pound *soba* noodles, or
    dried thin spaghetti
2 teaspoons cooking oil
3 cups coconut milk
2 cups chicken broth
1 stalk lemongrass, cut into 1-
    inch lengths (no leaves)
4 thin slices fresh galangal
    (laos) or ginger
3 tablespoons fish sauce
1 to 2 tablespoons curry
    powder
2 teaspoons grated or finely
    minced lime peel
2 tablespoons lime juice
4 hot red chilies, seeded and
    slivered, or 2 teaspoons
    Chinese chili sauce
4 skinless, boneless chicken
    breast halves
1 tablespoon Oriental
    sesame oil
8 button mushrooms
Salt to taste
Sprigs of cilantro (fresh
    coriander), for garnish

FOR THE GOURMET COOK IN A QUANDARY ABOUT WHETHER TO USE FRESH OR CANNED COCONUT MILK, CONSIDER THE FOLLOWING: FORCE A SHARP SKEWER INTO ONE OF COCONUT'S EYES. EACH TIME COCONUT SLIPS, REPOSITION AND TRY AGAIN. PLACE COCONUT IN 325°F. OVEN FOR 15 MINUTES. JUGGLING HOT COCONUT, RACE OUTSIDE TO DRIVEWAY. SMASH COCONUT DOWN AND DART ABOUT, RETRIEVING AS MANY PIECES AS POSSIBLE. (DO THIS VERY EARLY IN THE MORNING TO ESCAPE OBSERVING EYES.) NEXT, WITH A STURDY SCREWDRIVER, PRY HARD SHELL AWAY FROM MEATY WHITE INTERIOR. AFTER STRUGGLING 1 HOUR, DISCARD REMAINING PIECES. NOW TAKE A POTATO PEELER AND SLOWLY REMOVE THE BLACK SKIN ON EACH COCONUT FRAGMENT. BANDAGE YOUR FINGERS AS CUTS OCCUR. CHOP COCONUT IN FOOD PROCESSOR. ADD HOT WATER AND CHOP AGAIN. TIP INTO A CLEAN TOWEL AND SQUEEZE OUT COCONUT MILK. WASH, DRY, AND FOLD TOWEL. THROW RECIPE AWAY. OR PROCEED USING CANNED COCONUT MILK.

ADVANCE PREPARATION Bring 5 quarts of water to a rapid boil. Add the noodles and cook until just tender in the center, about 5 minutes. Immediately drain, rinse with cold water, and drain again. Mix in the cooking oil and set aside.

In a 3-quart saucepan, combine the coconut milk, broth, lemongrass, galangal or ginger, fish sauce, curry powder, lime peel and juice, and chilies or chili sauce. Set aside.

Cut the chicken into very thin bite-size pieces, then mix with the sesame oil. Thinly slice the mushrooms and set aside.

LAST-MINUTE COOKING Bring the soup to a simmer and cook over low heat for 20 minutes. Add the chicken and stir gently with a spoon to separate the pieces. Then add the mushrooms, noodles and salt. Turn into a soup tureen or individual bowls and garnish with cilantro sprigs. Serve at once.

Serves: 4 as an entrée, or 6 to 8 as the soup course.

Menu Ideas: Thai Chopstix dinner for 8—Spicy Marinated Mussels; Yummy Yam Gai, Coconut Curry Explosion (use ½ pound thinly sliced sea bass in place of chicken); Flower Blossom Squid served with steamed white rice; and Mango Ice Cream with Tequila Sauce.

For a fun variation on this recipe, pass small bowls of freshly grated coconut, minced green onion, minced cilantro, wedges of lime, and chili sauce so guests can create their own flavor combinations.

Coconut Curry Soup Explosion

CRYSTAL SOUP

6 cups chicken broth
⅓ pound skinless salmon filet
2 ounces enoki mushrooms
6 to 8 sprigs of basil, mint, or
  cilantro (fresh coriander)
2 teaspoons Oriental
  sesame oil
Salt to taste
⅛ teaspoon freshly ground
  white pepper

WITH ITS PAPER-THIN SLICES OF SALMON AND THREADS OF ENOKI MUSH-
ROOMS, THIS CLEAR SOUP IS BEST APPRECIATED AS A PERFECT INTER-
MISSION BETWEEN THE ENTRÉE AND A RICH DESSERT.

PREPARATION AND SERVING Set aside the broth. Thinly slice the salmon into
bite-size pieces. Discard the mushroom ends and separate the long
stems. Set the basil aside.

In each bowl, place a few slices of salmon, a few mushrooms, and
some basil. Bring the broth to a low simmer and add the sesame oil.
Add the salt and pepper, adjusting to taste. Ladle the broth into bowls
and serve at once.

Serves: 6 as the soup course.

Menu Ideas: A dinner for 6—Danny Kaye Shrimp (complete the preparation a day in advance); Crazy Coconut Noodle Toss (prepare the day of
the dinner); Tropical Paradise Salad (make the dressing several days
ahead); Crystal Soup (make the broth weeks in advance and freeze);
and Chopstix Tart with Raspberry Cabernet Sauvigon Sauce (make the
tart and sauce a day in advance).

THREE MUSHROOM SOUP

½ pound small fresh button
    mushrooms
¼ pound fresh shiitake
    mushrooms
¼ pound fresh chanterelle
    mushrooms
1 bunch chives
2 cloves garlic, minced
1 tablespoon finely minced
    fresh ginger
2 shallots, minced
8 tablespoons (1 stick)
    unsalted butter
6 cups chicken broth
¼ cup dry sherry
1 tablespoon Oriental
    sesame oil
¼ teaspoon white pepper
2 tablespoons cornstarch
salt to taste

THIS RICH-TASTING MUSHROOM SOUP IS EXCELLENT AS THE MAIN DISH ACCOMPANIED BY A GREEN SALAD AND A HEARTY DARK BREAD. VARIATIONS WE HAVE ENJOYED INCLUDE SUBSTITUTING DIFFERENT TYPES OF MUSHROOMS SUCH AS FRESH ENOKI OR FRESH OR DRIED MORELS AND PORCINI MUSHROOMS, ADDING THINLY SLICED LEFTOVER COOKED MEAT JUST TO REHEAT, OR TRANSFORMING THE SOUP INTO A MORE SUBSTANTIAL DISH BY STIRRING IN 3 CUPS OF COOKED PASTA. HOWEVER YOU MAKE THIS RECIPE, SAUTÉ THE MUSHROOMS WITH THE TOTAL AMOUNT OF BUTTER CALLED FOR, SINCE THIS CONTRIBUTES A WONDERFUL RICHNESS TO THE SOUP WITHOUT ANY HINT OF OILINESS; ALSO, SAUTÉ THE MUSHROOMS UNTIL ALL THE MOISTURE EVAPORATES, WHICH HEIGHTENS THE MUSHROOM TEXTURE AND INTENSIFIES THE FLAVOR.

PREPARATION AND COOKING Wipe the mushrooms with a damp cloth. Cut the button mushrooms into ⅛-inch slices. Discard the shiitake stems, and cut the caps into ¼-inch-wide strips. Cut the chanterelle mushrooms into spoon-size pieces, ⅛ inch thick.

Cut the chives into 1-inch lengths and set aside. Mince and combine the garlic, ginger, and shallots.

Use a sauté pan that has an 8- to 10-inch diameter and place over medium-high heat. Add the butter, garlic, ginger, and shallots. Sauté until the butter melts and the garlic sizzles, and then add the mushrooms. Sauté the mushrooms over medium-high heat until they soften and all the moisture evaporates, about 10 minutes.

Add the broth, sherry, sesame oil, and white pepper. Combine the cornstarch with an equal amount cold water, and stir this into the soup. Taste and adjust seasonings (with homemade broth I add about 1½ teaspoons salt). Stir in the chives, and serve at once.

Serves: 2 as the entrée, or 6 as the soup course.

Steamed Lobster with Oriental Butter Enrichments

Chapter 4

SEAFOOD AND MEATS: SIZZLING AND SMOKING

COOKING IS A JOYFUL, EDIBLE ART, EMBUED WITH THE SPIRIT OF CREATING AND THE GIFT OF SHARING. THE BEAUTIFUL FOODS USED IN THIS CHAPTER—SUCH AS LOBSTER, VEAL, LAMB, AND SALMON—ARE MATCHED WITH ASIAN SEASONINGS TO ACHIEVE FRESH, INNOVATIVE FLAVORS AND COLORS. COMBINATIONS OF TROPICAL INGREDIENTS GIVE A SPECIAL TASTE TO GRILLED TUNA, ADD AN EXCITING CONTRAST TO CRISP SOUTHERN FRIED CHICKEN, FORM A CARAMEL GLAZE AROUND BRAISED RABBIT, AND BECOME A CRUSTY SURPRISE ON BUTTERFLIED LEG OF LAMB.

NOWHERE IN THIS BOOK ARE SUCH DIVERSE ASIAN INGREDIENTS MATCHED SO OFTEN WITH FOODS THOUGHT OF AS TRADITIONALLY AMERICAN AS IN THIS CHAPTER. USING THESE RECIPES AS A GUIDELINE, TRY INVENTING YOUR OWN CROSS-CULTURAL ACCENTS TO EVERYDAY FOOD: ADD FRESH BASIL AND HOT CHILIES TO A BUBBLING POT ROAST; BROIL SOLE RUBBED WITH A DASH OF OYSTER SAUCE, SESAME OIL, AND GRINDS OF SICHUAN PEPPER; AND SAUTÉ SHIITAKE MUSHROOM CAPS IN BUTTER, THEN PLACE THEM ON CHARBOILED HAMBURGERS SANDWICHED BETWEEN TOASTED SESAME-SEED BUNS.

STEAMED LOBSTER WITH ORIENTAL BUTTER ENRICHMENTS

STEAMING LIQUID

½ cup dry white wine
4 thin slices fresh ginger
1 teaspoon *fines herbes*
10 basil leaves
10 sprigs cilantro (fresh coriander)
2 green onions
1 carrot, cut into 1-inch pieces
Salt and pepper

LEMON-GINGER BUTTER

½ cup unsalted butter, at room temperature
2 tablespoons finely minced fresh ginger
2 tablespoons finely minced fresh chives
4 teaspoons grated or finely minced lemon peel
½ teaspoon freshly ground black pepper
½ teaspoon Chinese chili sauce
¼ teaspoon salt

CILANTRO-BASIL BUTTER

½ cup unsalted butter, at room temperature
3 cloves garlic, finely minced
¼ cup finely minced cilantro (fresh coriander)
¼ cup finely minced basil leaves
½ teaspoon freshly ground black pepper

LOBSTER

2 live lobsters, 1½ pounds each
Salt and freshly ground pepper
Lemon wedges

WHEN MAKING THIS PHOTOGRAPH, I REMOVED THE LOBSTER FROM ITS SERVING CONTEXT TO CONCENTRATE ON ITS INTERESTING SHAPE, RICH COLOR, AND UNUSUAL BEAUTY. BY PLACING THE LOBSTER ON THE PLEXIGLAS TABLE LIGHTED FROM BOTH BELOW AND ABOVE, AND BY SURROUNDING IT WITH ONLY THE GLASS CANDLESTICKS, THE ODDLY CUT ENRICHED BUTTERS, AND SPRAYS OF HERBS, THE LOBSTER SEEMS TO BE WALKING ON THE SANDY OCEAN BOTTOM OF A MEDITERRANEAN SEA LITTERED WITH ARTIFACTS.

ADVANCE PREPARATION In a 12-quart saucepan, place the wine, ginger, *fines herbes*, basil, cilantro, green onions, carrot, a sprinkling of salt and pepper, and 2 cups of water. Bring to a low boil, reduce the heat to a simmer, cover, and cook for 20 minutes, then set aside.

Place the ingredients for each flavored butter in a food processor and process until thoroughly blended. Transfer each to a small container and refrigerate. Or form the butter into a ½-inch-thick block. Refrigerate, then cut the butter into whimsical shapes.

LAST-MINUTE COOKING Bring the simmering liquid to a rapid boil over highest heat. Add the lobsters, head first, and cover the pot tightly. Cook for 8 minutes, then remove the lobsters and cool for 5 minutes. Using a sturdy knife or poultry shears, cut the lobsters in half lengthwise. Crack the claws. Place each lobster on a heated dinner platter and season with salt and pepper. Accompany with the flavored butters and the lemon wedges. Eat at once.

Serves: 2 as the entrée.

Menu Ideas: Dinner for 4 friends newly reunited—Asian Red Pepper Salad (double the recipe), Steamed Lobster with Oriental Butter Enrichments (double the recipe), Champagne Rice Pilaf, and Coconut Flan Supreme.

SALMON MOUSSE IN BLACK-BEAN BUTTER SAUCE

MOUSSE

2 teaspoons finely minced
  fresh ginger
½ pound salmon filet,
  trimmed of all gray flesh
  and cut into 1-inch cubes
1 egg white
½ teaspoon salt
½ teaspoon Chinese chili
  sauce
1½ cups heavy (whipping)
  cream, very cold

SAUCE

1 tablespoon salted black
  beans
2 cloves garlic, finely minced
½ cup chicken broth
2 tablespoons dry sherry
1 tablespoon Oriental
  sesame oil
½ teaspoon sugar
⅛ teaspoon freshly ground
  white pepper

TO FINISH

1 tablespoon cornstarch
3 tablespoons unsalted butter
1 bunch chives, minced

THIS RECIPE IS A GOOD EXAMPLE OF HOW EXCITING NEW FLAVORS CAN BE ACHIEVED BY DRAWING ON TECHNIQUES FROM DIFFERENT CUISINES. THE SALMON MOUSSE, SPICED WITH FRESH GINGER AND A HINT OF CHILI SAUCE, IS STEAMED AND SERVED ON A PLATE GLAZED WITH A CLASSIC CANTONESE BLACK-BEAN SAUCE THAT HAS HAD SWEET BUTTER SWIRLED INTO IT. THE INTENSE SALMON FLAVOR, THE ETHEREAL TEXTURE OF THE MOUSSE, AND THE SILKY TASTE OF THE SAUCE CREATE A MAGICAL COMBINATION.

ADVANCE PREPARATION In a food processor place the ginger, salmon cubes, egg white, salt, and chili sauce. Purée until the mixture is completely smooth, then place the processor bowl in the refrigerator for 2 hours or in the freezer for 30 minutes.

Return the processor bowl to the machine, turn the machine on, and slowly pour the chilled cream down the feed tube in a thin stream. Scrape the sides of the processor and blend again until the mixture is completely homogeneous. You should have approximately 2¾ cups.

Generously grease 8 small (¼-cup) molds. Spoon the salmon mixture into the molds, then refrigerate for up to 8 hours.

Make the sauce. Place the black beans in a small sieve and rinse under cold water. Press out the excess water and chop coarsely. Add the garlic and set aside. In small bowl, combine the broth, sherry, sesame oil, sugar, and pepper; set aside.

LAST-MINUTE COOKING Bring the water to a rapid boil in a Chinese steamer. Place the molds on a steamer tray, cover the steamer, and steam for 10 minutes. The salmon is cooked when a knife inserted in the mousse comes out clean.

Combine the cornstarch with an equal amount of cold water. Set aside. Put 2 tablespoons of the butter in a small saucepan or skillet placed over medium-high heat. When the butter begins to sizzle, add the black beans and garlic. Sauté until the garlic sizzles, then add the rest of the sauce. Bring to a low boil, then stir in enough cornstarch mixture to lightly thicken the sauce. Remove from the heat and stir in the remaining tablespoon of butter until absorbed by the sauce.

Invert the salmon molds onto salad plates. Spoon the sauce so it surrounds each mousse. Sprinkle chives across the sauce. Serve at once.

Serves: 8 as a light first course, or 4 as a very rich entrée.

Menu Ideas: Champagne lunch for 4 served on the terrace—first course of Salmon Mousse in Black-Bean Butter Sauce, followed by Tropical Paradise Salad and Thai-High Barbecued Chicken (served hot or at room temperature), and for dessert, Lemon Ice Cream.

THAI SAUTÉED SHRIMP

1 pound raw medium shrimp
2 tablespoons cooking oil
4 cloves garlic, minced
3 small fresh hot chilies,
    minced
¼ cup chopped fresh basil
¼ cup chopped fresh mint
2 teaspoons lime zest
Juice from 1 lime
1 tablespoon fish sauce
2 teaspoons light brown sugar
½ teaspoon cornstarch

WELCOME TO BANGKOK—CITY OF *KLONGS* AND *WATS*, MODERN OFFICE BUILDINGS AND ANCIENT RUINS, SAFFRON-ROBED MONKS AND BUSY EXECUTIVES, GLEAMING SPIRES OF ROYAL BUILDINGS AND TIN SHACKS LINING WATER HYACINTH—CHOKED WATERWAYS, AND TERMINAL TRAFFIC GRIDLOCK—PLEASURE CAPITAL OF THE WORLD. OUR THREE-WHEELED *TUK TUK*, DECORATED WITH ORCHID GARLANDS AND ORNATE TIN MOLDING, SLIPPED BETWEEN DENTED TAXIS, RACED PAST DIESEL-BELCHING TRUCKS, AND DARED PEDESTRIANS TO CROSS SILOM ROAD. MOMENTS LATER, SHIELDED FROM THE CITY CHAOS BY A HIGH GARDEN WALL AT THANYING RESTAURANT, WE FEASTED ON A SPICY SEAFOOD SOUP, CHICKEN CURRY WITH GREEN EGGPLANT, TINY SPRING ROLLS WRAPPED WITH LETTUCE, AND FRESHWATER PRAWNS SAUTÉED WITH HERBS, CHILI, AND FISH SAUCE. AS A DINNER FOR TWO, CRAZY COCONUT NOODLE TOSS IS A GOOD ACCOMPANIMENT FOR THIS SHRIMP DISH.

ADVANCE PREPARATION Shell the shrimp, cut in half lengthwise, and rinse out the vein. Set aside.

Combine cooking oil with the garlic and minced chilies. Mince the basil with the mint, then set aside. In a small bowl, combine the lime zest, lime juice, fish sauce, brown sugar, and cornstarch.

LAST-MINUTE COOKING Place a 12-inch skillet over highest heat. When very hot, add the cooking oil with garlic and chilies; then sauté for 15 seconds. Add the shrimp and sauté over highest heat until the shrimp turn white, about 2 minutes. Add the herbs and cook for 15 seconds more. Stir in the lime juice mixture. Taste and adjust the seasonings. Serve at once.

Serves: 2 as the entrée.

Thai Sautéed Shrimp

GRILLED TUNA IN GINGER-CILANTRO BUTTER SAUCE

FISH

4 tuna filets, 6 ounces each
Marinade from Asian
**   Barbecued Salmon (page**
**   92)**

SAUCE

⅔ cup dry white wine
¼ cup white wine vinegar
1 tablespoon finely minced
**   fresh ginger**
1 small shallot, minced
1 cup unsalted butter, at room
**   temperature**
1 teaspoon grated or minced
**   lemon peel**
¼ cup finely minced cilantro
**   (fresh coriander)**
¼ teaspoon or more freshly
**   ground white pepper**
¼ teaspoon salt

WHEN WE DECIDED TO INCLUDE A PHOTOGRAPH OF GRILLED FISH IN THE BOOK, WE WANTED TO CAPTURE THE SURPRISE AND ADVENTURE THAT ARE SO IMPORTANT TO THE FLAVOR EXPERIENCE OF THIS RECIPE. TO DO THIS, THE DISH HAS BEEN TAKEN OUT OF ITS NORMAL CONTEXT AND IS SEEN FLOATING IN THE WAVES OF JEFF STILLWELL'S OCEAN SET. I PLACED THE CAMERA CLOSE TO THE PLATE AT A LOW ANGLE, AND ADDED A SUNNY SIDE LIGHT TO ACCENT THE LOOSELY ARRANGED BABY VEGETABLES AND TO FRAME THE TUNA STEAK WITH ITS UNUSUAL SAUCE.

ADVANCE PREPARATION Marinate the tuna in the marinade for 1 hour. Drain and reserve the marinade.

In a small noncorrosive saucepan, place the wine, vinegar, ginger, and shallot. Bring to a rapid boil over high heat and cook until just 4 tablespoons remain. Set aside. Cut the butter into 16 pieces and set aside.

LAST-MINUTE COOKING If using a gas barbecue, preheat to medium (350°F). If using charcoal or wood, prepare the fire. When the coals or wood are ash covered, place the fish in a grilling basket. Grill the fish over medium-high heat until it just begins to flake, about 8 minutes. Turn once during barbecuing and brush with the reserved marinade. Transfer the fish to heated dinner plates or a serving platter.

Bring the wine-vinegar sauce to a rapid boil over medium-high heat, then add the butter all at once and beat vigorously with a whisk. When just a few lumps of butter remain (about 20 seconds after adding), pour the sauce into a bowl. Stir in the lemon peel, cilantro, pepper, and salt. Taste and adjust seasoning adding more pepper if necessary. Spoon the sauce around the fish and serve at once.

Serves: 4 as an entrée.

Menu Ideas: Easter lunch for 8—Firecracker Dumplings, Rainbow Salad with Raspberry Vinegar, Grilled Tuna in Ginger-Cilantro Butter Sauce (double recipe), Wild Chinese Rice (double recipe), and Painted Coconut Cream with Fresh Berries. Accompany lunch with a white wine such as a Sauvignon Blanc or Champagne.

Grilled Tuna in Ginger-Cilantro Butter Sauce

Ingredients for Crab with Lemongrass and Basil

CRAB WITH
LEMONGRASS AND BASIL

CRAB

1 3-pound Dungeness crab,
    cracked and cleaned (yield
    about ½ pound crabmeat)
4 ounces oyster mushrooms
1 sweet red pepper or small
    fresh red chili
1 cup slivered basil leaves
2 cups bean sprouts
2 tablespoons finely minced
    fresh ginger
2 cloves garlic, minced
1 tablespoon minced
    lemongrass stem
    (optional)
2 tablespoons (¼ stick) butter
2 tablespoons cooking oil
2 ounces rice sticks
oil for deep-frying

SAUCE

4 tablespoons chicken broth
4 tablespoons dry sherry
2 tablespoons oyster sauce
2 teaspoons lemon zest
¼ teaspoon sugar
¼ teaspoon freshly ground
    black pepper

TO FINISH

1 tablespoon cornstarch
1 egg white

WHEN TERI AND I HAVE LED GROUPS TO THE FAR EAST ON EATING ADVENTURES, I HAVE SEEN AMERICANS DUMBFOUNDED WHEN A PLATTER OF SAUTÉED CRABS, WITH THE BODY AND LEGS CRACKED AND THE SHELLS GLISTENING WITH SOME DELECTABLE SAUCE, APPEARS AT THE BANQUET TABLE. HOW ARE THEY TO ATTACK THE CRAB? THERE IS NO WAY TO AVOID MESSY FINGERS, RICOCHETING SHELLS, SAUCE DRIPPING FROM CHINS, AND A HISTORY OF THE DISH RECORDED ON CLOTHES. WHILE THE CHINESE AND THAIS LOVE SPENDING AN HOUR LEISURELY PICKING EVERY FRAGMENT OF CRABMEAT FROM THE SHELL, AMERICANS OFTEN JUST MAKE A CURSORY ATTACK AT THE CRAB BEFORE IMPATIENTLY RUSHING ON TO THE NEXT DISHES. THIS RECIPE ANSWERS THOSE FRUSTRATIONS BY USING LUMP CRABMEAT. ALWAYS BUY FRESHLY COOKED DUNGENESS CRAB, NEVER FROZEN CRAB OR THE FAKE CRABMEAT (SEALEGS) SO PREVALENT NOW. HAVE THE CRABS CRACKED AND CLEANED AT THE MARKET SO THE MEAT IS EASILY REMOVABLE. OR YOU CAN SUBSTITUTE SOFT-SHELL CRABS. COOK THEM WITH THE SAUCE AND SEASONINGS IN A COVERED SAUTÉ PAN UNTIL THE CRABS TURN RED, ABOUT 3 MINUTES, THEN STIR IN THE VEGETABLES AND SERVE THE DISH.

ADVANCE PREPARATION Remove the crabmeat from the shells and refrigerate. Do this within 8 hours of cooking.

Cut the mushrooms into ½-inch slices. Seed, stem, and sliver the red pepper and set aside with the mushrooms. Set basil aside with the sprouts. Combine the ginger, garlic, and lemongrass with the butter and oil. Cook the rice sticks as described on page 52; after draining the rice sticks on paper towels, transfer them to a serving platter and break into small pieces. In a small bowl, combine the sauce ingredients.

LAST-MINUTE COOKING Combine the cornstarch with an equal amount of cold water. Lightly beat the egg white with 1 teaspoon water.

Place a sauté pan over highest heat and add the ginger-butter mixture. When the butter bubbles and the seasonings sizzle, about 1 minute, add the mushrooms and pepper. Sauté over high heat until the pepper brightens, about 30 seconds.

Add the crabmeat, basil, sprouts, and sauce. When the sauce comes to a low boil, stir in a little of the cornstarch mixture to lightly thicken. Stir in the egg white, then taste and adjust seasonings. Transfer to the rice sticks and serve at once.

Serves: 2 as the entrée.

Menu Ideas: As a special dinner for 2, serve this with a spinach salad, rice pilaf, a dessert from Chapter 7, and a fine white wine.

ASIAN BARBECUED SALMON

1 salmon filet with skin,
    approximately 2 pounds
¼ cup dry sherry
¼ cup light soy sauce
2 tablespoons oyster sauce
2 tablespoons lemon juice
2 tablespoons Oriental
    sesame oil
½ teaspoon freshly ground
    black pepper
1 bunch chives, minced
¼ cup finely minced fresh
    ginger
2 tablespoons cooking oil
Lemon wedges

TASTING THIS DISH RECALLS THE MEMORY OF THE GRILLED FISH SERVED AT THE HUGE PALM BEACH RESTAURANT, LOCATED INSIDE SINGAPORE'S MODERN NATIONAL SPORTS STADIUM. ON A WARM NIGHT, WITH GENTLE TRADE WINDS AND THE CHATTER OF CICADAS, WE PUSHED OUR WAY THROUGH THE CROWDS AT THE ENTRANCE AND CROSSED THE HUGE DINING ROOM TO THE CIRCULAR TABLES NEXT TO A FLOOR-TO-CEILING GLASS WALL LOOKING OUT ONTO THE SOCCER FIELD. AS THEIR NATIONAL TEAM PRACTICED JUST FEET AWAY, 800 ENTHUSIASTIC SINGAPOREANS CONSUMED PLATTERS OF CHILI CRAB, *LO HAY* RAW FISH SALADS, CRUNCHY FRIED SQUID, CRISP DUMPLING PURSES FILLED WITH SHELLFISH, AND BARBECUED POMFRET SERVED ON BANANA LEAVES. LITTLE CHILDREN POUNDED THE CRABS WITH METAL MALLETS, TOOTHLESS GRANDMOTHERS SLURPED FISH SOUP, A STAFF OF 70 RUSHED FROM TABLE TO KITCHEN, AND WE FANTASIZED ABOUT CONVERTING "DODGER DOGS" AND THE PRESS BOX AT CHAVEZ RAVINE INTO A SIMILAR RESTAURANT.

THIS IS ONE OF THE EASIEST RECIPES IN THE BOOK. IF YOU WISH TO BROIL THE FISH, HAVE THE SALMON SKINNED, AND THEN BROIL THE FILET 3 INCHES FROM THE HEAT FOR APPROXIMATELY 10 MINUTES.

PREPARATION AND COOKING Remove any remaining bones from the filet using tweezers or needle-nose pliers. Combine the sherry, soy sauce, oyster sauce, lemon juice, sesame oil, pepper, chives, and ginger. Marinate the salmon for 1 hour. Pour extra marinade into a saucepan, bring to a rapid boil, then set aside.

If using a gas barbecue, preheat to medium (350°F). If using charcoal or wood, prepare the fire. When the coals or wood are ash covered, brush the barbecue rack with the cooking oil and lay the salmon, skin side down, on top. Immediately cover and cook the salmon until the fish just begins to flake, about 12 minutes. (If the barbecue cannot be covered, place the salmon in a wire fish basket and turn the salmon once during cooking; total cooking time will be about 18 minutes.)

If the salmon filet is directly on the barbecue grill, carefully slide a spatula under the filet and transfer to a heated serving platter. The spatula will slide easily between the flesh and the skin (the skin remains on the grill). For a large filet, 2 people will be needed to transfer the fish to the serving platter. Pour the reserved marinade over the salmon. Serve immediately with lemon wedges.

Serves: 4 as an entrée.

Menu Ideas: Quick outdoor dinner for 4—Asian Barbecued Salmon, Wild Mushroom Pasta, Crazy Caesar Salad and Ginger Chocolate Petit Pots.

CRISP PAN-FRIED TROUT

2 green onions
1 tablespoon finely minced fresh ginger
½ cup chicken broth
2 tablespoons dry sherry
2 tablespoons oyster sauce
½ teaspoon sugar
¼ teaspoon freshly ground black pepper
¼ cup plus 1 tablespoon cornstarch
2 trout, 8 ounces each (preferably with bone in)
½ cup cooking oil

THIS TROUT IS AN EXAMPLE OF A DISH BEST SUITED FOR A SMALL DINNER PARTY. COUNT ON SERVING ONE SMALL TROUT PER PERSON, PERHAPS WITH AN ASIAN SALAD AND A RICE DISH. SINCE A 12-INCH SAUTÉ PAN ACCOMMODATES THREE EIGHT-OUNCE TROUT, YOU CAN SIMULTANEOUSLY COOK ENOUGH TROUT IN TWO SKILLETS FOR AN INFORMAL DINNER, WHILE FIVE FRIENDS GATHER IN THE KITCHEN TO ENJOY A GLASS OF WINE AND WATCH THE CRISP TROUT SKIN PICK UP THE BEAUTIFUL GLAZE OF THE SAUCE.

PREPARATION AND COOKING Mince the green onions. Set out the ginger. Combine the broth, sherry, oyster sauce, sugar, and pepper. Set aside.

Combine 1 tablespoon of the cornstarch with an equal amount of cold water and set aside. Place the trout on a layer of newspaper. Dust with the remaining cornstarch, shaking the trout to remove any excess. Place a heavy 12-inch skillet over medium-high heat. When very hot, add the oil. When the oil becomes very hot (it should appear thinner and give off a little haze), add the trout. Shake the pan to prevent the trout skin from sticking, and pan-fry for about 3 minutes on each side, regulating the heat so the oil always sizzles but does not smoke. The trout are cooked when the end of a chopstick easily sinks into the flesh.

Temporarily remove the trout to a layer of paper toweling. Tip the oil from frying pan, then return the pan to medium-high heat. Add the ginger and green onions. When the green onions brighten, add the sauce mixture and a little cornstarch mixture to lightly thicken the sauce. Immediately return the trout to the pan and turn the fish over in the sauce. Transfer the trout and sauce to a heated platter or plates. Serve at once.

Serves: 2 as the entrée.

Menu Ideas: Dinner party for 6 old college friends—Ginger Gravlox, Rainbow Salad with Raspberry Vinegar, Crisp Pan-Fried Trout accompanied by Wild Chinese Rice and followed by Mango Ice Cream with Tequila Sauce. Begin with the gravlox as an appetizer, served with assorted crackers, thinly sliced pumpernickel, and one or more dips with which to season the salmon. Given the informality of the evening, serve the gravlox and the salad in the living room. Next, encourage guests to accompany you into the kitchen (bringing their appetizer plates with them) so that you remain part of the conversation while the trout are sizzling in the frying pan. Make the rice ahead and then reheat it in the microwave in order to minimize your time in the kitchen. Once the main course is concluded, you might consider returning to the living room for dessert and coffee, and tales of epic adventures of long ago.

SMOKED RIB-EYE STEAKS WITH GINGER-MANGO SALSA

EVERYONE WILL HAVE FAR MORE FUN AT HOME PARTIES IF THE COOK MATCHES A SIMPLE MENU WITH RECIPES USING EASY PREPARATION TECHNIQUES AND COOKING METHODS. LET CHEFS SLAVE IN THEIR RESTAURANT KITCHENS DOING IMPOSSIBLE RECIPES WHILE THE REST OF US SERVE SIMPLE PREPARED FOODS WITH GLORIOUS TASTES THAT CAUSE SPIRITS TO SOAR. THE MENU FOR AN EASY FATHER'S DAY DINNER MIGHT BY CRAZY CAESAR SALAD, SMOKED RIB-EYE STEAKS WITH GINGER-MANGO SALSA (DAD DOES THE BARBECUING), NEW WAVE GARLIC BREAD, STIR-FRIED GARDEN VEGETABLES, AND STRAWBERRIES SIAM.

ADVANCE PREPARATION Trim the excess fat from the steaks. Rub the steaks with the barbecue sauce and marinate for 1 hour or longer.

In a small bowl, make the salsa. Combine the green onions, cilantro, ginger, lime juice, brown sugar, fish sauce, and chili sauce. Peel the mango, cut flesh off in large pieces, and then chop finely. If using the papaya, peel, cut in half, scoop out the seeds, and chop flesh; if using the peaches, drop in boiling water for 20 seconds, plunge in cold water, then peel, seed, and chop. Add to the bowl, then stir well to combine. Refrigerate. May be made a day in advance of using. Yields 2 cups.

SMOKING Soak the wood chips in water for 1 hour before using. If using a gas barbecue, preheat to medium (350°F.). If using charcoal or wood, prepare the fire. When the coals or wood are ash covered, drain the chips and place on a 6-inch square of aluminium foil, directly on the coals. When the wood begins to smoke, brush the rack with oil, lay the ribs on, and cover the barbecue. Roast at medium temperature for about 5 minutes on each side for medium-rare. Transfer to warmed dinner plates, spoon the salsa next to each steak, and serve at once.

Serves: 4 as the entrée.

Smoked Rib-Eye Steaks with Ginger-Mango Salsa

Barbecued Veal Chops with Macadamia Nuts

BARBECUED VEAL CHOPS WITH MACADAMIA NUTS

4 veal chops, 10 ounces each
4 cloves garlic, finely minced
1 tablespoon finely minced
  fresh ginger
1 tablespoon grated or finely
  minced lemon peel
1 tablespoon grated or finely
  minced orange peel
2 bunches chives, minced
⅓ cup lemon juice
¼ cup orange juice
3 tablespoons dry sherry
3 tablespoons extra-virgin
  olive oil
2 tablespoons Dijon-style
  mustard
2 tablespoons light soy sauce
½ teaspoon freshly ground
  black pepper
2 ounces macadamia nuts,
  roasted

To CREATE A VISUALLY DYNAMIC FOOD PRESENTATION FOR THIS PHOTO-GRAPH, WE USED A LAVENDER PLATTER AS A COLOR ACCENT AND A SOFT SIDE LIGHT TO MAKE THE MEAT LOOK JUICY. THEN WE BROKE UP THE SURFACE OF THE VEAL WITH THE CHOPPED MACADAMIA NUTS, LEMON ZEST, AND CHIVE BLOSSOMS. YELLOW, GREEN, AND MAUVE DETAILS IN THE BACKGROUND PASTEL DRAWING MIRRORED THE COLORS OF THE FOOD.

THIS IS ONE OF OUR FAVORITE RECIPES. THE MARINADE'S BLEND OF LEMON, ORANGE, DIJON MUSTARD, AND SOY SAUCE IS AN IDEAL FLAVOR COMBINATION WHEN MARINATING VEAL, CHICKEN, OR FISH IN PREPARATION BEFORE BARBECUING.

PREPARATION AND COOKING Place the chops in a single layer in a noncorrosive dish. Combine all the remaining ingredients except the nuts. Pour the marinade over the chops and marinate for 1 to 3 hours. Drain and reserve the marinade.

Coarsely chop the macadamia nuts with a knife (not in the food processor).

If using a gas barbecue, preheat to medium (350°F.). If using charcoal or wood, prepare fire. When the coals or wood are ash covered, brush the grilling rack with oil and place the chops on the grill. Grill the veal for about 10 minutes on each side, basting with some of the reserved marinade. The veal is done when the internal temperature reaches 150°F. and the meat feels firm when pressed with your fingers.

Place the chops on dinner plates. Transfer the marinade to a small saucepan, bring to a boil, and then spoon it over the chops. Sprinkle the macadamia nuts on top. Serve at once.

Serves: 4 as the entrée.

Menu Ideas: Labor Day dinner for 10 without the labor!—begin with simple appetizers of raw vegetables and chilled shrimp accompanied by 3 Chopstix dipping sauces; follow with Crunchy Baja Salad (triple the recipe), then Barbecued Veal Chops with Macadamia Nuts (triple the recipe) and Champagne Rice Pilaf (double the recipe); for the grand finale, have Mango Ice Cream with Tequila Sauce.

SICHUAN VEAL MEATLOAF

1 cup pine nuts
2 pounds ground veal
2 slices whole-wheat bread
½ cup chopped onions
5 cloves garlic, finely minced
1 tablespoon grated or finely
    minced tangerine peel
2 eggs
½ cup catsup
2 tablespoons oyster sauce
2 teaspoons Chinese chili
    sauce
South Seas Salsa (page 39) or
    Ginger Mango Salsa
    (page 94)

IT IS SO MUCH FUN TO ADD AN ASIAN ACCENT TO A TRADITIONAL AMERICAN FAVORITE SUCH AS MEATLOAF. STANDARD ASIAN INGREDIENTS THAT PERK UP AMERICAN FOOD MIGHT INCLUDE MINT, BASIL, LEMONGRASS, TANGERINE PEEL, GINGER, FISH SAUCE, COCONUT MILK, SOY SAUCE, OYSTER SAUCE, HOISIN SAUCE, SESAME OIL, AND CHINESE CHILI SAUCE. GIVE YOUR MOST CONSERVATIVE HOUSEGUESTS A HINT OF PACIFIC FLAVORS BY SERVING TEX-MEX WON TONS, A GENEROUS PORTION OF ASIAN AVOCADO ADVENTURE, THEN SPOONFULS OF SOUTH SEAS SALSA ON THICK SLABS OF SICHUAN VEAL MEATLOAF, ACCOMPANIED BY CRAZY COCONUT NOODLE TOSS AND A FINALE OF ORANGE GINGER BROWNIES. THEIR PALATES WILL BE FOREVER TRANS-FORMED.

PREPARATION AND COOKING Preheat the oven to 325°F., and then toast the pine nuts until golden, about 10 minutes. Turn the oven to 400°F. Place the veal in a large bowl; add the pine nuts. Trim and discard the crusts from bread. Put the bread in a food processor, mince until finely crumbled, and add to the veal. Add the onions, garlic, and tangerine peel to the mix, then add the eggs, catsup, oyster sauce, and chili sauce. Mix gently with your fingers until evenly combined. Gently pack into a 9-by-5-inch loaf pan.

    Bake the meatloaf for 30 minutes. Slice and serve with the salsa of your choice.

Serves: 4 to 6 as the entrée.

CHIU CHOW LEMON CHICKEN

CHICKEN

8 chicken breast halves, boned
    and skinned
1 cup slivered almonds
1 bunch chives
4 cloves garlic, finely minced
1 tablespoon finely minced
    fresh ginger

SAUCE

2 teaspoons grated or finely
    minced lemon peel
½ cup lemon juice
6 tablespoons sugar
¼ cup chicken broth
2 tablespoons light soy sauce
½ teaspoon salt

TO FINISH

2 tablespoons cornstarch
¼ cup cooking oil
Salt and pepper
1 cup all-purpose flour
4 tablespoons unsalted butter

PLATTERS LADEN WITH CHILLED CRACKED CRAB, THINLY SLICED SOY GOOSE, DOUBLE-BOILED DUCK SOUP WITH SALT LEMON; AN EXPRESSWAY NOISE VOLUME FROM 900 FELLOW DINERS; CHEFS IN THE DISPLAY KITCHEN CLEAVING STEAMED LOBSTER; JIM BEAM WHISKEY ENRICHING A SOUP AT A NEIGHBORING TABLE; FRIED SLICED POMFRET; AND TSING TAO BEER CONTRIBUTE TO A KALEIDOSCOPE OF IMPRESSIONS AT CITY CHIU CHOW RESTAURANT IN HONG KONG. THIS RECIPE ADAPTS ONE OF THE RESTAURANTS' DISHES BY USING THE SAUCE FOR PAN-FRIED CHICKEN BREASTS. OR YOU CAN DRIZZLE THE SAUCE OVER BARBECUED CHICKEN OR GRILLED SWORDFISH, OR USE THE LEMON SAUCE AS A DIP FOR CHILLED JUMBO SHRIMP.

ADVANCE PREPARATION Dip each chicken breast in water and then gently flatten with a meat pounder or rolling pin until the breast increases in size by about one-third. Set aside.

Toast the almonds in a 325°F. oven until light golden, then set aside. Mince the chives and set aside. Combine the garlic and ginger and set aside. In a small bowl combine the sauce ingredients and mix well.

LAST-MINUTE COOKING Combine the cornstarch with an equal amount of cold water. Preheat oven to warm.

Place a small noncorrosive skillet or saucepan over medium heat. Add 1 tablespoon cooking oil and then the garlic and ginger. Sauté briefly, then add the sauce. Bring to a low boil and reduce the heat to a simmer.

Sprinkle the chicken on both sides with a little salt and pepper. Dust with flour, shaking off any excess. Place a 12-inch skillet over high heat. When hot, add the butter and remaining 3 tablespoons of oil. When the butter bubbles, pan-fry 3 or 4 chicken pieces at a time. Cook for about 1 minute on each side. The chicken is done when the meat turns color and feels firm to the touch (do not overcook). Transfer the chicken to a heated platter or dinner plates and keep warm in the oven while you cook the remaining chicken.

Bring the sauce back to a low boil and stir in a little of the cornstarch mixture to lightly thicken it. Spoon the sauce over the chicken. Sprinkle the almonds and chives on top. Serve at once.

Serves: 4 as the entrée.

ASIAN ROAST CHICKEN GLAZED WITH MUSHROOMS

CHICKEN

2 chickens, about 3 pounds
    each, cut into 6 to 8
    pieces
5 tablespoons unsalted butter
5 cloves garlic, finely minced
2 shallots, minced
2 tablespoons finely minced
    fresh ginger
8 ounces fresh shiitake
    mushrooms
4 green onions

SAUCE

1 cup chicken broth
1 cup heavy (whipping) cream
½ cup dry sherry
2 tablespoons oyster sauce
2 tablespoons Oriental
    sesame oil
2 teaspoons sugar
1 teaspoon Chinese chili sauce

TO FINISH

2 tablespoons cornstarch

THE KEY TECHNIQUE IN THIS RECIPE IS TO ROAST THE CHICKEN IN A HEAVY, SHALLOW PAN SO THAT THE SKIN BECOMES CRISP (THE CHICKEN WILL STEAM IN A HIGH-SIDED PAN) AND PROVIDES LOTS OF PAN DRIPPINGS FOR ENRICHING THE MUSHROOM PAN GRAVY. AS AN ALTERNATIVE, MARINATE THE CHICKEN WITH THE MARINADE FROM BARBECUED VEAL CHOPS WITH MACADAMIA NUTS (PAGE 97), THEN BARBECUE THE CHICKEN AND MAKE THE MUSHROOM SAUCE IN A SAUTÉ PAN. CHOPSTIX ROAST CHICKEN GLAZED WITH MUSHROOMS, LITTLE BOILING POTATOES, AND A SPINACH SALAD WITH VINAIGRETTE DRESSING IS A QUICK AND MUCH APPRECIATED WORKDAY DINNER.

ADVANCE PREPARATION Rinse and dry chickens. Place in a shallow roasting pan, dot with butter, and set aside.

Combine the garlic, shallots, and ginger; set aside. Cut off and discard the mushroom stems, stack the caps, and cut them into ¼-inch-wide strips; set aside. Mince the green onions and set aside. In small bowl combine the sauce ingredients and mix well.

COOKING Preheat the oven to 350°F. If the chickens are cold, bring to room temperature, then roast for about 30 to 40 minutes, basting every 10 minutes with the pan juices. The chicken is done when the internal temperature reaches 165°F. and the juices no longer are tinged with pink when the chicken is pierced deeply.

Transfer the chicken pieces to a heated serving platter or dinner plates and keep warm in the oven. Discard all but 4 tablespoons of fat from roasting pan. Place the pan over highest heat, add the garlic, shallots, ginger and mushrooms. Sauté for about 3 minutes, then add the sauce and bring to a vigorous boil, scraping up the pan drippings. Cook over highest heat until the sauce reduces by about one-half, about 10 minutes.

Combine the cornstarch with an equal amount of cold water. Stir a little of this into the sauce to lightly thicken. Stir in the green onions and cook for 30 seconds more. Taste and adjust seasonings. Pour the sauce over the chicken and serve at once.

Serves: 4 as the entrée.

Asian Roast Chicken Glazed with Mushrooms

CHOPSTIX SOUTHERN FRIED CHICKEN

CHICKEN

3 cups all-purpose flour
3 tablespoons dried red chili
    flakes
3 tablespoons dried basil
2 tablespoons salt
2 eggs
1 cup milk
1 chicken, about 3 pounds,
    cut into pieces

SAUCE

2 tablespoons cooking oil
4 cloves garlic, finely minced
1 tablespoon finely minced
    fresh ginger
⅓ cup chicken broth
2 tablespoons dry sherry
2 tablespoons hoisin sauce
2 tablespoons light soy sauce
1½ tablespoons red wine
    vinegar
1 tablespoon Oriental
    sesame oil
1 tablespoon Chinese chili
    sauce
2 teaspoons sugar
¼ cup finely minced green
    onions
2 tablespoons finely minced
    cilantro (fresh coriander)

TO FINISH

4 cups cooking oil

GOLDEN FRIED CHICKEN, SOUTHERN STYLE, WITH ITS CRISP EXTERIOR AND MOIST MEAT, FORMS A DRAMATIC CONTRAST TO THE SPICY CILANTRO SAUCE DRIZZLED OVER THE PIECES. OTHER SAUCES TO CONSIDER SERVING WITH THE CHICKEN ARE SOUTH SEAS SALSA (PAGE 39), NEW AGE GUACAMOLE (PAGE 42), AND SINGAPORE SATAY SAUCE (PAGE 41). FOR A SPECIAL FAMILY DINNER TO WELCOME HOME COLLEGE KIDS AND THEIR FRIENDS, SERVE THAI FRIED DUMPLINGS, VEGETARIAN SPICY SHREDDED DUCK SALAD (OMIT THE DUCK), CHOPSTIX SOUTHERN FRIED CHICKEN, NEW WAVE GARLIC BREAD, AND CALORIE CHEESECAKE COUNTERATTACK.

ADVANCE PREPARATION Place flour, chili, basil, and salt in a paper bag. In a 2-quart bowl, beat eggs well, then add milk. Rinse chicken pieces and pat dry.

Prepare the sauce. Place a 10-inch skillet over medium-high heat and add the cooking oil. Add the garlic and ginger, sautéing until garlic sizzles. Then add remaining sauce ingredients except green onions and cilantro. Bring to a low boil, then pour into a small bowl. Stir in the green onions and cilantro; set aside.

LAST-MINUTE COOKING Place the cooking oil in a deep 12-inch skillet and heat to 365°F (bubbles will come out from the end of a wooden spoon when it is dipped into the oil at this temperature). Place the chicken in the paper bag with the flour and shake vigorously. Remove each piece, shaking it to remove any excess flour and transfer to the bowl with the eggs and milk. Let soak for 3 minutes, then return the chicken to the paper bag and shake again vigorously.

Place the chicken skin side down in the hot oil. Reduce the heat to medium, and fry the chicken until golden on one side (about 10 minutes). Turn the pieces and cook until golden on the other side (about 10 minutes more). Turn the chicken pieces once more and cook for about 5 minutes more. During cooking, adjust the heat so the oil is always bubbling around the pieces but is never smoking. The chicken is done when the internal temperature reaches 165°F., or when the juices run clear when the chicken is pierced deeply with a fork.

Drain the chicken on paper towels. Transfer to dinner plates and accompany with the sauce, which each person spoons over the chicken.

Serves: 2 to 3 people as the entrée.

THAI-HIGH
BARBECUED CHICKEN

2 frying chickens, about 3½
    pounds each, split in half
6 cloves garlic, minced
1 tablespoon minced fresh
    galangal or fresh ginger
8 small hot chilies (preferably
    serrano), minced
    including seeds
4 minced green onions
¼ cup minced cilantro (fresh
    coriander)
1 tablespoon grated or minced
    lime peel
Juice from 2 limes
¼ cup hoisin sauce
¼ cup red wine vinegar
¼ cup fish sauce
¼ cup honey
2 tablespoons dark soy sauce
2 tablespoons cooking oil

NEAR THE WHITE RECLINING BUDDHA IN AYUTHAYA, THE ANCIENT CAP-
ITAL OF THAILAND, IS A COURTYARD OF LARGE STONE BUDDHAS, ALL
DRAPED WITH SAFFRON ROBES, WHO WITNESS PERSPIRING TOURISTS CLIMB-
ING STEEP STAIRS TO THE TOP OF THE RUINS. SKINNY TEMPLE DOGS AND
LAUGHING CHILDREN PLAY BY AN OLD BULL AND DART PAST WOODEN SIGNS
INSCRIBED WITH BUDDHIST SAYINGS SUCH AS "VICTORY BEGETS REVENGE."
AT THE TEMPLE ENTRANCE, BAREFOOT COOKS BARBECUE CHICKEN ON SMALL,
OPEN, ELEVATED, RECTANGULAR PITS OF WOOD COALS. WITH EACH BITE THE
TASTE OF CHICKEN, GARLIC, FRESH CHILIES, AND LIME PROVIDES A MIDMORN-
ING SNACK BEFORE EXPLORING MORE RUINS.

ADVANCE PREPARATION Working with one chicken half, loosen a small area
of the skin along the top of the breast. Gently push your index finger
underneath the skin, moving it along the breast, thigh, and drumstick,
being careful not to dislodge the skin attached to the backbone. Repeat
with the remaining chicken halves.

Combine the remaining ingredients and stir well. Spoon about one-
eighth of the marinade under the skin of one chicken half and, with
your fingers, massage the outside of the skin to work the marinade over
the breast, thigh, and drumstick. Rub another one-eighth of the marinade over the entire outside surface of the chicken half. Repeat with
rest of the chicken halves, then refrigerate for at least 2 hours.

COOKING When ready to cook, bring the chicken to room temperature.
Pour any excess marinade into a small saucepan and bring to a boil for
3 minutes, then reserve.

If using a gas barbecue, preheat to medium (350°F). If using charcoal or wood, prepare a fire. When the coals or wood are ash covered,
brush the grill rack with oil, then grill the chicken halves over medium
heat for about 30 minutes, or until a meat thermometer reads 160°F.
when plunged deep into the chicken. When pierced with a fork, the
juices should run clear. Or roast the chicken halves meat-side up in a
425°F. oven for about 30 minutes.

Serve the chicken with the reserved barbecue sauce. Spoon a little of
the sauce over the chicken for added flavor. The chicken is excellent
eaten hot, at room temperature, or cold with the reserved barbecue
sauce. If you wield a Chinese cleaver with great dexterity, chop the
chicken into bite-size pieces before serving cold, as part of a picnic.

Serves: 4 as the entrée.

SMOKED BABY BACK RIBS
WITH CHOPSTIX BARBECUE SAUCE

RIBS

4 slabs baby pork back ribs, each with 6 ribs

BARBECUE SAUCE

3 tablespoons white sesame seeds

1 tablespoon chopped garlic

1 tablespoon finely minced fresh ginger

⅓ cup minced green onions

¼ cup minced cilantro (fresh coriander)

2 teaspoons grated or finely minced orange peel

5 tablespoons hoisin sauce

3 tablespoons plum sauce

2 tablespoons Oriental sesame oil

2 tablespoons distilled white vinegar

2 tablespoons oyster sauce

2 tablespoons dark soy sauce

2 tablespoons honey

2 tablespoons dry sherry

2 teaspoons Chinese chili sauce

FOR SMOKING

2 cups wood chips

Giving barbecued meat a smoky flavor is so easy and adds a complex taste. Among the many wood chips sold at gourmet shops and home-improvement centers are maple, cherry, hickory, mesquite, and our favorite—grape cuttings. Just soak the chips for a couple of hours, drain, and place on a layer of aluminium foil directly on the coals. When the chips begin to smoke, barbecue the meat or seafood. Keep the barbecue top closed during cooking to intensify the smoky flavor.

The following barbecue sauce lasts indefinitely refrigerated if you omit the green onions and cilantro, whose fresh taste quickly deteriorates. We give cooking friends this barbecue sauce packaged in jars with labels saying, "Good on all meats and seafood that you barbecue, broil or roast." The first time you try this recipe, serve it with corn on the cob, parsleyed potatoes, and lemon meringue pie.

ADVANCE PREPARATION On the underside of the ribs is a tough white membrane; using your fingernail or a sharp pointed knife, loosen the membrane along the bone at one edge, then, gripping the membrane with a paper towel, pull it away. Set ribs aside.

Place the sesame seeds in an ungreased 10-inch skillet and cook over high heat until they turn light golden, about 2 minutes. Tip out immediately. Mince the garlic and ginger in a food processor. Add the green onions and cilantro, mincing again. Transfer to a bowl, then add the sesame seeds and remaining sauce ingredients. Mix well. Yields 1½ cups.

SMOKING Soak the wood chips in water for 1 hour before using. Rub the ribs with barbecue sauce. If using a gas barbecue, preheat to medium (350°F.). If using charcoal or wood, prepare a fire. When the coals or wood are ash covered, drain the chips and place on a 6-inch square of aluminium directly on the coals. When the chips begin to smoke, brush the rack with oil, lay the ribs on, and cover the barbecue. Roast at medium temperature until the meat begins to shrink away from the ends of the rib bones, about 45 to 60 minutes. Brush the ribs with more barbecue sauce halfway through cooking. Serve hot or at room temperature. If eating these as an appetizer, cut into individual ribs before serving them.

Serves: 12 as an appetizer or 4 as the entrée.

Smoked Baby Back Ribs with Chopstix Barbecue Sauce
and Chopstix Noodle Magic (recipe on page 138)

THAI RABBIT

¼ cup chopped fresh basil
2 tablespoons chopped fresh mint
4 cloves garlic, finely minced
2 shallots, minced
2 small hot chilies, stemmed and minced
2 cups chicken broth
1 tablespoon grated or finely minced lime peel
6 tablespoons lime juice
¼ cup dry sherry
¼ cup honey
1½ tablespoons fish sauce
1 rabbit, about 3 pounds, cut into pieces
Chopped fresh basil or mint, or toasted sesame seeds as garnish

FRESH RABBIT, SKINNED AND CUT INTO PIECES, IS AVAILABLE AT MOST SUPER-MARKETS. ITS RICH TASTE CONTRASTS NICELY WITH A SAUCE MADE FROM BASIL, MINT, CHILIES, LIME, AND HONEY. AFTER THE MEAT BECOMES TENDER, THE RABBIT IS TEMPORARILY REMOVED FROM THE POT, THE SAUCE REDUCED TO A CARAMELIZED GLAZE, AND THEN THE RABBIT IS RETURNED FOR A FINAL MOMENT OF COOKING. A LATE SUNDAY LUNCH FOR GOOD FRIENDS MIGHT INCLUDE: COOKED CHILLED SHRIMP WITH 2 CHOPSTIX DIPPING SAUCES (PRE-PARED ON SATURDAY), CRAZY CAESAR SALAD, THAI RABBIT (GIVE VAGUE ANSWERS WHEN QUESTIONED ABOUT THE ENTREE), WILD CHINESE RICE (DO A DAY AHEAD AND REHEAT IN THE OVEN), AND CHOPSTIX TART WITH RASP-BERRY CABERNET SAUVIGNON SAUCE (MAKE A DAY AHEAD).

PREPARATION AND COOKING In a 2½-quart saucepan, combine the basil, mint, garlic, shallots, chilies, broth, lime peel and juice, sherry, honey, and fish sauce. Bring to a low boil.

Rinse the rabbit and pat dry, then add to the saucepan, fitting the pieces in tightly. There should be enough liquid to cover all the pieces. If not, add more broth or water. When the liquid returns to a low boil, reduce the heat to a simmer, cover the saucepan, and simmer for about 40 minutes; the meat should feel tender when prodded with a fork.

Remove the rabbit from the pan and keep warm. Transfer the sauce to a 12-inch skillet and place over highest heat. Rapidly boil the sauce, stirring occasionally, until it begins to thicken and to turn a caramel color, about 15 minutes. During the last few minutes, stir continually to prevent the sauce from scorching.

Place the rabbit in the skillet and coat the pieces with the sauce. Transfer to heated dinner plates and garnish with the herbs or sesame seeds. Serve at once.

Serves: 4 as the entrée.

MESQUITE BARBECUED LAMB, CHOPSTIX STYLE

LAMB

1 leg of lamb, about 5 pounds, boned and butterflied

BARBECUE SAUCE

1 cup hoisin sauce
¾ cup plum sauce
¼ cup distilled white vinegar
¼ cup dry sherry
3 tablespoons honey
2 tablespoons dark soy sauce
2 tablespoons Oriental sesame oil
1 tablespoon Chinese chili sauce
8 cloves garlic, finely minced
2 tablespoons salted black beans, rinsed and chopped
1 tablespoon grated or finely minced orange peel

FOR SMOKING

4 cups mesquite chips

ACCOMPANIMENTS

8 cups shredded salad greens
4 cups shredded carrots
3 bunches cilantro (fresh coriander)
3 bunches fresh mint
3 bunches fresh basil
South Seas Salsa (page 39)
Double recipe of Peking Chive Pancakes (page 150)

O N A WARM SUMMER NIGHT, FRIENDS MOVE SLOWLY ALONG THE OUT-DOOR BUFFET TABLE DECORATED WITH GIANT THAI UMBRELLAS, KOREAN BAMBOO PICNIC BOXES, AND FIERCE-LOOKING BALINESE MASKS. JUMBO COOKED SHRIMP SET IN A BOWL OF CRUSHED ICE AND ACCOMPANIED BY CHOPSTIX DIPPING SAUCES (PAGES 40–43), TEX-MEX WON TONS (PAGE 32) WITH NEW AGE GUACAMOLE (PAGE 42), SPROUTING NOODLE SALAD (PAGE 56) WITH SHREDDED VEGETABLES, THINLY SLICED MESQUITE BAR-BECUED LAMB, A BAMBOO STEAMER HIDING PEKING CHIVE PANCAKES (PAGE 150), AND A PLATTER OF CHOPSTIX BARBECUED VEGETABLES (PAGE 130) ARE ALL DISPLAYED ON COLORFUL PLATES. CHINATOWN NEWSPAPERS SERVE AS TABLE MATS, ORIENTAL WHISTLES AND PARTY FAVORS ADD TO THE RACKET. FRIENDS CONTINUE THEIR ATTACK ON THE BUFFET TABLE, AND ENTHUSIASM GROWS AS EVERYONE ANTICIPATES THE MANGO ICE CREAM, AND CHOCOLATE CHIP–MACADAMIA NUT COOKIES.

PREPARATION AND COOKING Trim off all thick sections of fat. Combine the ingredients for the barbecue sauce. Marinate the lamb for 4 hours, unrefrigerated.

If using a gas barbecue, preheat to medium (350°F.), add the mesquite in a disposable aluminum tray, and let the chips burn until ash covered. If using charcoal or wood, add the mesquite chips and prepare the fire. When the wood is ash covered, brush the barbecue rack with oil and add the lamb. Rotate the lamb occasionally, basting it with the barbecue sauce as it cooks. The lamb is done when the temperature on a meat thermometer reaches 140°F. for medium-rare or 160°F. for medium (about 30 to 45 minutes).

Place the greens, carrots, and herbs on separate serving plates or on one large platter. Have the salsa nearby.

Fold the pancakes in quarters and overlap on a Chinese steamer tray. Place over rapidly boiling water, cover, and steam for 2 minutes. Place the pancakes in a basket lined with a cloth napkin, then fold the napkin over the top and bring to the table. (If you steam the pancakes in a bamboo steamer, just bring the steamer to the table). If heating the pancakes in the oven, seal tightly in aluminum foil and reheat in a 350°F. oven for 8 minutes.

Remove the meat from grill and bring to the table. Thinly slice the lamb. Each person opens a pancake, adds a slice of meat, a sprinkling of greens and carrots and a choice of fresh herbs, then drizzles on the salsa and rolls the pancake into a cylinder to eat.

Serves: 10 as the entrée.

Thai Chicken Stir-Fry with Lettuce Cups

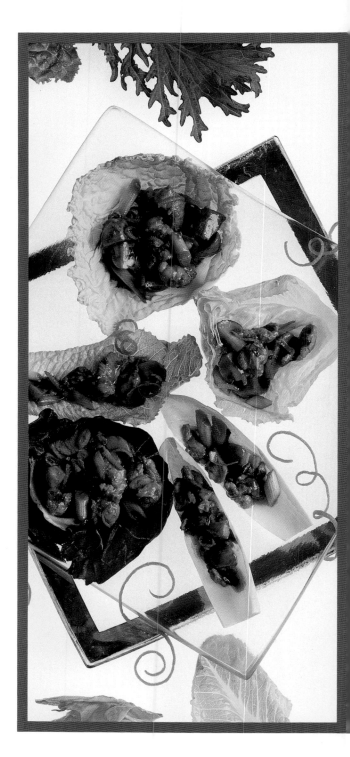

Chapter 5

MU SHU FANTASIES AND STIR-FRY TRIUMPHS

WITH TONGUE IN CHEEK, I AM FOND OF SAYING IN COOKING DEMONSTRATIONS, DIG A DEEP HOLE IN YOUR GARDEN AND BURY THE WOK. RUSH WITH YOUR COOKING FRIENDS TO THE NEAREST BODY OF WATER AND HAVE A CONTEST TO SEE WHO CAN THROW HIS OR HER WOK THE FARTHEST. GIVE YOUR WOK AWAY TO A NEIGHBOR WHO DOESN'T LIKE TO COOK. USE THE WOK AS A PLANTER. COVER YOUR HEAD WITH THE WOK DURING ACID-RAIN ATTACKS. THOUSANDS OF YEARS AGO THE CHINESE, WITH MALICIOUS INTENT, DESIGNED THE WOK TO RENDER USELESS A LARGE PART OF YOUR CUPBOARD.

SECURE IN THE PRIVACY OF YOUR OWN KITCHEN, DON'T WORRY ABOUT SUDDEN ACCUSATIONS OR REPRISALS WHEN YOUR FRIENDS DISCOVER THAT YOU ARE WOKLESS. ALL STIR-FRY RECIPES WORK JUST AS WELL WHEN COMPLETED IN A 12-INCH SKILLET!

TEST OUT THIS THEORY BY STIR-FRYING SHRIMP WITH CHILIES AND ORANGE ZEST—OR CLAMS IN A SINGAPORE CURRY SAUCE—AND THEN MOUNDING THEM ON CRISP PAN-FRIED NOODLES. OR FLASH-COOK GROUND MEAT, LOTS OF GARLIC, AND CHILIES, THEN USE THIS AS A STUFFING FOR A PACIFIC-STYLE BURRITO. ACCOMPANIED BY A SIDE DISH FROM THE NEXT CHAPTER AND A BIG GARDEN SALAD DRESSED WITH OIL AND VINEGAR, ANY OF THE RECIPES IN THIS CHAPTER WILL MAKE AN ENTRÉE SERVING FOUR.

THAI CHICKEN STIR-FRY WITH LETTUCE CUPS

CHICKEN

4 skinless, boneless chicken
    breast halves, trimmed of
    all fat
1 tablespoon dark soy sauce
1 tablespoon dry sherry
2 teaspoons cooking oil
4 green onions
¼ pound fresh button
    mushrooms
4 cloves garlic, finely minced
2 teaspoon finely minced fresh
    ginger
2 teaspoons grated or minced
    tangerine or orange peel
2 heads iceberg lettuce, or
    3 heads radicchio

SAUCE

3 tablespoons dry sherry
2 tablespoons light soy sauce
1 tablespoon Oriental
    sesame oil
2 teaspoons hoisin sauce
2 teaspoons red wine vinegar
1 teaspoon Chinese chili sauce
½ teaspoon sugar
¼ teaspoon salt
¼ cup chopped fresh basil

TO FINISH

1 tablespoon cornstarch
3 tablespoons cooking oil

IMAGINE SERVING THIS, OR ANOTHER FAVORITE STIR-FRY, CRADLED IN LETTUCE AS AN APPETIZER, OR AS THE OPENING COURSE FOR DINNER. SINCE THE RECIPE REQUIRES LAST-MINUTE COOKING, FOLLOW THIS COURSE WITH OTHER CHOPSTIX OR AMERICAN FARE ALREADY COMPLETED AND READY TO BE BROUGHT STRAIGHT FROM THE KITCHEN.

ADVANCE PREPARATION Cut the chicken into ¼-inch cubes and marinate with the soy sauce, sherry, and oil. Refrigerate until ready to use.

Cut the green onions on the diagonal into ½-inch pieces. Cut the mushrooms in half and then into quarters. Mix and set aside the garlic, ginger, and tangerine or orange peel.

Cut the top third off each head of lettuce. Carefully separate the leaves of the tops, or separate the radicchio leaves into cups; you should end up with about 14 lettuce cups, about 3 to 5 inches across. Refrigerate the leaves (reserve the rest of the lettuce for salads).

In a small bowl, combine the ingredients for the sauce. Set aside.

LAST-MINUTE COOKING Combine the cornstarch with an equal amount of cold water and set aside.

Place the wok over highest heat. When the wok is very hot, add 2 tablespoons of the oil to the center of the wok. Tilt the wok to coat the sides with oil. When the oil just begins to smoke, add the chicken and stir-fry until it just loses its raw outside color, about 1 minute. Transfer to a platter.

Immediately return the wok to highest heat. Add the remaining 1 tablespoon oil to the center, then add the garlic mixture. Sauté for a few seconds, then add the vegetables. Stir-fry until the onions brighten, about 2 minutes.

Return the chicken to the wok and pour in the sauce. When the sauce comes to a low boil, stir in a little of the cornstarch mixture so the sauce glazes the chicken. Taste and adjust the seasonings, then spoon onto a heated platter or individual plates. Serve at once with the lettuce cups. Each person puts some of the filling in a lettuce cup, gently cups the edges up, and eats it quickly!

Serves: 2 as the entrée.

Menu Ideas: Fourth of July party for 10, with the stir-fry cooked in a 22-inch wok (available in Chinese markets) placed on an outdoor barbecue—Thai Chicken Stir-Fry with Lettuce Cups (triple the recipe), Champagne Rice Pilaf (double the recipe), Rainbow Salad with Raspberry Vinegar (double the recipe), and homemade peach ice cream with Chocolate Chip–Macadamia Nut Cookies.

DANNY KAYE SHRIMP

1 pound medium to large
   shrimp, in the shell
2 tablespoons cooking oil
4 cloves garlic, finely minced
1 tablespoon finely minced
   fresh ginger
2 teaspoons grated or finely
   minced orange peel
4 small chilies, stemmed and
   minced
Dry sherry to taste
Oriental sesame oil to taste
Pinch of sugar

WAS DANNY KAYE A GOOD COOK? WAS EINSTEIN INTERESTED IN SCIENCE? DOES THE POPE KNOW HOW TO PRAY? TO EXPERIENCE A CHINESE DINNER AT DANNY KAYE'S HOME WAS TO TASTE CHINESE FOOD AS CLOSE TO PERFECTION AS POSSIBLE. FROM SCRIBBLED NOTES DATED OCTOBER 19, 1980, I RECALL WE FEASTED ON SHARK'S FIN DUMPLINGS, SCALLOP SOUP, PEKING DUCK, TOP SIRLOIN AND ONIONS WITH OYSTER SAUCE, CUCUMBER SOUP, HOMEMADE NOODLES WITH SICHUAN MEAT SAUCE, STIR-FRIED SEA SCALLOPS SMOKED WITH FRESH ORANGE PEEL, CRISP SICHUAN CHICKEN, VELVET SHRIMP AND OYSTERS, AND FRESH FRUIT.

STIR-FRYING SHRIMP IN THEIR SHELLS IS A TECHNIQUE DANNY DID BEAUTIFULLY. THIS COOKING METHOD KEEPS THE SHRIMP MOIST, ADDS FLAVOR, AND PROTECTS THE TENDER FLESH FROM THE SIDE OF THE HOT PAN. FOR AN EASY DINNER, ACCOMPANY DANNY KAYE SHRIMP WITH A TOSSED GREEN SALAD. OR SERVE THE SHRIMP CHILLED, AS AN APPETIZER.

PREPARATION AND COOKING Using a scissor or thin knife, cut along the top of the shrimp shell to expose the vein. Rinse out the vein, being careful to keep the shell intact.

Combine the oil, garlic, ginger, orange peel, and chilies.

Place a wok over highest heat. When very hot, add the oil mixture and sauté a few seconds. Add the shrimp, stir, and toss until shrimp shells turn pink (a few black scorch marks are fine). The shrimp are cooked when they feel firm to the touch. Or cut one in half; it should be white in the center. During the last minute of cooking, add a splash of dry sherry, drizzle the sesame oil on top, and add the sugar. Taste and adjust the seasonings. Transfer to a heated platter or plates.

Serve hot, at room temperature, or cold. Each person peels off the shells at the table.

Serves: 6 to 8 as an appetizer, or 3 as the entrée.

Scallops and Cashews in Tangerine Sauce

SCALLOPS AND CASHEWS IN TANGERINE SAUCE

SCALLOPS

2 cups raw cashews
2 cups cooking oil
4 green onions, chopped
4 cloves garlic, finely minced
1 pound bay scallops

SAUCE

¼ cup dry sherry
3 tablespoons tomato sauce
1 tablespoon oyster sauce
**1 tablespoon Oriental
  sesame oil**
1 teaspoon red wine vinegar
**½ teaspoon Chinese chili
  sauce**
**2 teaspoons grated or finely
  minced tangerine peel**

TO FINISH

1 tablespoon cornstarch

GIVING SCALLOPS, OR THINLY SLICED FILET MIGNON, OR SHRIMP, A BRIEF STIR-FRY IN A BLAZING WOK, WITH A SPLASH OF SAUCE ADDED TO GLAZE THE FOOD, IS THE EASIEST, MOST PRACTICAL WAY TO STIR-FRY AT HOME. THIS MEANS NO HOURS CUTTING DIFFERENT TYPES OF EXOTIC ORIENTAL VEGE-TABLES, NO FRANTIC RELAYS OF FOOD IN AND OUT OF THE WOK, NO EX-HAUSTION! MEAT OR SEAFOOD, STIR-FRIED AND ROLLED INTO HOT FLOUR TORTILLAS—OR PLACED ON A SNOW-WHITE BED OF DEEP-FRIED RICE STICKS, OR CUPPED IN CRISP LETTUCE POCKETS—MAKES A SATISFYING AND QUICK ENTRÉE.

ADVANCE PREPARATION Place the nuts and oil in a small saucepan over medium-high heat. Stir the nuts occasionally and when they turn very light golden, drain immediately and pat dry on paper towels. Pour off and reserve 2 tablespoons of the cooking oil for stir-frying.

Set aside in separate containers the green onions, garlic, and scallops. In a small bowl, combine the sauce ingredients and mix well.

LAST-MINUTE COOKING Combine the cornstarch with an equal amount of cold water. Set aside.

Place a wok over highest heat. When the wok is very hot, add the reserved oil to the center. Roll the oil around the sides of wok and add the garlic. When it just begins to turn white, in about 15 seconds, add the scallops. Stir-fry until the scallops just lose their raw outside color, about 1 minute.

Stir in the green onions and pour in the sauce. When the sauce comes to a low boil, stir in a little of the cornstarch mixture so the sauce glazes the scallops. Stir in the cashews, then taste and adjust the seasonings. Spoon onto a heated platter or individual plates. Serve at once.

Serves: 4 as the entrée.

Menu Ideas: A worknight dinner for 2—Scallops and Cashews in Tangerine Sauce, New Wave Garlic Bread, Melrose Mushroom Salad, and fresh fruit.

SINGAPORE CURRIED CLAMS

CLAMS

26 small steamer clams

2 tablespoons cornmeal

3 cloves garlic, finely minced

1 tablespoon finely minced fresh ginger

1 tablespoon salted black beans, rinsed and chopped

2 tablespoons cooking oil

¾ cup minced green onions

SAUCE

1 cup chicken broth

¼ cup tomato sauce

¼ cup dry sherry

2 tablespoons oyster sauce

1 tablespoon curry paste, or 2 tablespoons curry powder

1 tablespoon Oriental sesame oil

1 tablespoon light soy sauce

1 teaspoon Chinese chili sauce

½ teaspoon sugar

TO FINISH

2 tablespoons cornstarch

AT AN EATING PARADISE IN SINGAPORE, THE FAMOUS OUTDOOR HAWKER'S FOOD MALL AT NEWTON CENTRE, FRIENDS FEAST ON CHILI CRAB, OYSTER OMELETS, CRACKLING DEEP-FRIED SQUID, AND CRUNCHY PAN-FRIED NOODLES COOKED IN A HUGE WOK BY A WIZENED CHINESE LADY. ANOTHER ROUND OF BEER FORETELLS NEW FORAYS TO OTHER FOOD STALLS FOR HUGE BARBECUED PRAWNS, SPICY COCONUT CHICKEN SOUP, AND COURAGEOUS TASTINGS OF THE STINKY DURIAN FRUIT. GENTLE TRADE WINDS BLOW AND HAWKERS SHOUT THEIR TRIUMPHS, SUCH AS THIS DISH OF SINGAPORE CURRIED CLAMS.

TRY TO USE CURRY PASTE, AVAILABLE IN MANY SUPERMARKET GOURMET SECTIONS, WHICH ADDS A MORE COMPLEX TASTE THAN CURRY POWDER. FOR EXCITING VARIATIONS IN FLAVOR, INSTEAD OF THE CURRIED SAUCE SUBSTITUTE THE HERB-COCONUT SAUCE FROM CRAZY COCONUT NOODLE TOSS (PAGE 132).

ADVANCE PREPARATION Scrub the clams. Cover with cold water and stir in the cornmeal to make the clams spit out any sand. After 1 hour, discard any clams that are not tightly closed. Rinse off and refrigerate until ready to use.

Combine and set aside the garlic, ginger, black beans, and cooking oil. Set aside the green onions. Combine the sauce in a small bowl.

LAST-MINUTE COOKING Combine the cornstarch with an equal amount of cold water and set aside.

Place a wok over high heat. When hot, add the oil mixture. Sauté a few seconds, then add the clams and sauce. Bring the sauce to low boil. Cover and cook until all the clams pop open, about 5 minutes.

Discard any clams that do not open. Stir in enough cornstarch mixture to thicken the sauce, then add the green onions. Turn out onto a platter and serve at once.

Serves: 2 as the entrée.

Menu Ideas: On a hot summer night outdoors, serve these clams with steamed rice, Chopstix Barbecued Vegetables, and Sprouting Noodle Salad, with lots of Tiger beer to bring a taste of Singapore to your home.

FLOWER BLOSSOM SQUID

1½ pounds small squid
¼ cup chopped fresh basil, mint, or cilantro (fresh coriander)
½ red bell pepper, seeded
3 cloves garlic, finely minced
3 small chilies, minced
1 tablespoon lime zest
¼ cup chicken broth
¼ cup light brown sugar
¼ cup distilled white vinegar
1 tablespoon fish sauce
2 ounces rice sticks
Cooking oil for deep-frying
1 tablespoon cornstarch

WHEN WE SAW NANCY TOLER'S "ELEPHANT PLATTER" AT THE WILD BLUE GALLERY ACROSS THE STREET FROM CHOPSTIX ON MELROSE AVENUE, WE KNEW IT HAD TO MAKE AN APPEARANCE IN THIS COOKBOOK. HAVING BEEN RAISED IN SOUTHERN CALIFORNIA AND WORKED IN SUNNY LAGUNA BEACH, NANCY TOLER FEELS A NATURAL AFFINITY WITH TROPICAL THEMES AND BRIGHT COLORS. SHE IS ANOTHER LOCAL CERAMIC ARTIST WORKING WITH LOW-FIRE CLAYS AND GLAZES TO ACHIEVE RICH, SATURATED COLORS.

ADVANCE PREPARATION Clean the squid. Pull the head from squid and cut the tentacles off in one piece. If the black mouth is in the center of the tentacles, pull this away and discard. Discard the rest of head. Under cold running water, rub off the squid skin with your fingers. Run a thin knife inside the squid and cut open into a flat steak. Clean inside thoroughly. Make light lengthwise cuts ½ inch apart along the inside of the squid steak, being careful not to cut all the way through. Make light crosswise cuts ½ inch apart, creating a diamond pattern. Cut each steak into 4 quarters, then refrigerate, along with the tentacles, until ready to cook.

Set the basil or other herbs and the red pepper aside. In a small bowl, combine the garlic, chilies, lime zest, broth, brown sugar, vinegar, and fish sauce; set aside.

Deep-fry the rice sticks in cooking oil as described on page 52.

LAST-MINUTE COOKING Break the rice sticks into small pieces and place in a thin layer on a serving platter or on 4 dinner plates. Combine the cornstarch with an equal amount of cold water and set aside. In a large saucepot, bring 5 quarts of water to a rapid boil.

Place the sauce in a wok and bring to a rapid boil over highest heat. Stir occasionally. When the sauce, about 5 tablespoons, turns a caramel color, in about 8 minutes, stir the squid into the boiling water. As soon as the squid turns white in about 10 seconds, drain in a colander; shake the colander vigorously to thoroughly drain all the water. Immediately transfer the squid to the wok. Stir in the basil and red pepper. Add a little cornstarch mixture to lightly thicken the sauce so squid pieces are glazed. Turn out onto rice sticks and serve at once.

Serves: 2 to 4 as the entrée.

Menu Ideas: A squid festival—Chili Squid with Basil (variation of Chili Shrimp with Basil), Melrose Mushroom Salad with Squid (add ½ pound cooked and chilled squid), and Flower Blossom Squid (double the recipe); serve with Champagne Rice Pilaf and Strawberries Siam.

OVERLEAF: *Flower Blossom Squid on Rice Sticks*

BALI PAN-FRIED NOODLE CRUNCH

SHRIMP AND NOODLES

½ pound dried spaghetti-style
   noodles, preferably
   Chinese
1 bunch asparagus
½ pound medium button
   mushrooms
2 red bell peppers
⅓ cup chopped fresh basil
⅓ cup chopped fresh mint
⅓ cup chopped green onions
5 cloves garlic, minced
1 pound medium shrimp,
   shelled and deveined

SAUCE

1 cup coconut milk
¼ cup dry sherry
2 tablespoons oyster sauce
½ teaspoon Chinese chili
   sauce

TO FINISH

2 tablespoons cornstarch
½ cup cooking oil

Oh BALI—ISLAND OF FORESTS AND RICE PADDIES, SOARING VOLCANIC PEAKS AND PRISTINE BEACHES, ANCIENT HINDU TEMPLES AND CROWDED CITIES, BUNGALOWS FILLED WITH JAPANESE SURFING TOURS AND AUSTRALIAN FAMILIES, LAND OF EXQUISITE ARTS AND EXOTIC DANCE—DO NOT PASS TOO SWIFTLY INTO THE MODERN AGE. DINING AT A MOUNTAIN RESTAURANT, WE LOOKED FROM THE TEAK VERANDAH ACROSS DISTANT VALLEYS OF FLOODED RICE PADDIES SEPARATED BY RIDGES OF DENSE PALM GROVES. CRUNCHY PAN-FRIED NOODLES TOPPED WITH SEAFOOD IN A SPICY COCONUT SAUCE WAS ONE OF THE DISHES WE TASTED BEFORE CONTINUING UP MT. AGUNG TO VISIT BALI'S GREATEST TEMPLE.

HERE IS A CLOSE APPROXIMATION OF THE RECIPE. THE DRAMATIC CONTRAST BETWEEN THE SOFT INTERIOR AND CRUNCHY OUTER NOODLES, WHICH STAY CRISP WHEN SOAKED IN SAUCE, MAKES THIS A GREAT NOODLE BASE UPON WHICH TO SERVE EVEN SUCH NON-BALINESE SPECIALITIES AS POT ROAST, LAMB CURRY, OR IRISH STEW.

ADVANCE PREPARATION In a large pot, bring at least 4 quarts of water to a vigorous boil, then add the noodles. Cook until they lose their raw taste but are still firm, about 5 minutes. Immediately drain in a colander, shaking out any excess water.

Lightly oil the surface of a 12-inch round plate and spread the noodles evenly on top to a thickness of about ½ inch. Leave uncovered at room temperature for at least 2 hours, turning the noodle disk over once. (This can be done a day ahead and refrigerated, covered.)

Snap the tough ends off the asparagus; cut each stalk on a sharp diagonal, rolling the asparagus one-quarter turn toward you after each cut. Cut the mushrooms into ¼-inch slices. Stem, seed, and cut the red peppers into ½-inch cubes. Combine the asparagus, mushrooms, and peppers, then refrigerate. Combine the basil, mint, and green onions and set aside. Set aside the garlic and the shrimp separately. In small bowl, combine the sauce ingredients and mix well.

LAST-MINUTE COOKING Mix the cornstarch with an equal amount of cold water and set aside. Preheat the oven to 200°F.

Place a 12-inch cast-iron skillet over medium heat for 5 minutes. Add ¼ cup of the cooking oil. When the oil gives off a wisp of smoke, carefully transfer the noodle disk to the skillet. Turn the heat to medium-high and fry the noodles until golden on one side, about 6 minutes. Then turn over, add 2 more tablespoons of the oil around the sides of the pan, and fry until the noodles are golden on the other side, about 6 more minutes. Transfer the noodles to a layer of paper towels placed on a cutting board. Pat the noodles to absorb any excess oil, then with a long knife, cut the noodle disk into wedges. Transfer the noodle wedges to a round serving plate and place in the warm oven.

Place the wok over highest heat. When the wok is very hot, add 1 tablespoon of the cooking oil to the center of the wok. Tilt the wok to coat the sides with oil. When the oil just begins to smoke, add the shrimp. Stir-fry just until they turn white, about 2 minutes. Transfer the shrimp to a work platter.

Immediately return the wok to highest heat. Add the remaining 1 tablespoon oil to the center, then add the garlic and sauté for a few seconds. Add the vegetables and stir-fry until the asparagus brightens, about 2 minutes.

Return the shrimp to the wok; add the sauce and the herb mixture. When the sauce comes to a low boil, stir in a little of the cornstarch mixture so that the sauce glazes the food. Taste and adjust the seasonings. Pour the topping across the surface of noodles. Serve at once.

Serves: 4 as the entrée.

Menu Ideas: Since pan-fried noodles require about 15 minutes of attention to complete, serve this for just a few close friends who can observe the cooking. Perhaps a guest will volunteer to complete the cooking of the noodles while you finish the stir-fry topping. Yummy Yam Gai salad and Orange Ginger Brownies with fresh fruit would nicely round out the menu.

LAMB FAJITAS

LAMB
1 pound boneless leg of lamb,
    trimmed of all fat
1 tablespoon hoisin sauce
2 teaspoons dark soy sauce
2 tablespoons plus 2
    teaspoons cooking oil
1 red bell pepper
3 green onions
4 cloves garlic

SAUCE
1 tablespoon dry sherry
1 tablespoon dark soy sauce
1 tablespoon Oriental
    sesame oil
2 teaspoon red wine vinegar
1 teaspoon Chinese chili sauce
¼ teaspoon sugar
¼ teaspoon salt

TO FINISH
South Seas Salsa (page 39)
New Age Guacamole (page 42)
8 eight-inch flour tortillas
1 tablespoon cornstarch

A FOOD PHOTOGRAPHER FACES MANY CREATIVE PROBLEMS. FOR EXAMPLE, HOW COULD I EXPRESS THE FUN AND SENSORY EXCITEMENT OF A RECIPE SUCH AS LAMB FAJITAS, SIZZLING AND SPITTING ON THE TABLE IN FRONT OF THE DINER, EMITTING BURSTS OF SPICY AROMAS? HOW CAN THIS APPETITE APPEAL BE CAPTURED ON A TWO-DIMENSIONAL SHEET OF EKTACHROME?

TO CREATE A PHOTO THAT WAS AS BIG AND COLORFUL AS THIS LIVELY ASIAN-MEXICAN RECIPE, I FIRST ASKED ARTIST JEFF STILLWELL TO DO A BLACK-AND-WHITE "LAMB PAINTING" IN HIS DISTINCTIVE STYLE. THEN I SELECTED BOLD PLATTERS BY LOS ANGELES CERAMIC ARTIST LUNA GARCIA, WHO USES A RED CLAY AND BRIGHT SOUTHWESTERN GLAZES. WE FINISHED THE "PORTRAIT" OF LAMB FAJITAS BY ADDING MUGS OF THE POPULAR MEXICAN RICE DRINK, *HORCHATA*.

ADVANCE PREPARATION Cut the lamb into ⅛-inch slices, then cut the slices into very thin slivers. Place the meat in a bowl and mix in the hoisin sauce, soy sauce, and 2 teaspoons of the cooking oil.

Stem, seed, and cut the pepper into 1-inch-long slivers. Cut the green onions into the same length slivers. Mince the garlic and set aside. In a small bowl, combine the sauce ingredients and mix well.

LAST-MINUTE COOKING Place the salsa and guacamole in decorative bowls. Wrap the tortillas in foil and heat for 8 minutes in a 350°F. oven.

Combine the cornstarch with an equal amount of cold water. Set aside.

Place a wok over highest heat. When the wok is very hot, add the remaining 2 tablespoons cooking oil and the garlic. Tilt the wok to coat the sides with the oil. When the garlic just begins to turn white, in about 15 seconds, add the lamb. Stir-fry until the lamb just loses its raw outside color, about 1 minute.

Stir in the red pepper and green onions. Pour in the sauce. When the sauce comes to a low boil, stir in a little of the cornstarch mixture so the sauce glazes the lamb. Taste and adjust the seasonings, then spoon onto a heated platter or individual plates. Serve with the salsa, guacamole, and hot flour tortillas.

Serves: 4 as the entrée.

Menu Ideas: A fun Chopstix dinner for 4 might be—Lamb Fajitas, Crystal Soup with thin slices of salmon or swordfish, Yummy Yam Gai (use ½ pound cooked, shelled, and deveined shrimp in place of the chicken), and Chocolate Chip–Macadamia Nut Cookies with seasonal fruit marinated in kirsch.

Lamb Fajitas with New Age Guacamole,
South Seas Salsa, and the Mexican rice drink horchata

PHANTOM BEEF ON VEGETABLE THRONES

LIVER

1 pound calf's liver
2 white medium turnips
½ pound snow peas
3 cups slivered red cabbage
4 cloves garlic, finely minced
2 shallots, minced

SAUCE

3 tablespoons dry sherry
3 tablespoons tomato sauce
1 tablespoon Oriental
**   sesame oil**
1 tablespoon oyster sauce
2 teaspoons distilled white
**   vinegar**
1 teaspoon Chinese chili sauce
½ teaspoon sugar
¼ teaspoon salt

TO FINISH

2 tablespoons cornstarch
2 tablespoons cooking oil
1 tablespoon Oriental
**   sesame oil**
Freshly ground black pepper

I N A NATIONAL POLL, AMERICANS CHOSE LIVER AS THEIR NUMBER ONE FOOD ENEMY. EVIDENTLY THEY HAD NOT TRIED STIR-FRIED LIVER, COOKED IN A VERY HOT WOK AND PLACED ON A BED OF VEGETABLES SHIMMERING WITH OYSTER SAUCE. TRY THIS DELICACY ON THE UNSUSPECTING, CALLING IT BY THE POETIC CHINESE NAME PHANTOM BEEF. FOR ANOTHER VEGETABLE THRONE POSSIBILITY, USE A FRESH SEASONAL COMBINATION SUCH AS THE CLASSIC CHINESE AUTUMN DUO OF BABY BOK CHOY AND FRESH SHIITAKE MUSHROOMS.

ADVANCE PREPARATION Cut the calf's liver into ¼-inch slices, then cut the slices into bite-size pieces. Refrigerate until ready to use.

Peel the turnips. Cut into ¼-inch slices, stack the slices, and cut into ¼-inch slivers. Stem the snow peas, stack, and cut into ¼-inch crosswise slivers. Mix the turnips, snow peas, and cabbage until blended, then refrigerate.

Mix the garlic and shallots, and set aside. In a small bowl, combine the ingredients for the sauce, mix well and set aside.

LAST-MINUTE COOKING Preheat the oven to warm (200°F.). Combine the cornstarch with an equal amount of cold water and set aside.

Place the wok over highest heat. When the wok is very hot, add 1 tablespoon of the cooking oil to the center. Tilt the wok to coat the sides with oil. When the oil just begins to smoke, add the vegetables and stir-fry until they brighten, about 1 minute. Add the sesame oil and black pepper, then turn out onto a heated serving platter or dinner plates and spread in an even layer. Keep warm in the oven.

Immediately return the wok to highest heat and add the remaining 1 tablespoon cooking oil to the center. Add the garlic and shallots and sauté for a few seconds. Add the liver and stir-fry until the meat loses its raw outside color but each piece is still pink in the center, about 2 minutes. Pour in the sauce. When the sauce comes to a low boil, stir in a little of the cornstarch mixture so the sauce glazes the food. Taste and adjust the seasonings. Spoon the liver onto the platter or into the center of each dinner plate and serve at once.

Serves: 4 as the entrée.

Menu Ideas: For an early Sunday night dinner serving 4—Chopstix Barbecued Vegetables (barbecue these in the afternoon, then toss with the salad dressing from Crunchy Baja Salad, and serve this as the salad course), Phantom Beef on Vegetable Thrones with Wild Chinese Rice, and Lemon Ice Cream with Chocolate Grand Marnier Sauce.

MU SHU BEEF BONANZA

FILLING AND PANCAKES

½ pound beef filet, trimmed of
all fat
2 teaspoons hoisin sauce
2 teaspoons dry sherry
2 teaspoons Oriental
sesame oil
2 cups slivered carrots
2 cups slivered red cabbage
3 cups bean sprouts
4 eggs
3 cloves garlic, minced
2 teaspoons grated or finely
minced orange peel
12 Peking Chive Pancakes
(page 150)

SAUCE

3 tablespoons chicken broth
2 tablespoons dry sherry
1 tablespoon dark soy sauce
1 tablespoon oyster sauce
¼ teaspoon freshly ground
black pepper

TO FINISH

1 tablespoon cornstarch
5 tablespoons cooking oil
¾ cup hoisin sauce, for serving

MU SHU IS THE MOST POPULAR CHINESE RESTAURANT DISH IN THE UNITED STATES. TENDER PEKING PANCAKES, CRUNCHY SHREDDED VEGETABLES, TENDER MEAT, AND ACCENTS OF HOISIN SAUCE CREATE A TASTE BONANZA. SINCE THE PEKING CHIVE PANCAKES FREEZE WELL, COMPLETE THIS TASK FAR AHEAD OF THE EVENT. THIS DISH IS JUST AS GOOD WHEN YOU REPLACE THE BEEF WITH SHREDDED CHICKEN, PORK TENDERLOIN, LAMB, OR VEGETABLES.

ADVANCE PREPARATION Cut the meat into ¼-inch slices, stack the slices and cut into 2-inch slivers. Combine the meat with the hoisin sauce, sherry, and sesame oil; mix well and set aside.

Combine the carrots, cabbage, and sprouts; set aside. Break the eggs into a small bowl and set aside. Combine the garlic and orange peel and set aside. Set the pancakes aside. Combine the ingredients for sauce and set aside.

LAST-MINUTE COOKING Beat the eggs well. Combine the cornstarch with an equal amount of cold water and set aside. Fold the pancakes into quarters. Overlap them in a Chinese steamer tray and cover. Steam over rapidly boiling water for 2 minutes. Keep warm.

Place a wok over highest heat. When the wok is very hot, add 2 tablespoons of oil to the center. Tilt the wok to coat the sides with oil. When the oil just begins to smoke, add the eggs. Stir-fry, scrambling the eggs until they become firm, about 1 minute. Place the cooked eggs in a bowl.

Immediately return the wok to highest heat. Add 1 tablespoon of the oil to the center and tilt the pan to coat the sides. Add the beef and stir-fry until the meat just loses its·raw outside color, about 2 minutes. Transfer the beef to the bowl with the eggs.

Immediately return the wok to highest heat. Add the remaining 2 tablespoons oil to the center, then add the garlic and orange. Sauté for a few seconds, then add the vegetables, stir-frying until the cabbage brightens, about 2 minutes.

Return the eggs and beef to the wok, then pour in the sauce mixture. When the sauce comes to a low boil, stir in a little of the cornstarch mixture so the sauce glazes the food. Taste and adjust the seasonings, then transfer to a heated platter. Serve with the hot pancakes and a dish of hoisin sauce. Each person spreads a little hoisin sauce across the center of a pancake, places about ½ cup filling on top of the sauce, then rolls the pancake into a cylinder, folding the bottom end upward to keep the filling from escaping. Filled pancakes are eaten with the fingers.

Serves: 4 as the entrée.

THAI CHICKEN TACOS

Meat from one Thai-High
  Barbecued Chicken (page
  103)
½ hothouse cucumber
2 bunches cilantro (fresh
  coriander)
South Seas Salsa (page 39)
  or Ginger-Mango Salsa
  (page 94)
12 taco shells

FROM THE PHOTOGRAPHER'S POINT OF VIEW, THE EMPHASIS IN THIS PHOTO IS ON THE LIGHT, HEALTHFUL WAY OF EATING THAT HUGH PROMOTES. MUCH OF THIS EFFECT IS ACHIEVED THROUGH THE GREEN AND WHITE COLOR COMPOSITION, NANCY TOLER'S DELICATE BAMBOO-PATTERN PLATTER, AND THE WATERCOLOR PAINTING BEHIND IT. BUT THE NEXT EMPHASIS IS ON THE CRUNCHY TEXTURAL EXPERIENCE OF EATING THESE ASIAN TACOS. THE JULI-ENNED CUCUMBERS ARE ARRANGED TO CATCH THE LIGHT AND SHOW DIS-TINCTLY ON FILM, AND THUS GIVE THE VIEWER THE IMPRESSION OF CRISPY FRESHNESS.

ADVANCE PREPARATION Cut the meat and crisp skin from the barbecued chicken into shreds, then refrigerate until ready to use.

Cut the cucumber on a sharp diagonal into ¼-inch slices. Stack the slices and cut into shreds. Set aside. Wash and thoroughly dry the cilantro. Set aside.

LAST-MINUTE ASSEMBLING Place the chicken, salsa, cucumber, cilantro, and taco shells on separate plates. Each person assembles his or her own taco, first placing a layer of chicken in the bottom of the shell, followed by layers of salsa, cucumber, and a few cilantro sprigs.

Serves: 3 to 4 people as the entrée.

Note: The chicken can be prepared a day in advance, as can the salsa.

Menu Ideas: South of the border party with a mariachi band and homemade Margaritas—Tex-Mex Won Tons with New-Age Guacamole, Crunchy Baja Salad, Thai Chicken Tacos accompanied with California Cornbread and served piping hot with plenty of sweet butter and wild clover honey, and Mango Ice Cream with Tequila Sauce.

Thai Chicken Tacos with Ginger-Mango Salsa

ORIENTAL BURRITOS

FILLING AND TORTILLAS
1 pound ground pork
1 tablespoon oyster sauce
1 tablespoon Oriental
   sesame oil
5 cloves garlic, finely minced
1 medium onion, finely minced
2 ears corn
1 avocado
Lemon juice (optional)
8 flour tortillas, 8 inches in
   diameter

SAUCE
½ cup chicken broth
2 tablespoons dry sherry
1½ tablespoons hoisin sauce
1½ tablespoons oyster sauce
1 tablespoon bean sauce
1 tablespoon Oriental
   sesame oil
1 tablespoon red wine vinegar
1½ teaspoons Chinese chili
   sauce

TO FINISH
2 tablespoons cornstarch
3 tablespoons cooking oil

WHEN THE MEXICAN PREP CREW AT CHOPSTIX RESTAURANTS MEETS THE CHINESE CHEFS FOR STAFF MEALS, EAST MEETS WEST AND CULINARY FIREWORKS OCCUR: STIR-FRIED CHICKEN WITH SALSA, CHINESE ROAST PORK WITH BEANS, THAI CHARBROILED MEAT WRAPPED IN HOT FLOUR TORTILLAS WITH AN ACCENT OF GUACAMOLE.

THE FERMENTATION OF CROSS-CULTURAL CUISINES AMONG THE PEOPLES OF THE PACIFIC, PARTICULARLY IN LOS ANGELES, RESULTS IN A STORM OF NEW DISHES. IN THE FOLLOWING RECIPE EACH PERSON STUFFS LARGE FLOUR TORTILLAS WITH A RICH CHINESE MEAT SAUCE REMINISCENT OF AN OAXACAN *MOLE*, ADDS SHREDDED LETTUCE AND SLICED AVOCADO, AND ROLLS IT INTO A CYLINDER FOR A NEW-STYLE BURRITO.

ADVANCE PREPARATION Combine the meat, oyster sauce, and sesame oil; mix well and set aside. Mix garlic and onion, then set aside. Shuck the corn, stand ear on end, cut off kernels, and set aside. Pit the avocado, scoop out the flesh, and thinly slice; if done more than 30 minutes in advance of serving, sprinkle with a little lemon juice. Stack the tortillas and wrap in aluminum foil. In a small bowl, combine the sauce ingredients and mix well.

LAST-MINUTE COOKING Preheat the oven to 350°F. Place the tortillas in the oven for 10 minutes to warm. Meanwhile, combine the cornstarch with an equal amount of cold water and set aside.

Place the wok over highest heat. When hot, add 2 tablespoons of the oil to the center. Tilt the wok to coat the sides with oil. When the oil just begins to smoke, add the pork. Stir-fry, pressing meat against the sides of the wok, until it loses all of its raw color and breaks apart into little grains, about 5 minutes.

Immediately return the wok to highest heat. Add the remaining 1 tablespoon oil to the center, then add the garlic and onion. Stir-fry until the onion becomes translucent, about 2 minutes. With a slotted spoon, return the pork to the wok. Add the corn kernels and sauce, then bring to a low boil. Thicken the sauce with a little of the cornstarch mixture. Cook for 1 more minute over high heat. Turn onto a serving dish.

Arrange the meat filling, sliced avocado, and heated tortillas on the dining table. Each person assembles his or her own burrito. Place about ⅓ cup of filling across the bottom third of the tortilla, along with a few slices of avocado. Fold the sides of the tortilla part way over the filling, then roll the tortilla into a cylinder. Eat with fingers.

Serves: 4 as the entrée.

STIR-FRIED VEAL LOIN
WITH MUSHROOMS

VEAL
1 pound boneless veal loin
1 tablespoon light soy sauce
1 tablespoon dry sherry
1 teaspoon vegetable oil
¼ pound fresh shiitake
    mushrooms
¼ pound fresh chanterelle
    mushrooms
3 green onions
3 cloves garlic, minced
1 tablespoon finely minced
    fresh ginger

SAUCE
½ cup heavy (whipping) cream
¼ cup dry sherry
1 tablespoon oyster sauce
1 tablespoon Oriental sesame
    oil
1 teaspoon sugar
¼ teaspoon freshly ground
    black pepper

TO FINISH
3 tablespoons cooking oil
4 tablespoons (½ stick)
    unsalted butter

IN THIS RECIPE VERY THINLY SLICED VEAL LOIN IS STIR-FRIED IN A BLAZING HOT WOK. THE RICH CREAM-BASED SAUCE WITH ACCENTS OF OYSTER SAUCE AND SESAME PROVIDES A DYNAMIC TASTE CONTRAST WITH THE WILD FLAVORS OF THE FRESH SHIITAKE AND CHANTERELLE MUSHROOMS AND THE DELICACY OF THE VEAL.

ADVANCE PREPARATION Cut the veal into spoon-size pieces, ⅛ inch thick. Marinate in the soy sauce, sherry, and oil. Discard the stems from shiitake mushrooms, then cut the caps into ¼-inch-wide strips. Cut the chanterelles into ⅛-inch-thick slices. Cut the green onions on a diagonal into 1-inch pieces. Combine the garlic and ginger. In a small bowl, combine the sauce ingredients.

LAST-MINUTE COOKING Place a wok over highest heat. When very hot, add 2 tablespoons of oil to the center of the wok. Roll the oil around the sides of the wok. When the oil begins to smoke, add the veal and stir-fry until it just loses its raw outside color, about 1 minute. Transfer to a platter.

Immediately return the wok to high heat. Add the remaining oil and the butter to the center, then add the garlic and ginger and sauté until the garlic sizzles, about 15 seconds. Add the mushrooms and stir-fry until the mushrooms soften, about 2 minutes.

Add the sauce, bring to a vigorous boil, and cook until it thickens and turns golden brown, about 4 minutes. Add the green onions, cook 30 seconds, and then stir in the veal. Taste and adjust seasonings. Transfer to a heated platter or dinner plates and serve at once.

Serves: 2 as the entrée.

Menu Ideas: A special mushroom fantasy feast for mushroom hunters newly returned from a morning tramping up and down moist hills— Shiitake Yaki, Three Mushroom Soup, Stir-Fried Veal Loin with Mushrooms, Wild Mushroom Pasta, and for dessert, mushroom shaped meringues on homemade ice cream.

Chopstix Barbecued Vegetables

Chapter 6

MAGICAL SIDE DISHES FOR ANY ENTREE

THE CHOPSTIX APPROACH TO SIDE DISHES IS TO KEEP THE FOOD SIMPLE, INNOVATIVE, AND FULL OF FLAVOR. WHY IS IT THAT MOST SIDE DISHES HAVE NO MORE TASTE THAN THE FOOD SERVED AT A HOSPITAL OR CONVALESCENT HOME? FOOD SHOULD NEVER TASTE "DELICATE" (NOT MUCH FLAVOR), OR "SUBTLE" (NO FLAVOR). TASTE, TASTE, AND TASTE AGAIN THROUGHOUT THE COOKING. FINGERS DIP INTO SAUCES, THE PEPPER GRINDER RATTLES OVER A BUBBLING SOUP, HANDS MOVE QUICKLY TO CHOP EXTRA BASIL, AND A DASH OF OYSTER SAUCE PROVIDES THAT SOUGHT-AFTER RICH FLAVOR. DANNY KAYE WAS FOND OF SAYING, "IF YOU GIVE TEN PEOPLE THE SAME RECIPE, TEN DIFFERENT DISHES ALWAYS RESULT." COOKING IS NOT A SCIENCE, AND EVEN A COOK WHO HAS JUST DISCOVERED THAT ROOM CALLED "THE KITCHEN" CAN ADD A NEW CULINARY CHAPTER, WITH DRAMATIC LAST-MINUTE SEASONING ADDITIONS. THE RESULTS MAY NOT BE PERFECT, BUT THESE SPONTANEOUS PERSONAL TOUCHES MAKE COOKING AN ADVENTURE AND CREATE MAGIC FOR THE TABLE.

CHOPSTIX BARBECUED VEGETABLES

VEGETABLES

asparagus, broccoli, carrots,
cauliflower, eggplant,
green beans, green onions,
mushrooms, peppers,
summer squash

VEGETABLE BARBECUE SAUCE

¼ cup minced green onions,
fresh basil, or cilantro
(fresh coriander)
1 tablespoon finely minced
fresh ginger
3 cloves garlic, finely minced
1 tablespoon grated or finely
minced lemon peel
⅓ cup lemon juice
3 tablespoons dry sherry
3 tablespoons extra-virgin
olive oil
2 tablespoons light soy sauce
¼ teaspoon freshly ground
black pepper

BARBECUED VEGETABLES TASTE SENSATIONAL! SERVE THEM HOT OR CHILLED AS APPETIZERS, ADD THEM TO SALADS, TAKE THEM STRAIGHT FROM THE BARBECUE AND ROLL IN HEATED FLOUR TORTILLAS WITH ADDED SPOONFULS OF GINGER MANGO SALSA (PAGE 94), OR USE THEM AS A BOLD-TASTING VEGETABLE ACCOMPANIMENT TO MEAT AND SEAFOOD ENTRÉES.

CHOOSE VEGETABLES THAT LIE FLAT ON THE BARBECUE AND ARE LARGE ENOUGH NOT TO FALL THROUGH THE GRILL. LONGER COOKING VEGETABLES SUCH AS BROCCOLI AND CAULIFLOWER SHOULD BE BLANCHED FIRST, AND THEN BARBECUED JUST TO PICK UP THE WONDERFUL BARBECUE TASTE.

THE FOLLOWING RECIPE GIVES A SIMPLE OLIVE OIL, LEMON, AND SOY SAUCE BARBECUE SAUCE TO BRUSH ACROSS THE VEGETABLES AS THEY COOK. BUT FOR A DIFFERENT FLAVOR TRY THE MARINADES FROM BARBECUED VEAL CHOPS WITH MACADAMIA NUTS (PAGE 97) AND ASIAN BARBECUED SALMON (PAGE 92).

PREPARATION Prepare your choice of vegetables. Snap off the tough bottoms of the asparagus stems. Cut the broccoli into long pieces including some of the stem, then drop into 4 quarts of boiling water and cook until the color brightens; transfer immediately to ice water, chill, and pat dry. Peel the carrots; if large, split in half lengthwise. Cut the cauliflower into long pieces and follow the directions for cooking broccoli, but blanch for 2 minutes. Cut the eggplant into ½-inch slices. Cut off the stems from the green beans. Discard the root ends and ragged green tips from the green onions. Trim the tough stems from mushrooms. Stem and seed the peppers; cut into 2-inch-wide strips. Trim the stem end from the squash, then cut into long ½-inch-thick pieces.

In small bowl, combine all the ingredients for the sauce and mix well.

BARBECUING VEGETABLES If using a gas barbecue, preheat to medium (350°F.). If using charcoal or wood, prepare the fire. When the coals or wood are ash-covered, brush the vegetables with the sauce and place on the grill. Barbecue the vegetables until they are tender, turning them over occasionally and brushing with more of the barbecue sauce.

STEAMED VEGETABLES WITH ASIAN ACCENTS

VEGETABLES

asparagus (4 minutes), broccoli (5 minutes for the florets, 8 minutes for the whole head), Brussels sprouts (14 minutes when cut in half), carrots (4 to 10 minutes depending on size), cauliflower (5 minutes for the florets, 12 minutes for the whole head), Chinese long beans (4 minutes), corn (2 minutes), green beans (10 minutes), new potatoes (15 minutes sliced), squash (6 minutes)

ASIAN BUTTER SAUCE

½ cup unsalted butter
2 cloves garlic, finely minced
1 tablespoon finely minced fresh ginger
1 bunch finely minced chives, basil, or cilantro (fresh coriander)
2 tablespoons lemon juice
1 tablespoon light soy sauce
Salt and freshly ground black pepper to taste

BEAUTIFUL GARDEN VEGETABLES, PERFECTLY STEAMED, SPARKLING WITH COLOR, AND SEASONED TO HEIGHTEN THEIR NATURAL FLAVOR, ARE IDEAL ACCENTS TO MEAT AND SEAFOOD ENTREES. CHOOSE ONE OR MORE VEGETABLES THAT TAKE THE SAME AMOUNT OF TIME TO COOK, AND CUT THEM INTO THE SAME SHAPE AND SIZE. OR, IF YOU ARE COMBINING VEGETABLES THAT TAKE VARYING TIMES TO COOK, EITHER CUT THE LONGER-COOKING VEGETABLES INTO SMALLER SHAPES OR ADD THE SHORTER-COOKING VEGETABLES DURING THE STEAMING PROCESS. BE CAREFUL NOT TO STACK THE VEGETABLES OR TO COVER THE ENTIRE STEAMER TIER, WHICH HINDERS STEAM CIRCULATION.

IN THE LIST OF VEGETABLES AT LEFT, ALL LEAFY VEGETABLES ARE OMITTED (THEY WILT TOO FAST), AS WELL AS BOK CHOY, CABBAGE, EGGPLANT, MUSHROOMS, ONIONS, PEPPERS, AND SNOW PEAS. WHILE IT IS POSSIBLE TO STEAM THESE, THEY TASTE FAR BETTER STIR-FRIED OR BARBECUED.

THIS RECIPE GIVES A SIMPLE ASIAN BUTTER SAUCE TO DRIZZLE OVER THE COOKED VEGETABLES, BUT THE STEAMED VEGETABLES TASTE GREAT JUST SERVED WITH LEMON WEDGES, LOW-SODIUM SOY SAUCE, AND FRESHLY GROUND PEPPER, OR WITH CHOPSTIX DIPPING SAUCES.

PREPARATION AND COOKING Choose one or more of the vegetables and cut to the same size pieces. Count on serving at least 1 cup of vegetables per person.

Place the butter, garlic, and ginger in a small saucepan over medium heat. When the garlic sizzles, tip the contents into a small bowl. Add the chives, lemon juice, soy sauce, salt, and pepper. Set aside at room temperature.

Place 3 inches of water in a Chinese steamer, put over high heat, and bring to a rapid boil. Scatter the vegetables over the surface of the Chinese steamer tray, cover, and steam the vegetables according to the cooking times given, until they brighten but are still crisp. Transfer the vegetables to a heated serving platter or dinner plates, drizzle the butter sauce on top, and serve at once.

CRAZY COCONUT
NOODLE TOSS

NOODLES

½ **pound dried spaghetti-style noodles (plain or one of the flavored types)**

¼ **cup cooking oil**

1 **cup thinly sliced fresh button mushrooms**

1 **sweet red pepper, seeded and slivered**

1 **cup slivered red cabbage**

1 **cup stemmed and slivered snow peas**

¼ **cup chopped fresh basil**

⅓ **cup chopped fresh mint leaves**

⅓ **cup chopped green onions**

SAUCE

¾ **cup unsweetened coconut milk**

2 **tablespoons dry sherry**

1 **tablespoon oyster sauce**

1 **tablespoon light soy sauce**

1 **teaspoon Chinese chili sauce**

¼ **teaspoon salt**

TO FINISH

1 **tablespoon cornstarch**

CRAZY COCONUT NOODLE TOSS IS A SIGNATURE DISH AT THE CHOPSTIX RESTAURANTS. THE FRESH FLAVORS AND EASE OF PREPARATION SHOW THE SUCCESSFUL MERGING OF THAI, CHINESE, AND CALIFORNIAN INGREDIENTS AND COOKING STYLES. IN THE PHOTO, THE DISH IS HOVERING IN FRONT OF THE CHOPSTIX ON MELROSE AVENUE, WITH LOS ANGELES' FAMOUS "HOLLYWOOD" SIGN ON THE HILLS IN THE BACKGROUND. JEFF STILLWELL RE-CREATED THE CHOPSTIX RESTAURANT SCENE FOR THIS PHOTO, AND FOOD STYLIST STEPHEN SHERN PRODUCED THE GRACEFUL PRESENTATION OF THE NOODLES TOSSED WITH BASIL, MINT, AND CHILI.

ADVANCE PREPARATION Drop the noodles into 4 quarts of rapidly boiling water. Cook until they lose their raw taste but are still firm, about 5 minutes. Drain, rinse with hot water, and drain again. Toss the noodles with 2 tablespoons of the peanut oil.

Toss the vegetables and herbs with the noodles until evenly mixed.

In a small bowl, combine the sauce ingredients.

LAST-MINUTE COOKING Combine the cornstarch with an equal amount of cold water and set aside.

Place a skillet over highest heat. Add the remaining 2 tablespoons of cooking oil. When very hot, add the noodle mixture. Sauté for about 3 minutes, until the noodles begin to heat.

Add the sauce and bring to a low boil. Stir in a little of the cornstarch mixture and continue cooking until the noodles are well heated. Turn out onto a heated platter or onto individual plates. Serve at once.

Serves: 4 as the pasta dish with any meat or seafood entrée.

Menu Ideas: A quick family meal—broiled fish, Crazy Coconut Noodle Toss, and a tossed green salad.

Crazy Coconut Noodle Toss

STIR-FRIED GARDEN VEGETABLES

LONG-COOKING VEGETABLES

asparagus (thick stalks), broccoli, Brussels sprouts, carrots, cauliflower, eggplant (see Note), green beans

SHORT-COOKING VEGETABLES

asparagus (thin stalks), cabbage (bok choy, celery cabbage, green and red head cabbage), celery, Chinese long beans, corn kernels, mushrooms (button, enoki, oyster, shiitake), onions (green onions, yellow onions, red onions), peas (shelled sweet peas, snow peas, sugar-snap peas), peppers (all types of sweet peppers and chilies), squash (pattypan, yellow summer squash, zucchini), fresh water chestnuts

STIR-FRIED VEGETABLES—BRILLIANTLY COLORED, CRISP, AND GLISTENING WITH A SAUCE—ARE ONE OF THE HEALTHIEST, EASIEST VEGETABLE SIDE DISHES TO ACCOMPANY ANY AMERICAN OR ASIAN ENTRÉE. KEEP THE VEGETABLE STIR-FRY SIMPLE BY LIMITING YOURSELF TO NO MORE THAN THREE VEGETABLES. CUT THE VEGETABLES TO THE SAME SHAPE AND SIZE SO THEY COOK EVENLY. STIR-FRY NO MORE THAN FIVE CUPS OF VEGETABLES OR THE VEGETABLES WILL TURN TO MUSH AS THEY BEGIN TO BOIL IN THEIR OWN JUICES. THUS, IF YOU WANT TO SERVE A STIR-FRIED VEGETABLE DISH TO EIGHT PEOPLE, DOUBLE THE AMOUNT, AND, AIDED BY A FRIEND, COOK THE VEGETABLES IN TWO WOKS SIMULTANEOUSLY.

FOLLOW THE OUTLINE LISTING VEGETABLES COMMONLY FOUND IN OUR SUPERMARKETS OR EXPERIMENT WITH THE GROWING NUMBER OF ORIENTAL VEGETABLES FOUND IN ASIAN MARKETS. WHILE THE FOLLOWING RECIPE GIVES ONLY ONE SAUCE, TO VARY THE FLAVOR SUBSTITUTE ANY OF THE SAUCES USED FOR STIR-FRIED DISHES IN THIS BOOK.

PREPARATION Cut one or more vegetables to the same shape and size, not to exceed a total of 5 cups. The smaller the vegetables are cut, the quicker they will cook and the better the dish will look.

If choosing long-cooking vegetables, once these are cut, drop one vegetable type at a time into 2 quarts rapidly boiling water. As soon as the vegetable brightens in color (1 to 2 minutes), immediately transfer to ice water. Repeat process with other types of long-cooking vegetables. Pat dry, then combine with any short-cooking vegetables you have chosen.

Set aside any fragile vegetables.

In a small bowl, combine the sauce ingredients. Mince garlic or ginger.

**bean sprouts, torn leafy greens
(lettuce, spinach)**

SAUCE

**(or choose a sauce from one of
your favorite stir-fry
dishes)
¼ cup dry sherry
2 tablespoons oyster sauce
1 tablespoon Oriental sesame
oil
½ teaspoon sugar
¼ teaspoon freshly ground
black pepper**

TO FINISH

**1 tablespoon cornstarch
2 tablespoons cooking oil
Few cloves garlic and/or 1
tablespoon finely minced
fresh ginger**

LAST-MINUTE COOKING Combine the cornstarch with an equal amount of cold water and set aside.

Place a wok over highest heat. When the wok is very hot, add the cooking oil to the center, then add the garlic and/or ginger. Sauté for a few seconds, then add the blanched long-cooking vegetables and the short-cooking vegetables. Stir-fry until the long-cooking vegetables re-heat and the short-cooking vegetables brighten, about 2 minutes.

Pour in the sauce. When it comes to a low boil, stir in a little of the cornstarch mixture so the sauce lightly glazes the vegetables. Stir in any fragile vegetables. Taste and adjust the seasonings, then spoon onto a heated platter or individual plates. Serve at once.

Serves: 4 as the vegetable dish with any meat or seafood entrée.

Note: Eggplant is an exception, for it should be neither blanched nor stir-fried in an open wok. Set aside 3 to 5 cups eggplant cut into ¼-inch-thick spoon-size pieces. When the oil in the wok is hot, first stir-fry the eggplant (and plenty of minced garlic) for 2 minutes, then add the sauce and a splash of dry sherry, broth, or water. Cover and cook over highest heat until the eggplant softens (about 5 minutes), adding more liquid if necessary to prevent scorching. If you want, add just a few blanched long-cooking vegetables and/or a few short-cooking vegetables. Stir-fry for about 1 minute to heat, then tip onto platter or plates and serve.

FIRECRACKER NOODLES

NOODLES

8 ounces rice sticks
¼ pound ground lamb
3 cloves garlic, finely minced
2 teaspoons finely minced fresh ginger
8 dried black Chinese mushrooms
2 medium carrots
1 cup shredded green cabbage

SAUCE

⅓ cup chicken broth
¼ cup dry sherry
1 tablespoon light soy sauce
1 tablespoon Chinese chili sauce
2 teaspoons dark soy sauce
2 teaspoons Oriental sesame oil
¼ teaspoon sugar
½ cup finely minced green onions
¼ cup minced cilantro (fresh coriander)

TO FINISH

1 tablespoon cornstarch
8 Peking Chive Pancakes (page 150), optional
3 tablespoons cooking oil
½ cup hoisin sauce

WHEN I SAW THIS PLATTER BY "ARTQUAKE," I KNEW IT WAS PERFECT FOR THIS COOKBOOK. AS HUGH'S RECIPES BECOME MORE AND MORE IN-FLUENCED BY THE FOODS OF TROPICAL COUNTRIES, CHILIES PLAY AN EXPAND-ING ROLE. VISUALLY AND TASTE-WISE, THE CHILI IS THE FIRECRACKER ADDING THE BANG TO YOUR RECIPE!

ADVANCE PREPARATION Soak the rice sticks in hot water until soft, about 30 minutes. Drain thoroughly and then cut into 6-inch lengths. There should be 4 cups of rice sticks.

Combine the lamb with the garlic and ginger, mixing thoroughly. Set aside.

Soak the dried mushrooms in hot water until soft, about 20 minutes. Discard the stems, stack the caps, and cut into slivers. Sliver the carrots. Mix the rice stick noodles, mushrooms, carrots, and cabbage until evenly combined, then set aside.

In a small bowl, combine the ingredients for the sauce and mix well.

LAST-MINUTE COOKING Combine the cornstarch with an equal amount of cold water and set aside.

If using the Peking pancakes, fold in quarters and steam for 5 minutes.

Place a wok over highest heat. Add the oil. As it begins to heat, add the lamb and stir-fry, pressing the meat against the sides of the wok, until it loses its raw color and separates into small pieces, about 3 minutes.

Add the rice stick noodle mixture and stir-fry until the noodles and meat are evenly combined, about 2 minutes. Pour in the sauce. Bring to a low boil, then stir in a little cornstarch mixture to lightly thicken. Turn out onto a heated platter or individual plates. If using the pan-cakes, rub each pancake with 1 tablespoon hoisin sauce, then add 1 cup of the noodles and roll into a cylinder. Serve at once.

Serves: 4 as the pasta dish with any meat or seafood entrée.

Firecracker Noodles wrapped in Peking Chive Pancakes (recipe on page 150)

CHOPSTIX NOODLE MAGIC

VEGETABLES

3 cloves garlic, minced

1 shallot, minced

1 cup basil leaves, slivered

2 cups short-cooking
    vegetables (see Stir-Fried
    Garden Vegetables, page
    134)

2 tablespoons white sesame
    seeds

1 tablespoon cornstarch

SAUCE

3 tablespoons dry sherry

3 tablespoons tomato sauce

2 tablespoons light soy sauce

2 tablespoons lime juice

2 tablespoons dark brown
    sugar

1 teaspoon lime peel, grated or
    finely minced

½ teaspoon Chinese chili
    sauce

salt to taste

TO FINISH

salt

½ pound dried spaghetti-style
    noodles (plain or flavored)

2 tablespoons cooking oil

L**ATE ONE AFTERNOON, WE RACED ALONG THE CHAO PHYA RIVER IN A LONG, NARROW "SPEEDY BOAT" PROPELLED BY A GIANT OUTBOARD ENGINE. JUST PAST THE TEMPLE OF DAWN, THE TURMOIL OF BANGKOK SLIPPED AWAY AS THE BOAT DISAPPEARED INTO A MAZE OF NARROW CANALS. THE PINK LIGHT OF A SETTING SUN CAST AN ETHEREAL LIGHT ON ORCHID FARMS, TROPICAL PALM FORESTS, TEAKWOOD HOUSES ON STILTS, CHILDREN SWIMMING AMONG THE WATER HYACINTHS, AND ANCIENT LADIES PROPELLING VEGETABLE-LADEN BOATS.**

INTERRUPTING OUR RETURN TO THE HOTEL, WE STOPPED AT A WATERFRONT RESTAURANT TO SNACK ON QUICKLY STIR-FRIED NOODLES WITH BASIL, CHILI, AND LIME. THIS SIMPLE RECIPE, WITH ITS MAGICAL FLAVORS, IS A GOOD PASTA DISH TO SERVE ALONGSIDE EITHER AN AMERICAN OR ASIAN ENTRÉE. USING A "DESIGNER" PASTA SUCH AS LEMON BASIL FETTUCCINI, RATHER THAN PLAIN DRIED SPAGHETTI, ADDS AN EXTRA DIMENSION.

PREPARATION AND COOKING Prepare the garlic, shallot, and basil. Referring to the list of short-cooking vegetables, choose one or more vegetables and set aside 2 cups of these cut into slivers.

Place an ungreased skillet over high heat, add the sesame seeds, and toast until lightly golden. Set aside. Mix the cornstarch with an equal amount of cold water. Combine sauce ingredients. Set aside.

Bring at least 4 quarts of water to a vigorous boil. Lightly salt the water and add the noodles. Cook the noodles until they lose their raw taste but are still firm, about 5 minutes. Immediately drain in a colander.

Place a 12-inch sauté pan over high heat. Add the oil, garlic, and shallots and sauté for 15 seconds; when the garlic begins to sizzle, add the vegetables. Sauté the vegetables until they brighten, about 1 minute.

Transfer noodles to a sauté pan and add the basil, sesame seeds, and sauce. Stir and toss, mixing the vegetables evenly with the noodles. Add a little of the cornstarch solution and cook until the noodles are glazed with the sauce. Taste and adjust the seasonings, especially for salt, then serve at once.

Serves: 2 as the pasta dish with any meat or seafood entrée.

Menu Ideas: Quick Chopstix dinner for 4 on a weekday night—Thai-High Barbecued Chicken (chicken marinates during the day), Chopstix Noodle Magic (double the recipe), and Tropical Paradise Salad (dressing made a day in advance).

JADE NOODLES

NOODLES

½ pound dried spaghetti-style noodles (plain or one of the flavored types)
2 tablespoons cooking oil
3 ounces enoki mushrooms
1 sweet red pepper

SAUCE

12 ounces spinach leaves, washed and dried
2 cloves garlic, minced
¼ cup cilantro (fresh coriander) sprigs
10 basil leaves
1 green onion
½ cup heavy (whipping) cream
2 tablespoons dry sherry
2 tablespoons distilled white vinegar
2 tablespoons Oriental sesame oil
1 tablespoon light soy sauce
2 teaspoons sugar
½ teaspoon chili sauce

TO FINISH

1 tablespoon cornstarch
2 tablespoons cooking oil

THE BRILLIANT GREEN OF THIS ASIAN VARIATION ON PESTO SAUCE MAKES A PASTA DISH THAT CAN BE THE VISUAL CENTERPIECE OF A MEAL. THE GREEN COLOR IS MOST INTENSE WHEN A BLENDER RATHER THAN A FOOD PROCESSOR IS USED. THIS EASY, ROBUST NOODLE RECIPE IS A GREAT ACCOMPANIMENT TO GRILLED FISH OR BARBECUED MEAT. A CHOPSTIX MENU WELCOMING HOME WORLD TRAVELERS MIGHT BE ASIAN RED PEPPER SALAD, BARBECUED VEAL CHOPS WITH MACADEMIA NUTS ACCOMPANIED BY JADE NOODLES, AND FOR DESSERT, COCONUT FLAN SUPREME.

ADVANCE PREPARATION Drop the noodles into 4 quarts of rapidly boiling water. Cook until they lose their raw taste but are still firm, about 5 minutes. Drain, rinse with hot water, and drain again. Toss the noodles with the cooking oil.

Cut off and discard the bottom ends of the mushroom stems, then separate the stems. Stem, seed, and sliver the red pepper. Toss the mushrooms and pepper with the noodles until evenly mixed.

Prepare the sauce. Place the spinach in a food processor and finely mince. Add the garlic, cilantro, basil, and green onion and finely mince. Add the remaining ingredients and blend for 1 minute. Pour the sauce into an electric blender and blend the sauce until thoroughly puréed (about 20 seconds). Transfer to a small bowl.

LAST-MINUTE COOKING Combine the cornstarch with an equal amount of cold water and set aside.

Place a sauté pan over highest heat. Add the cooking oil. When very hot, add the noodle mixture. Sauté for about 3 minutes, until the noodles begin to heat.

Add the sauce and bring to a low boil. Stir in a little of the cornstarch mixture to lightly thicken the sauce. Turn out onto a heated platter or individual plates. Serve at once.

Serves: 4 as the pasta dish with any meat or seafood entrée.

PACIFIC-STYLE TAMALES

12 dried corn husks
1 tablespoon finely minced
    fresh ginger
½ pound filet of Chilean sea
    bass, white fish, or sole,
    cut in 1-inch cubes
1 egg white
¾ teaspoon salt
⅛ teaspoon Chinese chili
    sauce
1½ cups heavy (whipping)
    cream, very cold
2 ears corn, husked
South Seas Salsa (page 39)
New Age Guacamole (page 42)

AT THE AUTHENTIC CAFE, LOS ANGELES'S VERSION OF THE SPACE BAR FROM *STAR WARS*, BUSINESSMEN IN THREE-PIECE SUITS READING THE *WALL STREET JOURNAL*, YOUNG COUPLES IN DREADLOCKS, AND STARS FROM TELEVISION SOAP OPERAS SIT ELBOW-TO-ELBOW EATING EVERYTHING FROM TAMALES TO SPICY CHINESE DUMPLINGS. THIS RECIPE WAS INSPIRED BY ONE OF CHEF-OWNER ROGER HAYOT'S CREATIONS. THE SEAFOOD MOUSSE, STUDDED WITH FRESH CORN KERNELS, LIES HIDDEN INSIDE THE CORN HUSKS. THIS IS A GREAT SIDE DISH TO SERVE WITH ONE OF THE SOUPS FROM CHAPTER 3 AND A BIG GARDEN SALAD.

ADVANCE PREPARATION Soak the corn husks in cold water for 1 hour, then pat dry. In a food processor, add the ginger, fish cubes, egg white, salt, and chili sauce. Purée until the mixture is smooth, then place the processor bowl in the refrigerator for 2 hours or in the freezer for 30 minutes.

Return the processor bowl to the machine, turn the machine on, and slowly pour the chilled cream down the feed tube in a thin stream. Scrape the sides of the processor bowl and blend again until the mixture is homogeneous.

Stand the ears of corn on one end and cut off the kernels. You should have approximately 3 cups. Stir the kernels into the mousse. Open a corn husk flat on a surface. Place approximately ¼ to ⅓ cup mousse in the center of the husk and fold the edges inward. Fold the husk over to close. (The mousse will expand a little during steaming, so do not overfill the husk.) Tie the husk closed with string or thinly sliced corn husk. Fold the remaining tamales. (This may be done hours in advance and the tamales refrigerated.)

LAST-MINUTE COOKING Bring the water to a low boil in a Chinese steamer. Place the tamales on the steamer tier, place the tier over boiling water, cover the steamer, and cook about 12 minutes over high heat. Serve the tamales with South Seas Salsa and New Age Guacamole.

Serves: 8 as an appetizer or 4 as a side dish with salad and soup.

Pacific-Style Tamales with New Age Guacamole
and South Seas Salsa

WILD MUSHROOM PASTA

MUSHROOMS
1 ounce dried porcini
    mushrooms
¼ pound fresh shiitake
    mushrooms
½ pound small fresh button
    mushrooms
1 bunch chives, chopped
4 cloves garlic, minced
2 shallots, minced

SAUCE
½ cup chicken broth or heavy
    cream
½ cup dry sherry
2 tablespoons green
    peppercorns, rinsed of
    brine and drained
    (optional)
1 tablespoon oyster sauce
1 tablespoon Oriental
    sesame oil
½ teaspoon sugar
¼ teaspoon freshly ground
    black pepper
salt to taste

TO FINISH
1 tablespoon cornstarch
salt
½ pound dried spaghetti-style
    noodles (plain or
    mushroom flavored)
6 tablespoons (¾ stick)
    unsalted butter

NAPA: FIELDS OF MUSTARD GROWING AMONG THE GRAPEVINES, PINE-COVERED HILLS RISING FROM THE VALLEY FLOOR, OLD STONE WINERIES, GREAT HOMES AT THE END OF LONG DRIVES LINED WITH LIQUIDAMBAR TREES, HOT-AIR BALLOONS SILHOUETTED AGAINST THE BLUE SKY ON EARLY WINTER MORNINGS, GREAT RESTAURANTS, AND SPIRITED WINE AUCTIONS. NOWHERE ELSE IN AMERICA IS THERE SUCH PASSION FOR MAKING FINE WINES AND MATCHING THEM WITH GREAT FOOD. THIS IS A WINTER DISH I PARTICULARLY LOOK FORWARD TO PREPARING AFTER AN ADVENTURE HUNTING FOR MUSHROOMS IN THE HILLS BEHIND OUR HOME IN NAPA. A MIXTURE OF STORE-BOUGHT MUSHROOMS CREATES EQUALLY GOOD RESULTS.

ADVANCE PREPARATION Soak the porcini mushrooms in 2 cups hot water for 1 hour; rinse, drain, and sliver. Discard the stems for the shiitake mushrooms, and sliver the caps. Cut the button mushrooms into very thin slices. Set aside the chives. Combine the garlic and shallots. In a small bowl, combine all of the sauce ingredients except salt.

LAST-MINUTE COOKING Mix the cornstarch with an equal amount of cold water.

Bring at least 4 quarts of water to a vigorous boil. Lightly salt the water and add the noodles. Cook until they lose the raw taste but are still firm, about 5 minutes. Immediately drain in a colander.

Place a 12-inch sauté pan over high heat. Add the butter, garlic, and shallots. When the garlic sizzles, in about 15 seconds, add the mushrooms and sauté until they soften, about 5 minutes. Add the sauce and bring to a vigorous boil.

Transfer the noodles to the sauté pan. Stir in a little of the cornstarch mixture, and then toss the noodles with the mushrooms until evenly combined and the noodles are glazed with the sauce. Taste and adjust seasonings, particularly for salt. Transfer to a heated platter or dinner plates, sprinkle on chives, and serve at once.

Serves: 2 as the pasta dish with any meat or seafood entrée.

Menu Ideas: Wild Mushroom Pasta is a wonderful dish served with barbecued or roasted meats, with broiled fish, or as a vegetarian dinner accompanied by a big garden salad.

CHAMPAGNE RICE PILAF

RICE

1½ cups long-grain white rice
(not instant or converted)
4 cloves garlic, finely minced
2 shallots, minced
3 tablespoons unsalted butter
1 sweet red pepper, seeded and
chopped
¼ cup white sesame seeds

SAUCE

1 cup chicken broth
1½ cups champagne
2 tablespoons light soy sauce
1 teaspoon freshly grated
nutmeg
½ teaspoon Chinese chili
sauce
½ teaspoon salt
¼ teaspoon ground cloves

TO FINISH

1 cup dark raisins
½ cup minced green onions
⅓ cup chopped fresh basil

PERHAPS MORE APPROPRIATELY CALLED DRUNKEN RICE, THIS IS A WONDERFUL DISH FOR ENTERTAINING. EVERY STEP OF THE RECIPE CAN BE COMPLETED A DAY IN ADVANCE: RINSE THE RICE IN COLD WATER TO REMOVE THE GLUTEN; SAUTÉ IT IN BUTTER, WHICH KEEPS EVERY RICE GRAIN SEPARATE; SIMMER THE RICE IN A SEASONED BROTH; AND THEN, REHEAT THE RICE A DAY LATER IN THE OVEN OR MICROWAVE.

AS A FESTIVE WAY TO SERVE THE RICE, PRESS THE PILAF FIRMLY INTO OILED RAMEKINS, AND AFTER REHEATING THE RICE, INVERT THE RAMEKINS ON EACH DINNER PLATE. THIS IS SUCH A FUN RECIPE TO MAKE THAT IT WOULD BE A SHAME TO RUIN THE DISH USING INSTANT RICE. MAKE A STATEMENT FOR GOOD TASTE AND PURCHASE LONG-GRAIN WHITE RICE.

ADVANCE PREPARATION Place the rice in a sieve. Wash under cold water, stirring with your fingers, until the rinse water is no longer cloudy, about 2 minutes. Drain thoroughly.

Set aside the garlic and shallots with the butter. Set aside the red pepper. In a small ungreased skillet set over high heat, stir the sesame seeds until light golden, about 2 minutes. Immediately tip out and set aside. In a small bowl, combine the sauce ingredients.

COOKING Place a 3-quart saucepan over medium-high heat. Add the garlic, shallots, and butter and sauté until the butter sizzles. Add the rice and stir until coated with butter and heated through, about 5 minutes.

Add the raisins and sauce mixture. Bring to a low boil, stirring. Cover, reduce the heat to the lowest setting, and simmer until all the liquid is absorbed, about 18 to 25 minutes. If making the rice ahead, cool and refrigerate. Reheat in a 325°F. oven until piping hot, about 15 minutes.

Remove the cover. Stir in the pepper, green onions, basil, and sesame seeds. Serve at once.

Serves: 6 as the rice dish for any meat or seafood entrée.

Menu Ideas: A wonderful dinner for 12—shelled, deveined, and chilled shrimp (2 pounds) served with 3 Chopstix dipping sauces as the main appetizer; Smoked Baby Back Ribs with Chopstix Barbecue Sauce (count on 6 ribs per person), accompanied by Champagne Rice Pilaf (double the recipe); then the salad course of Rainbow Salad with Raspberry Vinegar (double the recipe); conclude with Lemon Ice Cream with Chocolate Grand Marnier Sauce.

REALLY RISQUE RICE

RICE

4 cups cold cooked rice (about
    1 cup raw)
1 cup dark raisins
½ cup rice vinegar
6 dried black Chinese
    mushrooms
1 sweet red pepper
3 green onions
½ cup pine nuts

SAUCE

3 tablespoons tomato sauce
2 tablespoons dry sherry
1 tablespoon oyster sauce
1 tablespoon Oriental
    sesame oil
½ teaspoon sugar
½ teaspoon Chinese chili
    sauce (optional)

TO FINISH

3 eggs
¼ cup cooking oil

WHEN I BEGAN PLANNING HOW I COULD CAPTURE THE PLAYFUL LOOK AND TASTES OF REALLY RISQUÉ RICE, I IMMEDIATELY THOUGHT OF THE UNIQUE SERVING PIECES MADE BY LAGUNA BEACH CERAMIC ARTIST BARBARA SCHUPPE, WHOSE ART ALSO APPEARS ELSEWHERE IN THIS BOOK. HER WORK IS FILLED WITH PLAYFUL IMAGERY AND HUMOROUS SYMBOLS, ESPECIALLY THE FIFTIES AND THE MUSIC SCENE. AS ONE CAN SEE ON OTHER PAGES, THE SHAPES OF HER TABLETOP ARTWARE DERIVE FROM BOTH WESTERN AND ASIAN CERAMIC TRADITIONS.

WHEN WE SERVE THIS RECIPE AT HOME, HUGH NEVER TRIES TO SQUEEZE A DOUBLE BATCH INTO ONE WOK. INSTEAD, FOR A LARGE PARTY, A GUEST STIR-FRIES A DUPLICATE PORTION IN A NEIGHBORING WOK WHILE THE REST OF OUR GUESTS ENJOY THE COOKING THEATRE.

ADVANCE PREPARATION Place the cooked rice in a plastic food bag and then squeeze the bag to break the rice into little pieces.

Soak the raisins in the rice vinegar for at least 1 hour. Soak the mushrooms in hot water until they soften, about 20 minutes; then discard the stems and chop the mushroom caps. Stem, seed, and chop the red pepper. Coarsely chop the green onions. Toast the pine nuts until golden in a 325° F. oven for about 8 minutes.

Combine the sauce ingredients and mix well.

LAST-MINUTE COOKING Drain and discard the vinegar from the raisins. Combine the eggs and beat well. Place a wok over highest heat. When the wok is very hot, add 1 tablespoon of the oil to the center. Tilt the wok to coat the sides of the wok and then add eggs. Scramble the eggs, and when well scrambled, transfer to a work platter.

Return the wok to highest heat and add the remaining 3 tablespoons oil. Add the vegetables and stir-fry until the pepper turns a brighter color, about 1 minute. Add the rice and raisins. Stir-fry the rice and mix it evenly with the vegetables, about 1 minute.

Add the sauce. Stir-fry for 30 seconds, then add the eggs and the pine nuts. Break the eggs into smaller pieces with the edge of the stir-fry spoon and continue stir-frying until everything is evenly combined and well heated. Spoon onto a heated platter or individual plates. Serve at once.

Serves: 4 as the side dish to any meat or seafood entrée.

Menu Ideas: Really Risqué Rice is excellent served with barbecued chicken, corn on the cob, and an American-style salad.

Really Risque Rice

WILD CHINESE RICE

SAUCE

3½ cups chicken broth
¼ cup dry sherry
2 tablespoons light soy sauce
½ teaspoon Chinese chili
    sauce
½ teaspoon salt
1 teaspoon grated or finely
    minced orange peel

RICE

3 tablespoons unsalted butter
½ cup minced onion
3 cloves garlic, finely minced
1½ cups brown rice, wild rice,
    red rice, or a multigrain
    rice mix
⅔ cup dried currants
½ cup chopped cilantro (fresh
    coriander) or fresh basil
¾ cup pecan halves

THIS IS A BEAUTIFUL RICE DISH ALIVE WITH THE FLAVORS OF GARLIC, PECANS, CILANTRO, CHILI, AND GRATED ORANGE PEEL. SOMETIMES GOURMET SHOPS SELL A BLEND OF BROWN RICE, RED RICE, AND WILD RICE WHICH WORKS WONDERFULLY IN THIS RECIPE. BUT SINCE DIFFERENT TYPES OF RICE VARY IN COOKING TIME, UNLESS YOU CAN FIND THE PACKAGED MULTIGRAIN MIX, USE JUST ONE TYPE.

CHECK THE RICE DURING COOKING, AND IF THE LIQUID DISAPPEARS BEFORE THE RICE IS TENDER, ADD A LITTLE MORE CHICKEN BROTH. FOR A WILD CHOPSTIX DINNER PARTY SERVE: CRAZY CAESAR SALAD, A SOUP OF ASIAN AVOCADO ADVENTURE, THAI RABBIT WITH WILD CHINESE RICE, AND CALORIE CHEESECAKE COUNTERATTACK.

PREPARATION AND COOKING In a small bowl, combine the sauce ingredients and mix well.

Place a 2½-quart saucepan over medium-high heat. Add the butter and sauté the onion and garlic until the onion is translucent, about 3 minutes. Add the rice and cook, stirring, until heated through, about 5 minutes.

Add the currants and sauce. Bring to a low boil, stirring occasionally. Cover, reduce the heat to low, and simmer until the rice is tender, about 45 minutes. If necessary, add a few tablespoons of water or broth toward the end of the cooking if rice seems about to scorch. Either proceed to the next step and serve the rice now, or cool at room temperature and refrigerate. (May be done a day prior to serving.)

LAST-MINUTE REHEATING Reheat the rice in a 325°F. oven for 20 minutes, or in the microwave oven for a few minutes. Then stir in the cilantro and pecans. Serve at once.

Serves: 6 as the side dish for any meat or seafood entrée.

NEW WAVE GARLIC BREAD

½ cup unsalted butter
1 teaspoon Chinese chili sauce
½ teaspoon ground Sichuan pepper
8 cloves garlic, finely minced
1 bunch chives, minced
⅓ cup minced cilantro (fresh coriander)
French bread, 1-foot loaf
½ cup grated Parmesan cheese

I F YOU THOUGHT THERE WAS NO WAY TO MAKE A BETTER GARLIC BREAD, TRY THIS RECIPE. USING FRESH GARLIC, HERBS, AND THE BEST-QUALITY PARMESAN CHEESE HELPS CREATE A TREAT THAT WILL HAVE HUNGRY TEENAGERS LINING UP AT YOUR FRONT DOOR. A REALLY EASY MENU WITH EVERYTHING DONE ON THE BARBECUE WOULD BE: SMOKED RIB-EYE STEAKS WITH GINGER-MANGO SALSA, CHOPSTIX BARBECUE VEGETABLES, NEW WAVE GARLIC BREAD, AND PERHAPS GRILLED BANANAS SERVED WITH A COCONUT CREAM (PAGE 167).

PREPARATION AND COOKING In a small saucepan, place the butter, chili sauce, Sichuan pepper, and garlic. Melt the butter over low heat until it bubbles around the edges of the pan. Remove from the heat and stir in the chives and cilantro.

Split the bread in half lengthwise. Brush on a thin layer of the butter sauce. Add a generous amount of cheese to one half. Shake the bread to evenly coat with the cheese. Repeat with the second half.

Toast the bread on a barbecue or in the broiler until golden. Cut into slices and serve.

Serves: 8 as a side dish.

OVERLEAF: *Ingredients for Wild Chinese Rice*

PEKING CHIVE PANCAKES

2 cups unbleached all-purpose
  flour
1 bunch chives, finely minced
2 teaspoons crushed dried red
  pepper flakes (optional)
¾ cup plus 2 tablespoons
  boiling water
½ cup Oriental sesame oil

PEKING PANCAKES ARE NORTHERN CHINA'S EQUIVALENT OF THE FLOUR TORTILLA. BUT WHAT FUN IT IS TO ADD MINCED CHIVES, DRIED CHILI FLAKES, OR ORANGE ZEST SO THE PLAIN SURFACE IS SPOTTED WITH COLOR ACCENTS AND FLAVOR SURPRISES. WHEN THE INSIDE SURFACE IS RUBBED WITH A LITTLE HOISIN SAUCE OR ANOTHER CONDIMENT, PEKING CHIVE PANCAKES WORK WONDERFULLY AS A WRAPPING FOR STIR-FRY DISHES, BARBECUED MEATS, AND ASIAN SALADS.

THE SECRET TO MAKING THESE PANCAKES WITHOUT DIFFICULTY LIES, FIRST, IN ROLLING THE DOUGH OUT IN A THIN SHEET, AND CUTTING OUT CIRCLES WITH A WINE GLASS. THIS MAKES EVERY PANCAKE AN IDENTICAL SIZE. SECOND, IF YOU ROLL THE CIRCLES OF DOUGH ON AN OILED RATHER THAN FLOURED SURFACE, THE PANCAKES ENLARGE EFFORTLESSLY. BE SURE TO USE A ROLLING PIN WITH HANDLES SO THE ROLLING PROCESS GOES QUICKLY.

SINCE THERE IS NO DETERIORATION IN THE QUALITY OF THE PANCAKES AFTER REPEATED FREEZING AND THAWING, STORE EXTRA BATCHES IN THE FREEZER FOR SPONTANEOUS MEALS.

ADVANCE PREPARATION Place the flour, chives, and dried red pepper flakes in a bowl. Add the boiling water and stir briefly. Turn the dough out onto a lightly floured board or smooth countertop and knead until smooth and elastic. Cover for 15 minutes.

Roll the dough out on a lightly floured surface until ¼ inch thick, occasionally turning the dough over. Then, with a 3-inch wine glass or round cookie cutter, cut the dough into 14 to 18 disks.

Thoroughly clean the work surface and lightly rub ½ tablespoon sesame oil over it. Place a disk on the oiled counter and rub about ½ teaspoon sesame oil over the top of the dough. Lay another disk on top. Using your palm, gently press the 2 disks together. Roll the pair into an 8-inch round. Always roll from the center of the disk out to the edge, changing directions after each rolling motion in order to stretch the dough into a large disk. Do not turn the dough during this process.

Heat a 12-inch skillet over medium heat. Add the double pancake and cook for about 45 seconds on one side. Flip the pancake over and cook for about 15 seconds on the other side. The pancake is done when it loses its raw color. The pancake should not have any brown spots; this is a sign of too high heat or too long cooking time.

Remove the double pancake from the pan and, starting on one edge, gently pull the 2 layers apart. Do this while the pancake is still hot. Stack them directly on top of each other (they will not stick together) and cover with a towel. Repeat the rolling and cooking process with the rest of the dough. Wrap the stack of Peking Chive Pancakes with plastic wrap or foil. Refrigerate for up to 5 days or freeze indefinitely.

- **LAST-MINUTE REHEATING** If frozen, thaw the pancakes at room temperature.
- Refreeze any extra pancakes you do not intend to use. Within 4 hours
- of serving, fold each pancake in half and then into quarters, shaped
- like a wedge. Overlap the pancakes on a plate. Cover with plastic wrap
  until ready to reheat.
- To reheat, bring water to a vigorous boil in a Chinese steamer. Put the
  plate on the steamer tier, cover, and reheat for 3 minutes. Or, seal the
- pancakes tightly in a foil package. Place in a 325°F. oven for 10 minutes.
- Do not reheat in a microwave; it toughens the dough. Serve imme-
- diately.

- **Makes: 14 to 18 large pancakes.**

CALIFORNIA CORNBREAD

1½ cups yellow cornmeal
½ cup all-purpose flour
2 teaspoons baking powder
1 teaspoon salt
3 eggs, well beaten
1¼ cups milk
⅓ cup unsalted butter, melted
¼ cup honey
½ cup dried currants
3 cloves garlic, finely minced
1 teaspoon grated or minced
   tangerine peel
Corn kernels from 1 ear of
   corn
¼ cup minced cilantro (fresh
   coriander)

ON OUR FIRST TRIP OUTSIDE OF CALIFORNIA, WE WERE SHOCKED TO DISCOVER THAT WHAT MOST AMERICANS CALL CORNBREAD HAS NO GARLIC, NO BEAUTIFUL FLECKS OF TANGERINE ZEST, NO CRUNCHY SWEET KERNELS OF CORN, NO GREEN SPECKS OF CILANTRO, AND NO CURRANTS! WHAT HAS HAPPENED TO GOOD COOKING? WHAT AN OUTRAGE THAT A GREAT RECIPE HAS BEEN SO SIMPLIFIED IT IS CURRENTLY FIT ONLY FOR ST. JOHN'S HOSPITAL OR THE BEVERLY MANOR CONVALESCENT HOME. HERE IN CALIFORNIA, THE ORIGINAL CORNBREAD, NURTURED BY GENERATIONS OF OUR COOKS, WARMS OUR TUMMIES. SERVE CALIFORNIA CORNBREAD WITH PLENTY OF HONEY BUTTER AND ACCOMPANY IT WITH BARBECUED MEAT OR A DISH WITH LOTS OF SAUCE.

PREPARATION AND COOKING Preheat the oven to 400°F.

In a large mixing bowl, place the cornmeal, flour, baking powder, and salt. Mix well. In a separate bowl, combine the eggs, milk, butter, and honey. Mix well. Add the remaining ingredients and mix well. Then stir into the cornmeal mixture. Mix just until the dry ingredients are moistened, leaving plenty of lumps.

Butter a 9-by-5-inch loaf pan, then pour in the batter. Bake for about 50 minutes. The cornbread is done when a knife pushed deep into the center comes out clean.

Cut into slices and serve with butter and honey.

Serves: 6 as the side dish to any meat or seafood entrée.

Magic Mousse and Chocolate Chip-Macadamia Nut Cookies

Chapter 7

SINFUL SWEETS

GOD CREATED DESSERTS AND, AS AN AFTERTHOUGHT, ADDED THE PRELIMINARY DISHES. BUT NOT ALL DESSERTS WERE CREATED EQUAL, FOR IT IS SAID THAT ON THE LONG DESSERT TABLES CRISSCROSSING THE GARDEN OF EDEN, "CHOCOLATE WAS KING." IN THE TIME OF DARKNESS AND TURMOIL THAT FOLLOWED THE APPLE AFFAIR, NO LONGER DID DAYS COMMENCE WITH CHOCOLATE, CONTINUE WITH CHOCOLATE, AND CONCLUDE WITH CHOCOLATE. CHARLATANS SPREAD MYTHS ABOUT CALORIES, PREACHED THE EVILS OF FAT, AND ESTABLISHED DIET CENTERS. GUILT WAS EVERYWHERE.

NOW A GREAT PERIOD OF ENLIGHTENMENT COMES UPON US, FORETELLING OF A JUDGEMENT DAY, WHEN ONCE AGAIN A PERSON'S WEALTH WILL BE DETERMINED BY THE AMOUNT OF CHOCOLATE STORED IN HIS OR HER CHOCOLATE CELLAR. FATHERS WILL THRUST LITTLE CHUNKS OF CHOCOLATE INTO THE UPRAISED HANDS OF THEIR NEWBORN. OUR LIVES WILL BE ENRICHED BY CHOCOLATE LOTTERIES, CHOCOLATE HOLIDAYS, AND CHOCOLATE CURRENCY. CHOPSTIX, THE RESTAURANTS AND THE BOOK, ANTICIPATES THIS GLORIOUS AGE WITH LUSCIOUS HOMEMADE ICE CREAMS, BUTTERY CHOCOLATE-CHIP COOKIES, AND EXTRA-RICH CHOCOLATE DESSERTS. SERVE THESE SWEETS ANYTIME, AND SIN AGAIN.

MAGIC MOUSSE

¼ cup freshly ground espresso
    coffee beans
2 ounces semisweet chocolate,
    cut into small pieces
4 eggs, separated
⅓ cup sugar
¼ cup Grand Marnier
1 tablespoon unflavored
    gelatin
1 cup heavy (whipping) cream
Raspberry Cabernet Sauvignon
    Sauce (page 160),
    thoroughly chilled.
Fresh raspberries, chocolate
    shavings, and whipped
    cream, for garnish

THE CHOCOLATE MOUSSE IN JULIA CHILD'S *MASTERING THE ART OF FRENCH COOKING*, WITH THE FLAVORS OF RICH CHOCOLATE, GRAND MARNIER, AND ESPRESSO, HAS A LINGERING ETHEREAL TASTE. THE SAME FLAVOR COMBINATIONS ARE USED TO MAKE THIS VERY EASY MOUSSE. LAYERS OF MOUSSE, PIPED THROUGH A PASTRY TUBE INTO WINE GLASSES, ALTERNATE WITH RASPBERRY CABERNET SAUVIGNON SAUCE. WITH THE MOUSSE GARNISHED WITH FRESH RASPBERRIES, WHIPPING CREAM, AND CHOCOLATE SHAVINGS, YOUR FRIENDS WILL MURMUR "MAGICAL . . . MAGICAL!"

ADVANCE PREPARATION Place the coffee in a cup, add ½ cup of boiling water, stir, cover, and steep for 10 minutes. In a small saucepan, add ¼ cup of the coffee, 2 teaspoons of the coffee grounds, and the chocolate. Melt over simmering water, stir until thoroughly blended, and then keep warm over hot water.

In a stainless-steel or copper mixing bowl, vigorously beat the egg yolks and sugar until the mixture turns pale yellow, about 3 minutes. Now beat in the Grand Marnier and gelatin. Place the mixing bowl over simmering water and stir the mixture until it becomes hot to the touch, about 4 minutes. Remove from the simmering water and stir in the chocolate mixture.

Beat the egg whites until stiff peaks form. Stir one-fourth of the egg whites into the chocolate mixture, then gently fold in the remaining egg whites one-third at a time. Beat the cream until stiff, and then gently fold into the mousse.

Transfer the mousse to a pastry bag fitted with a large tube. Pipe a little of the mousse into the bottom of 8 wine glasses. Add a very thin layer of raspberry sauce, then a thick layer of mousse, a thin layer of sauce, and finish with another thick layer of mousse. Refrigerate for at least 3 hours. This can be made a day ahead.

SERVING Garnish the top of each mousse with one or any combination of the following: chocolate shavings, fresh raspberries, or stiffly beaten whipped cream piped through a pastry tube.

Serves 8

CHOCOLATE CHIP–
MACADAMIA NUT COOKIES

4 ounces roasted macadamia
    nuts
½ cup (1 stick) unsalted
    butter, softened
½ cup light brown sugar
¼ cup granulated sugar
1 egg
1 teaspoon vanilla extract
¾ teaspoon baking powder
½ teaspoon baking soda
½ cup chopped crystallized
    ginger
8 ounces white or dark
    chocolate chips or chunks
1½ cups all-purpose flour

WHAT HAPPIER CHILDHOOD MEMORIES REMAIN THAN THOSE OF SCOOP-ING CHOCOLATE-CHIP COOKIE BATTER FROM THE MIXING BOWL, OR SURREPTITIOUSLY SEIZING HOT COOKIES FROM THE BAKING SHEET—OR LAZ-ING ON YOUR BED IN THE HEAT OF A SUMMER AFTERNOON, CONDUCTING A QUALITY-CONTROL TEST ON MOUNDS OF COOKIES? CREATE A LITTLE CHILD-HOOD MAGIC AND WHIP UP A BATCH OF THESE COOKIES, FILLED WITH CHOCO-LATE, MACADAMIA NUTS, AND CRYSTALLIZED GINGER CANDY. AS A FUN VARI-ATION, FORM THE BATTER INTO ONE GIANT COOKIE AND BAKE IN A 350°F. OVEN FOR 30 MINUTES. SERVED ON A HUGE COOKIE PLATE, THIS MEGA-COOKIE ALWAYS EVOKES LAUGHS FROM DINNER GUESTS AS THEY BREAK OFF SECTIONS.

PREPARATION If the nuts are salted, rinse briefly and pat dry; chop. Combine the butter and sugars in a large bowl; stir with a spoon until thoroughly blended. Add the egg, vanilla, baking powder, and baking soda. Stir well. Add the crystallized ginger, chocolate chips, and nuts, then stir again. Add the flour one-third at a time and mix thoroughly. The cookie dough can now be refrigerated for up to a week or frozen indefinitely.

BAKING Preheat oven to 350°F. Butter a baking sheet or line it with parchment paper. Scoop out the cookie dough 2 tablespoons at a time, and place 1 inch apart on the baking sheet. Bake until light golden, about 12 minutes. Let cool on a rack. They can be served later, or eaten at once.

Makes: 24 cookies

MANGO ICE CREAM
WITH TEQUILA SAUCE

ICE CREAM

6 egg yolks
1 cup sugar
2 cups half and half
2 cups heavy (whipping)
cream
2 cups mango fruit purée
2 teaspoons vanilla extract

TEQUILA SAUCE

6 egg yolks
⅔ cup sugar
2 cups half and half
5 tablespoons tequila

TO SERVE

Chocolate Grand Marnier
Sauce (page 159)
(optional)
Mint sprigs

HIGH ABOVE THE OUTDOOR BARBECUE AT THE ORIENTAL HOTEL, BURSTS OF FIREWORKS ILLUMINATE BANGKOK'S SKYLINE, WHILE ALONG THE CHAO PHYA RIVER THOUSANDS OF LOTUS-SHAPE "BOATS," EACH CONTAINING A LIGHTED CANDLE, INCENSE, AND FLOWERS, BOB IN SWIRLING PATTERNS. AS THE THAIS CELEBRATE THE MOST ENCHANTING OF ALL THEIR FESTIVALS AND GIVE THANKS TO THE MOTHER OF WATER, A FEW FEET AWAY OUR BAND OF AMERICANS, PILGRIMS ABROAD, JOIN TOGETHER FOR THANKSGIVING. LONG AFTER PLATTERS OF BARBECUED LOBSTER, PAD THAI NOODLE SALAD SEASONED WITH LIME, CRISP BANANA FRITTERS, AND MANGO ICE CREAM, WE WATCH THE FESTIVAL OF LIGHTS.

IN THIS RECIPE, MANGO ICE CREAM IS SERVED WITH A MEXICAN TEQUILA SAUCE, BUT THE ICE CREAM IS ALSO VERY GOOD PLAIN OR TOPPED WITH GENEROUS SPOONFULS OF CHOCOLATE GRAND MARNIER SAUCE.

ADVANCE PREPARATION Make the ice cream. In a copper or stainless-steel mixing bowl, vigorously beat the egg yolks and sugar with a whisk until the mixture turns a pale yellow, about 3 minutes. Fill a large bowl or sink with cold water and add a generous amount of ice. Put the half and half in a 3-quart saucepan and heat until bubbles appear around the edges. Slowly whisk the half and half into the egg mixture. Briefly beat the mixture and pour it back into the saucepan. Place the empty mixing bowl in the ice water.

Place the saucepan over high heat. Beat the mixture quickly with a whisk until it becomes thick enough to lightly coat a spoon and nearly doubles in volume, about 4 minutes. (Be sure to stir vigorously and do not overcook the custard, or the yolks will curdle). Immediately tip the custard into the chilled mixing bowl and stir slowly with a whisk for 2 minutes. Refrigerate for at least 2 hours.

When the custard is thoroughly chilled, stir in the cream, mango purée, and vanilla. Place in an ice cream maker and freeze according to manufacturer's directions. Makes 2 quarts of ice cream.

Make the sauce. Following the same procedure as for the ice cream custard, beat the yolks and sugar. Heat the half and half, then stir it into the egg mixture. Pour back into the saucepan, and cook over high heat, beating constantly with a whisk until the custard thickens enough to coat a spoon. Chill in an ice-water bath. Stir in tequila, and refrigerate.

ASSEMBLING Lightly coat each dessert plate with some tequila sauce. Place 1 large scoop or 3 small scoops of ice cream in the center of each plate. If desired, drizzle some Chocolate Grand Marnier Sauce on top, and then make little swirls with the end of a skewer to create a painted sauce. Garnish with mint sprigs. Serve at once.

Serves 12

Mango Ice Cream
with Tequila Sauce and
Orange Ginger Brownies
(recipe on page 158)

ORANGE GINGER BROWNIES

1 cup chopped pecans,
walnuts, or macadamia
nuts
½ pound (2 sticks) unsalted
butter
4 ounces semisweet chocolate
4 eggs
1¼ cups sugar
2 teaspoons vanilla extract
1 tablespoon grated or finely
minced orange peel
4 ounces crystallized ginger
candy, slivered
½ cup all-purpose flour
Raspberry Cabernet Sauvignon
Sauce (page 160) or
Coconut Cream (page 167)
(optional)

WHEN WE WERE WORKING ON A BROWNIE RECIPE, SOMEONE SUGGESTED WE TRY WHITE CHOCOLATE. WE THOUGHT, "A BROWNIE MADE FROM WHITE CHOCOLATE IS A CONTRADICTION! ONLY INVALIDS EAT WHITE CHOCO- LATE!" NOW, THESE ARE "REAL" BROWNIES MADE WITH DARK CHOCOLATE, MINCED ORANGE RIND, CRYSTALLIZED GINGER, AND PECANS. SERVE ORANGE GINGER BROWNIES WITH FRUIT OR ICE CREAM, OR PLACE ON DESSERT PLATES WITH A GLAZE OF RASPBERRY CABERNET SAUVIGNON SAUCE OR COCONUT CREAM.

PREPARATION AND BAKING Preheat the oven to 350°F. Butter a 9-by-12-inch baking dish. Place the nuts on a baking sheet and toast for 10 minutes. Melt the butter, then let cool to room temperature. Cut the chocolate into small chunks, place in a small saucepan, and melt over simmering water.

In a mixing bowl, combine the eggs and sugar, beating well with a whisk. Add the melted butter and chocolate, mixing again. Stir in the vanilla, orange peel, crystallized ginger, and nuts. Add the flour and mix well.

Pour the batter into the prepared baking dish. Bake in the middle of the oven until the brownies are just set in the center, about 20 to 25 minutes. Cool, cut into squares, and store in an airtight container.

If offering brownies as the main dessert, serve with one of the sauces. Glaze the surface of each dessert plate with the sauce. Place a brownie in the center of each plate, then serve.

Makes: 28 brownies

LEMON ICE CREAM WITH CHOCOLATE GRAND MARNIER SAUCE

ICE CREAM
4 cups heavy (whipping) cream
2 cups sugar
1 cup lemon juice

CHOCOLATE GRAND MARNIER SAUCE
8 ounces semisweet chocolate
½ cup heavy (whipping) cream
½ cup Grand Marnier

TO SERVE
Mint sprigs or candied lemon

THE SUPER-DELUXE IL GELATIO ICE CREAM MACHINE, MAKING 2 QUARTS EVERY 30 MINUTES, JUST KEEPS PACE WITH THE QUANTITY OF ICE CREAM REQUIRED BY TRUE ICE CREAM ADDICTS. TO FORESTALL ANY INTERRUPTIONS PRODUCING THE FOOD ESSENTIAL FOR DAILY LIFE, AN ELECTRIC GENERATOR SITS ON OUR FRONT LAWN READY TO GO INTO ACTION WHEN THE "BIG ONE" ROCKS LOS ANGELES. THIS DELICIOUS ICE CREAM, FROM COOKING FRIEND GRANT SHOWLEY, MAY HELP CALM SHAKEN NERVES. IF YOU DO NOT HAVE A FANCY ELECTRIC ICE CREAM MAKER, THE SMALL HANDCRANK DONVIER IS INEXPENSIVE AND EASY TO USE.

ADVANCE PREPARATION Beat the cream with the sugar until well mixed. Stir in the lemon juice and mix well (ignore curdled look!). Place the mixture in an ice cream maker and freeze according to the manufacturer's directions. Makes 2 quarts.

Cut the chocolate into small chunks. Place the chocolate and cream in a small saucepan and melt over simmering water. Stir until thoroughly blended, then stir in the Grand Marnier. Set aside at room temperature.

LAST-MINUTE ASSEMBLING If the chocolate sauce is a little too thick to pour evenly over the dessert plates, warm over simmering water. Then glaze each dessert plate with a thin layer of the sauce. Place 1 large scoop or 3 small scoops of ice cream in the center of each plate. Garnish with mint sprigs or twists of candied lemon. Serve at once.

Serves 12

CHOPSTIX TART WITH RASPBERRY CABERNET SAUVIGNON SAUCE

PASTRY DOUGH

1¼ cups all-purpose flour
½ teaspoon salt
½ cup (1 stick) unsalted
    butter, cut into small
    pieces
2 to 4 tablespoons ice water
4 ounces semi-sweet
    chocolate, chopped

PASTRY CREAM

6 egg yolks
⅔ cup sugar
1 tablespoon vanilla extract
3 tablespoons finely minced
    vanilla bean
2 tablespoons all-purpose flour
2 tablespoons cornstarch
2 cups milk

RASPBERRY CABERNET SAUVIGNON
    SAUCE

1 bottle reasonably good
    Cabernet Sauvigon or
    other red wine
12 ounces frozen raspberries,
    defrosted
1 cup sugar
½ teaspoon freshly ground
    black pepper

AT OUR HOME IN NAPA, WE ALWAYS MAKE A POINT OF DRIVING "UP VALLEY" TO MARK DIERKHISING'S ALL SEASONS' RESTAURANT IN THE QUAINT TOWN OF CALISTOGA. HIS RASPBERRY CABERNET SAUVIGNON SAUCE IS EXCELLENT ON CHEESECAKE, ICE CREAM, PANCAKES, PIES AND TARTS, AND CHILLED ROAST CHICKEN. WHILE THE SAUCE TAKES ONLY A FEW MINUTES OF YOUR ATTENTION, THE TART REQUIRES ABOUT ONE HOUR OF PREPARATION.

ADVANCE PREPARATION (CAN BE DONE A DAY AHEAD) Prepare the pastry dough. Place the flour, salt, and butter in a food processor. Place in the freezer for 45 minutes. When very cold, process until the mixture resembles cornmeal. Add a little ice water, processing again until the dough holds together when pressed between your fingers. Turn out onto plastic wrap, press into a circle, wrap, and refrigerate for 1 hour.

Preheat the oven to 375°F. After 1 hour, on a lightly floured board or chilled pastry cloth, roll out the dough into a ¼-inch thin circle. Gently fit the dough into the tart pan and press the dough up the sides. Cover with buttered foil and place a layer of pastry weights or beans on top of the foil. Bake for about 15 minutes, until the edges are light golden. Remove the foil and bake for about 15 minutes more, until deep golden. Remove from the oven and let cool to room temperature.

Place the chocolate in a small saucepan and melt over simmering water. Stir until blended, then brush across the pastry shell and around the sides. Do not refrigerate.

Prepare the pastry cream. Beat the egg yolks and sugar until pale yellow. Beat in the vanilla, vanilla bean, flour, and cornstarch. In a saucepan, heat the milk until bubbles appear around edges, then stir into the egg mixture. Pour back into the saucepan and place over medium-high heat. Beat with a whisk until the mixture becomes very thick, about 2 minutes. Pour into a bowl and refrigerate for at least 1 hour. Then fill the tart pan with the pastry cream and refrigerate for at least 4 hours.

Prepare the raspberry sauce. In a large stainless-steel saucepan or skillet, combine the wine, raspberries, sugar, and pepper. Bring to a vigorous boil over high heat and cook until only 2 cups remain, about 30 minutes of rapid boiling. As the sauce begins to thicken, stir with a spoon to prevent scorching. Strain the liquid through a sieve to remove the seeds. Refrigerate for at least 3 hours. (It will last for a month refrigerated.) Makes 1⅔ cups sauce.

ASSEMBLING Add ½ cup sauce to the top of the tart, and tilt the tart back and forth to glaze the top. (It can be refrigerated for 1 day.) Remove the sides of the tart pan. Cut the tart into wedges and serve with the remaining sauce.

Serves 8

Chopstix Tart with Raspberry Cabernet Sauvignon Sauce

GINGER PUMPKIN PIE
WITH PECAN PRALINE CRUST

CRUST
Pastry Dough (page 160)
2 tablespoons unsalted butter
½ cup dark brown sugar
½ cup chopped pecans

FILLING
2 eggs
¾ cup dark brown sugar
1 teaspoon ground cinnamon
½ teaspoon ground ginger
½ teaspoon ground allspice
½ teaspoon freshly ground
black pepper
½ teaspoon salt
¼ teaspoon ground cloves
¼ teaspoon freshly grated
nutmeg
1¾ cups canned pumpkin
purée
1⅔ cups evaporated milk
2 tablespoons brandy

TO SERVE
1 cup heavy (whipping) cream
⅓ cup slivered crystallized
ginger

TRY THE ULTIMATE GASTRONOMIC SURPRISE: A CHOPSTIX THANKSGIVING DINNER. CHILLED SHRIMP WITH 3 CHOPSTIX DIPPING SAUCES (PAGES 40–43), TEX-MEX WON TONS WITH NEW AGE GUACAMOLE (PAGE 42), ASIAN PARTY FAVORS, BALLOONS, AND PAPER TURKEYS BEGIN THE DAY OF PILGRIM THANKS. SOUND THE CHINESE GONG AS YOU ENTER WITH THAI-HIGH BARBECUED TURKEY (VARIATION OF THAI-HIGH BARBECUED CHICKEN, PAGE 103), CALIFORNIA CORNBREAD (PAGE 151) THICKLY COATED WITH HONEY BUTTER, AND RAINBOW SALAD WITH RASPBERRY VINEGAR (PAGE 46). IGNORE PERIODS OF UNEASY QUIET, COMMENTS ABOUT FOREIGN INFLUENCES ON AMERICA, OR SEARCH TEAMS LOOKING FOR TURKEY STUFFING. KEEP THE DESSERT-FANTASY TABLE A SECRET, THEN TREAT YOUR GUESTS TO CHOCOLATE CHIP–MACADAMIA NUT COOKIES (PAGE 155), AND THIS PUMPKIN PIE WITH A PECAN PRALINE CRUST.

ADVANCE PREPARATION Roll out the dough and fit into a 10-inch pie plate. Melt the butter and sugar, then add the pecans. Press the pecan mixture against the bottom of the pie crust, then refrigerate until the filling is ready.

BAKING Preheat the oven to 425°F. Slightly beat the eggs, then add the sugar, cinnamon, ginger, allspice, pepper, salt, cloves, and nutmeg. Stir well and add the pumpkin, milk, and brandy; mix well. Pour into the pastry shell.

Bake for 15 minutes, then reduce the temperature to 350°F. and bake for 40 to 50 minutes more, or until a knife inserted in the center of the pie comes out clean. Let cool to room temperature.

SERVING Beat the cream until stiff. Place in a pastry bag and pipe onto the surface of the pie. Decorate with slivered ginger and serve.

Serves 8

CALORIE CHEESECAKE COUNTERATTACK

CRUST
1½ cups crumbled ginger snaps, approximately 6 ounces
½ cup (1 stick) unsalted butter

FILLING
3 (8-ounce) packages cream cheese, at room temperature
1 cup sugar
2 tablespoons all-purpose flour
2 tablespoons grated or finely minced lemon peel
1 teaspoon vanilla extract
3 eggs plus 2 egg yolks
¼ cup heavy (whipping) cream

TOPPING
1¼ pints sour cream
1 tablespoon sugar
1 teaspoon vanilla extract

THIS RECIPE WAS SENT TO US YEARS AGO BY A STUDENT IN SAN JOSE, WHOSE HANDWRITTEN RECIPE CARD SAID "BEST EVER CHEESECAKE." IF YOU MAKE THIS LEMON-SCENTED CHEESECAKE A DAY OR TWO IN ADVANCE, THE TEXTURE IMPROVES AND THE LEMON FLAVOR BECOMES MORE PRONOUNCED. FOR A BEAUTIFUL PRESENTATION, TRY GLAZING DESSERT PLATES WITH RASPBERRY CABERNET SAUVIGNON SAUCE (PAGE 160), AND THEN POSITION A SLICE ON TOP OF THE SAUCE. AFTER ALL THE CAREFUL DIETING AND HEALTHFUL RECIPES IN THE PREVIOUS CHAPTERS, YOU'LL FIND THE CALORIES IN THIS DESSERT REALLY COUNTERATTACK, ESPECIALLY WITH SECOND HELPINGS.

ADVANCE PREPARATION Preheat the oven to 400°F. Grind the ginger snaps in a food processor. Melt the butter and mix with the crumbs. Sprinkle about half the mixture across the bottom of a 12-inch tart pan and press into a thin layer using your fingers. Press the crumbs against the side of the pan. Bake for 10 minutes, then let cool to room temperature.

Increase the oven temperature to 500°F. Make the filling in a food processor. Cut each package of cream cheese into 6 pieces and add to the processor. Add the sugar and process until thoroughly mixed. Add the flour, lemon peel, and vanilla, and blend again. Add the eggs and yolks a few at a time, mixing well with each addition. Lastly, add the cream and stir.

Place the tart pan on a baking sheet, then pour the filling into tart pan. Bake for 8 minutes, then reduce heat to 200°F. and bake 10 minutes more. Remove from the oven and cool in the pan at room temperature for 3 hours.

Preheat the oven to 350°F. Temporarily remove the sides of the tart pan, carefully cut away any crust that rises above the top of the cheesecake, and then resecure sides of the pan. Combine and mix well the sour cream, sugar, and vanilla. Spread evenly over the top of the cheesecake. Bake for 5 minutes, then let cool. Refrigerate the cake for several hours or overnight before serving.

Serves 12

COCONUT FLAN SUPREME

1 coconut
2½ cups heavy (whipping)
    cream
1 cup plus 4 tablespoons sugar
4 egg yolks
1½ teaspoons vanilla extract
Chocolate Grand Marnier
    Sauce (page 159)

LEAVING OUR FRIENDS SHOPPING IN HONG KONG, WE SPED BY JETFOIL ACROSS THE SOUTH CHINA SEA TOWARD MACAO. OUR DESTINATION WAS THE DINING ROOM OF THE POUSADA DE SAO TIAGO, BUILT ON THE RUINS OF A SEVENTEENTH-CENTURY FORTRESS, WHICH FEATURES A UNIQUE COMBINATION OF PORTUGUESE AND ASIAN FOOD. PÂTÉ WITH SICHUAN PEPPER, GRILLED CRAB SAFFRON SOUP, AFRICAN CHICKEN, AND DUCK WITH STRAW MUSHROOMS PROVIDED A START BEFORE ANOTHER BOTTLE OF WINE AND FURTHER EXAMINATIONS OF THE MENU LED TO NEW TASTE DISCOVERIES. ONE OF THE DISHES WAS THIS FLAN.

ADVANCE PREPARATION AND COOKING Puncture one of the coconut "eyes." Hold the coconut in your palm and firmly tap the coconut along the circumference with a hammer, rotating the coconut slightly after each hit. After a few minutes of gentle tapping, a hairline crack will appear around the circumference and the coconut will separate into 2 equal spheres. Using a screwdriver, pry away the coconut flesh, then place in food processor and coarsely chop.

Heat the cream until hot but not boiling, then add to the processor and process again for 15 seconds. Transfer the coconut and cream to the center of a layer of cheesecloth placed over a bowl, and squeeze the cheesecloth vigorously to extract all the coconut cream. You will need 2 cups of coconut cream.

Place 1 cup of the sugar and 2 tablespoons of water in a saucepan. Bring to a vigorous boil, never stirring, and cook until the sugar turns dark brown. Immediately pour into 8 small Pyrex custard cups or ramekins, and roll the caramelized sugar around to coat the bottom.

Preheat the oven to 350°F. Beat the egg yolks with the remaining 4 tablespoons sugar with a whisk until the mixture turns pale yellow and the sugar is absorbed, about 3 minutes. Beat in the cream and vanilla.

Pour the mixture into the custard cups, then place the cups in a roasting pan and add enough hot water to come halfway up the cups. Place the roasting pan in the oven and bake the custards for 50 minutes, or until the tops are golden brown and a knife blade, when inserted, comes out clean. Refrigerate the flans for at least 3 hours. This can be done up to 4 days in advance of serving.

LAST-MINUTE ASSEMBLING Warm the chocolate sauce over simmering water, then glaze 8 dessert plates with the sauce. Carefully run a knife around each custard and gently invert, sliding each flan onto the center of each plate. Serve at once.

Serves 8

GINGER PEACH SORBET

⅔ cup sugar
2 tablespoons finely minced
    fresh ginger
about 6 tree-ripened peaches
1 tablespoon lemon juice

GREAT SORBETS DEPEND ON THE VERY FRESHEST FRUIT, AND THIS IS PARTICULARLY TRUE OF PEACH SORBET. SINCE THE TASTE OF SUPERMARKET PEACHES IS SO DISAPPOINTING, IF YOU DON'T HAVE ACCESS TO TREE-RIPENED PEACHES PICKED WITHIN TWO DAYS OF MAKING THIS DESSERT, SUBSTITUTE ANOTHER SEASONAL FRUIT OR BERRY AT THE PEAK OF FLAVOR. YOU WILL NEED TWO CUPS OF FRUIT PURÉE.

PREPARATION In a small saucepan, combine the sugar, 1½ cups water, and ginger. Bring to a low boil, stirring until the sugar is dissolved. Transfer to a bowl and chill at least 2 hours.

Bring 2 quarts of water to a vigorous boil. Add the peaches for 15 seconds, then remove from the boiling water. The peach skins should easily slip off. Cut off the fruit, purée enough to make 2 cups, stir in the lemon juice and set aside.

When the sugar syrup is thoroughly chilled, stir in the peach purée. Churn in an ice-cream freezer, following manufacturer's directions.

Serves: 8 as a refreshing dessert accompanied by little cookies and chocolates.

GINGER CHOCOLATE PETIT POTS

8 ounces semisweet chocolate
2 cups heavy (whipping) cream
1 egg plus 2 yolks
¼ cup Grand Marnier
4 thin slices crystallized ginger
Whipped cream or fresh raspberries, for garnish (optional)

WE ARE HAPPY TO BE PART OF A GROWING NUMBER OF PEOPLE CONVINCED THAT, WHEN "WE SLIP OFF THE RAFT," WE WILL BE GREETED ON THE OTHER SIDE WITH A CHOCOLATE-DESSERT-FANTASY TABLE EXTENDING FAR INTO THE DISTANCE. THIS SHOULD BE PART OF THE FEAST!

ADVANCE PREPARATION Place the chocolate and cream in a metal mixing bowl. Put over simmering water and melt the chocolate. Beat with a whisk, then let cool to room temperature.

Beat the egg and yolks with a whisk until thickened, about 1 minute, then stir into the chocolate mixture. Add the Grand Marnier.

Sliver the ginger, then place a few slivers in each of 8 small pots or ramekins and add the chocolate mixture. Refrigerate for at least 2 hours. May be made a day ahead.

SERVING Decorate the tops with whipped cream or raspberries.

Serves 6

STRAWBERRIES SIAM

COCONUT CREAM

1 coconut

2 cups heavy (whipping)
    cream

TO SERVE

2 pints strawberries, perfectly
    ripe

¼ cup confectioners' sugar

¼ cup kirsch

STRAWBERRIES SIAM, PRACTICALLY THE NATIONAL DESSERT OF THAILAND, WAS ADAPTED BY COUNT ROMANOFF FOR THE TSARIST COURT IN NINE-TEENTH-CENTURY RUSSIA. BUT HE FORGOT THE COCONUT! THE ORIGINAL RECIPE IS, OF COURSE, FAR BETTER WITH ITS SUBTLE BLEND OF FRESH STRAWBERRIES, KIRSCH, AND COCONUT CREAM.

AS A VARIATION, AT THE BOTTOM OF TALL-STEMMED WINE GLASSES, PLACE CRUSHED ALMOND COOKIES, LADYFINGERS, OR VERY THIN SLICES OF POUND CAKE MOISTENED WITH A LIQUEUR. THEN ADD THE STRAWBERRIES SIAM, SPRINKLE ON A FEW TOASTED SLIVERED ALMONDS, AND GARNISH WITH MINT.

CANNED COCONUT MILK IS GREAT FOR MOST ASIAN RECIPES, WHEN OTHER FLAVORS QUICKLY OVERWHELM THE SUBTLETY OF FRESH COCONUT MILK. BUT FOR DESSERTS, FRESH COCONUT MILK CREATES A TASTE CLEARLY SUPERIOR TO CANNED. COCONUT MILK IS HIGHLY PERISHABLE AND DOES NOT FREEZE WELL, SO PLAN ON USING IT WITHIN 3 DAYS.

ADVANCE PREPARATION Puncture one of the coconut "eyes." Hold the co-conut in your palm and firmly tap along the circumference with a hammer, rotating the coconut slightly after each hit. After a few min-utes of gentle tapping, a hairline crack will appear around the circum-ference and the coconut will separate into 2 equal spheres. Using a screwdriver, pry away the coconut flesh. Grate one-fourth of the co-conut on the largest setting of a cheesegrater (do not be too thorough about this since you need only a small amount to sprinkle across the top of the dessert). Place the grated coconut in a small bowl and refrigerate. Place the remaining coconut flesh in a food processor and coarsely chop. Add the cream and process again for 10 seconds. Tip into a bowl and refrigerate for 3 hours.

Transfer the chilled coconut and cream into a bowl lined with a single layer of cheesecloth. Squeeze the cheesecloth with all your strength to extract as much cream as possible. Discard the coconut flesh and refrigerate the coconut cream. This can be done a day in advance.

ASSEMBLING Before dinner, stem the strawberries, cut in half, and refrig-erate. Beat the coconut cream until stiff. Add the sugar and beat briefly again. After dinner, stir the kirsch into the coconut cream and gently fold in the strawberries. Spoon the berries and cream into dessert bowls or wine glasses. Sprinkle the reserved grated coconut on top, and serve at once.

Serves 6 to 8

PAINTED COCONUT CREAM WITH FRESH BERRIES

1 coconut
3 cups half and half
6 egg yolks
⅔ cup sugar
6 cups fresh berries
½ cup kirsch
Chocolate Grand Marnier
    Sauce (page 159)
Raspberry Cabernet Sauvignon
    Sauce (page 160)

DESSERT PLATES GLAZED WITH COCONUT CREAM AND MOUNDED WITH FRESH BERRIES, LITTLE CUPS OF CAPPUCCINO, AND EXTRA HELPINGS OF CHOCOLATE CHIP–MACADAMIA NUT COOKIES (PAGE 155) CONCLUDE A SIMPLE MENU FEATURING NEW TASTE SENSATIONS. NOW A DIFFERENT TYPE OF FEAST DRAWS TO A CLOSE. JUST AS THE RECIPE FOR SALMON RIBBONS, WHICH BEGAN THIS BOOK, WELCOMED YOU TO OUR LOVE OF FOOD AND ENTERTAINING, SO THIS DELICIOUS DESSERT SERVES AS OUR FOND FAREWELL.

ADVANCE PREPARATION AND COOKING Puncture one of the coconut "eyes." Hold the coconut in your palm and firmly tap the coconut along the circumference with a hammer, rotating the coconut slightly after each hit. After a few minutes of gentle tapping, a hairline crack will appear around the circumference and the coconut will separate into 2 equal spheres. Using a screwdriver, pry away the coconut flesh, then place in a food processor and coarsely chop. Add the half and half and chop again for 1 minute. Transfer the coconut and liquid to a saucepan and heat to just below the boiling point. Then turn off heat and set aside for 1 hour. Transfer the coconut and cream to the center of a layer of cheesecloth placed over a bowl, and squeeze the cheesecloth to extract all the coconut liquid. You will need 2 cups coconut cream.

Vigorously beat the egg yolks and sugar with a whisk until the mixture turns pale yellow, about 3 minutes. Fill a large bowl or sink with cold water and add a generous amount of ice. Put the coconut cream in a 3-quart saucepan and heat until bubbles appear around the edges. Pour slowly into the egg mixture, stirring with a whisk. Briefly beat the mixture and pour back into the saucepan. Place the empty mixing bowl in the ice water.

Place the saucepan over high heat. Beat quickly with a whisk until the mixture becomes thick enough to lightly coat a spoon and nearly doubles in volume, about 4 minutes. (Be sure to stir vigorously and do not overcook the custard, or the yolks will curdle). Immediately tip the custard into the chilled mixing bowl and stir slowly with a whisk for 2 minutes. Refrigerate for at least 2 hours.

LAST-MINUTE ASSEMBLING Toss the berries with the kirsch. Glaze 8 dessert plates with the coconut cream. Warm the chocolate sauce over simmering water. Using 2 pastry bags fitted with fine piping tubes, alternate thin lines or circles of raspberry and chocolate sauces across the surface of the coconut cream. With the tip of a skewer, cut across the lines of raspberry and chocolate sauces to create swirls; or take a chef's knife and make little cuts across the sauces. Drain the berries and carefully position them in the center of each plate. Serve at once.

*Painted Coconut Cream
with Fresh Berries*

Serves 8

ALL ABOUT WOKS AND STIR-FRYING

WOKS *Wok* is the Cantonese word for a practical, multipurpose, concave Chinese cooking utensil used to create a vast range of delicious Chinese dishes. Spring rolls slide down the sides into hot oil without a splash. Fish placed on an elevated rack above rapidly boiling water, and covered by the domed top, steams to perfection. Stews bubble gently over low heat. The sloping sides mean the wok requires less oil than Western frying pans. When given a swish, stir-fried ingredients automatically fall to the bottom, the hottest part of the wok, for quick, even cooking. Because of the pan's shape, Chinese foods—particularly stir-fried dishes—*taste better* than recipes made in another utensil.

Woks range from the inexpensive, traditional heavy steel type sold by Asian markets to deluxe stainless-steel and nonstick woks available at gourmet shops. I prefer the heavy steel woks because they distribute the heat evenly. After frequent use, they acquire a beautiful black luster; it is this black seasoning that makes them nonstick and contributes a special wok flavor to stir-fried dishes. However, steel woks need to be specially seasoned, used frequently, and carefully cleaned. If this does not appeal to you, purchase a stainless-steel, Calphalon, or nonstick wok. But avoid the electric wok. Even at its highest setting, the electric wok never becomes hot enough for stir-frying, so the food just boils in its own juices.

Buy a 14- or 16-inch wok with a long wooden handle. For stir-frying on a gas stove, get a wok with a round bottom. Remove the grill from the burner and place the round bottom wok directly on the jets so the flames leap up around the sides of the wok. (Stir-fried dishes cook quickly and taste more succulent this way than if the wok is placed on the grating or elevated above the burner by using a wok ring.) For electric stoves, buy a flat-bottom wok. The flat bottom rests on the largest electric coil, so the high heat is conducted directly from the coil to the surface of the utensil. Using a flat-bottom wok on an electric stove produces food just as delicious as that made with a round-bottom wok on a gas stove.

The heavy steel woks sold in Asian markets require special care. These come coated with a thin layer of oil. Scrub the wok thoroughly inside and out with hot soapy water, using a scouring pad. The wok is clean when the gray coating no longer comes off on your hands. Dry the wok, then place it over high heat. When the wok becomes hot to the touch, "season" it by adding ¼ cup of cooking oil to the center. With a paper towel and spoon, coat the inside surface with oil; as the oil begins to smoke slightly, remove the wok from the heat. Let it cool completely, then wipe the oil from wok. With repeated use, the wok seasoning gradually turns black, creating a nonstick surface—provided no one scrubs the seasoning off or boils water in the wok for steaming, which removes the seasoning.

Clean your steel woks as you would any good omelet pan. Place it in the sink and fill with hot water. After a few minutes, or after dinner, use hot water and a sponge to rub off all food particles sticking to the sides. Never use soap or an abrasive pad, since this removes the wok seasoning. Dry the wok over medium heat, then store for future use. Do not add oil to the inside surface, since this eventually turns into a sticky, rancid layer that must be scrubbed off.

PRINCIPLES FOR STIR-FRYING If stir-frying is new to you, review these principles to ensure success.

- Cut the food into smaller pieces than you think are necessary. The smaller the food is cut, the more quickly it will cook and the better it will taste.

- Cut all ingredients for a recipe to the same shape and size. This ensures even cooking and a more attractive dish.

- Never stir-fry more than 1 pound of meat or seafood in the wok. If you double a recipe, have a friend stir-fry the second portion in another wok, following the same procedure.

- Do all stir-frying over highest heat, with the temperature never reduced. This is true even if you have a commercial stove.

- Place the ingredients next to the wok in the order in which they will be cooked.

- Whenever an ingredient changes color, proceed to the next step. For example, when the stir-fried meat loses its raw color, remove it from the wok. As soon as the ginger and garlic turn white, add the vegetables. When the stir-fried vegetables brighten, pour in the sauce.

- Undercook everything. If you find yourself saying, "I'll just cook this a little longer," it probably already has been overcooked.

- When the sauce comes to a boil, stir in *a little* of the cornstarch mixture. Add only enough thickener so the sauce lightly glazes the food.

- Serve the finished dish *immediately*.

ASIAN INGREDIENTS AND SHOPPING INFORMATION

The recipes in this book use a small number of Asian herbs, spices, and condiments. Since most Asian supplies sold in our supermarkets are mediocre products, it is worth the effort to acquire the same brands chefs from Asia use. This section describes each of these products and lists the best brands. With the huge influx of Asians during the last decade, nearly every large town across the United States has an Asian market where these products are available. Just check your Yellow Pages under "Markets" or "Asian Markets" to locate the nearest one. Or if this proves unsuccessful, ask your local Asian restaurant where these supplies are available.

If you are beginning an adventure with Asian cooking, start with the following items, which are the basis for nearly all the recipes in this book. They cost only a few dollars and last indefinitely.

Chinese chili sauce
unsweetened coconut milk
fish sauce
hoisin sauce
light and dark soy sauce
oyster sauce

plum sauce
red sweet ginger
rice sticks
salted black beans
Oriental sesame oil

BEAN CURD: Known as tofu and referred to by the Chinese as "meat without bones," this is a protein-rich, low-calorie food made from soy beans. The production of bean curd involves adding a coagulant to soy milk, which causes the milk to separate into white curds and clear whey. Gently transferred to cheesecloth-lined boxes, the bean curd is pressed to extract the whey and to form the bean curd into a solid mass. Sold in one-pound blocks immersed in water, Chinese bean curd differ from the Japanese by being more dense and usually cut into four cakes. Bean curd is available in the deli section of most supermarkets, at health food stores, and at all Asian markets. *Storage*: Kept in the refrigerator and submerged under a new change of fresh water daily, bean curd will keep for about one week. With longer storage, it begins to take on an unpleasant sour taste. *Best brand*: No preference.

BEAN SAUCE: Sometimes called brown bean sauce, bean sauce is a pungent condiment made from yellow beans, flour, salt, and water. It is used as an ingredient for sauces, such as in Oriental Burritos. While this condiment is sold in the puréed form called "ground bean sauce," purchase only bean sauce containing parts of the beans since this guarantees that top-quality beans have been used to make the sauce. The sauce's unusual taste is not immediately appealing to all, and preparations containing it always include a little sugar to counter the slight salty taste. *Storage*: Sold in both cans and glass jars. If canned, transfer to a jar and seal tightly. Will keep indefinitely refrigerated.

Substitute: None. *Best brand*: Koon Chun Bean Sauce, or Yuet Heung Yuen Bean Sauce.

BEAN SPROUTS: Called "vegetables for the teeth" by the Chinese, these are three-day-old mung bean sprouts. They are highly perishable, so if they do not look pearly white, do not buy them. Very fresh bean sprouts add a marvelous crunchy taste in salads or in stir-fry dishes added at the very end of the cooking process. *Storage*: Will keep for two days refrigerated in a plastic food bag lined with paper towels. *Substitute*: Matchstick-cut hothouse cucumber or jicama.

BEAN THREADS: Also known as cellophane noodles, glass noodles, transparent noodles, and Chinese vermicelli, these are thin, nearly translucent dried noodles made from ground mung beans. Wrapped tightly together in small bundles, they are first soaked in hot water before being cut into shorter lengths and added to soups or spring roll fillings. Bean threads put directly into hot oil from the package will puff up dramatically in size similar to rice sticks. (However, since bean threads acquire a stale taste unless eaten immediately, rice sticks are a better choice when you need masses of light deep-fried noodles to mix into Asian salads.) Bean threads are increasingly stocked in the gourmet section of most supermarkets. *Storage*: Keeps indefinitely at room temperature. *Substitute*: Rice sticks. *Best brand*: No preference.

BLACK BEANS, SALTED: Also called fermented black beans, these are small, wrinkled, salted black beans that add a fragrant flavor to sauces. They are always rinsed, coarsely chopped, and then combined with ginger and garlic for stir-fry dishes or rubbed across the surface of fish filets. *Storage*: Keeps indefinitely at room temperature. *Substitute*: None. *Best brand*: Yang Jiang Preserved Beans with Ginger, or Mee Chun and Koon Chun brands, both of which are available in 8-ounce plastic packages. There is also an excellent brand of black beans already processed into a paste, called Black Bean Garlic Sauce, made by Lee Kum Kee.

BOK CHOY: Known as Chinese cabbage, or Chinese chard, bok choy is called "white vegetable" by the Chinese. Its tender, long white stalks and bright green leaves add a subtle flavor to soups and stir-fried dishes. This is one of the Chinese vegetables increasingly stocked by supermarkets across the country. *Storage*: Will keep for one week in the refrigerator. *Substitute*: Chard, tender celery ends, or other quick-cooking vegetables.

CHICKEN BROTH: While recipes in this book taste best made with unsalted homemade broth, when necessary canned broth can be substituted. Or, soak four dried Chinese mushrooms in two cups of hot water for one hour. Strain the liquid and use in place of broth. *Best canned brand*: Swanson Chicken Broth.

CHILI SAUCE, CHINESE: Used in this book to make Chinese and Southeast Asian food spicy, this condiment is made with chilies, garlic, salt, and oil. A teaspoon is sufficient to transform a dish from mild to fiery intensity. The dozen imported brands are variously labeled "chili paste with garlic," "chili sauce," and simply "chili paste or sauce." They are superior in flavor to the spicy Chinese condiment made from soybeans called "hot bean sauce." *Storage*: Keeps indefinitely in the refrigerator. *Substitute*: None. *Best brands*: Cock Brand Delicious Hot Chili Garlic Sauce, sold in nine-ounce clear plastic jars with green tops; and Szechuan Chili Sauce, sold in a six-ounce black-labeled can.

CHILIES, FRESH: Recipes using fresh chilies in this book usually refer to the jalapeño or serrano chilies. Keep in mind that the smaller the chili, the hotter it tastes. The most potent part of the chili is its seeds, so if you want to lessen the spiciness of the dish, either reduce the number of chilies or remove the seeds. To remove the seeds, place your hands in plastic food bags to avoid getting the volatile oil on your skin. Fresh chilies are available at most supermarkets and all Asian markets. *Substitute*: To achieve the same type of spice, substitute ½ teaspoon or more of Chinese chili sauce.

CILANTRO: Called accurately by the Chinese "fragrant greens," this leafy, small, parsleylike plant with a distinct pungent flavor takes some people several exposures before really appreciating the delicious taste. Cilantro is sold in Italian, Spanish, and Mexican markets, and increasingly in supermarkets across the country as "fresh coriander," "Chinese parsley," and "cilantro." *When available*: Always. *Storage*: Cilantro is highly perishable. Do not wash until ready to use. Wrap roots in a dampened paper towel before refrigerating in a plastic bag. Will last for about five days. *Substitute*: Fresh cilantro has a completely different taste from ground coriander seeds. When unavailable, or for those who do not care for the taste, fresh mint is a good substitute.

COCONUT, FRESH: Several of the dessert recipes in this book use fresh coconut milk, which has a subtlety of flavor not present in even the best canned coconut milk from Thailand. Mature coconuts, with a hard brown shell, are available at most supermarkets and all Asian markets. Shake the coconut; it should feel heavy and be filled with liquid (this is coconut water, not milk). After cracking the shell (see a description on page 164), taste a little of the coconut. If it does not have a lovely sweet flavor, and instead has a sour taste, it is spoiled and must be discarded. *Storage*: Keep uncracked coconut at room temperature for at least one month, and cracked coconut in the refrigerator for one week. *Substitute*: Canned unsweetened coconut milk from Thailand.

COCONUT, SHREDDED: Recipes using this ingredient refer to the sweetened shredded coconut sold in supermarkets.

COCONUT MILK: Excellent canned unsweetened coconut milk is sold in every Asian market. Purchase a Thai brand whose ingredients are just coconut, water, and a preservative. Occasionally, the coconut milk is so thick it needs to be diluted with a little water. *Storage*: Once opened, it keeps for only a few days in the refrigerator before it takes on a sour flavor. Do not freeze coconut milk since the oil separates and gives the coconut milk a curdled look. *Substitute*: Fresh coconut milk. *Best brands*: Since there is some variation in flavor among brands, if you live near an Asian market purchase the different brands, then open each, taste, and make a note about the one you prefer. Two good brands are A.C. Products Coconut Milk and Chaokoh Coconut Milk, both sold in 5.6-ounce cans.

COOKING OIL: Use any tasteless oil that can be heated to very hot without smoking. Good choices are avocado oil, corn oil, grapeseed oil, peanut oil, safflower oil, and soybean oil.

CORNSTARCH: Many of these recipes use a mixture of cornstarch dissolved with cold water to thicken sauces. This ensures that the sauce glazes all the ingredients and prevents any watery liquid from collecting on the bottom of the serving platter. The cornstarch mixture is an equal amount of cold water and cornstarch. If you stir in a few drops of oil to the cornstarch mixture, this will help prevent the cornstarch from giving the sauce a starchy taste or causing the sauce to lump. Never add all the cornstarch mixture to thicken a sauce. Just add a very small amount and let the sauce come to a low boil; if the sauce does not thicken enough to lightly coat a spoon, then stir in a little more of the mixture. *Substitute*: Any starch such as tapioca starch, rice starch, or potato starch.

CURRY PASTE: A blend of many different seasonings mixed with oil, curry paste has numerous advantages over curry powder, including a much more complex taste and a longer shelf life. *Storage*: Once opened, keeps indefinitely at room temperature. *Substitute*: The flavor will not be as complex, but an adequate substitution is to use curry powder and double the amount. *Best brand*: Koon Yick Wah Kee Factory Best Curry, made in Hong Kong, and any good Indian curry paste sold in supermarkets.

CURRY POWDER: Trying to achieve a special taste from curry powder is about the same as expecting a lot of flavor from store-bought ground pepper. *Storage*: Keep away from heat and on a dark shelf in order to retard its gradual loss of flavor. *Best brands*: In general, curry powders sold by cookware stores and gourmet shops have a superior flavor to brands sold in supermarkets.

DRY SHERRY: While working with Chinese chefs, I have heard some insist on using dry Chinese rice wine, while others adamantly say that the Chinese rice wine imported into this country is of very low quality and it is better to use dry sherry. No one will notice whether you use Chinese rice wine or a moderately priced domestic sherry.

EGGPLANT, ORIENTAL: This slender purple- to white-skinned vegetable, about four to eight inches long, tastes far superior to the large globe European eggplant. Its tender skin makes peeling unnecessary; the virtually seedless interior has no bitter taste; and when sautéed, the eggplant does not absorb large amounts of oil. *Available*: Spring through fall in all Asian markets. Choose the smallest firm eggplants with shiny skins. *Storage*: Lasts for two weeks refrigerated. *Substitute*: Improve all European eggplant recipes by substituting Oriental eggplant, and for Asian recipes substitute large globe eggplant only as a last resort.

FISH SAUCE: This condiment is used in Thai and Vietnamese cooking the way the Chinese use soy sauce. Made by layering fresh anchovies or squid with salt in wooden barrels, it is fermented for several months to produce a watery but very flavorful liquid. Always buy fish sauce produced in Vietnam or Thailand; it is superior to those from other countries. Look at each bottle and purchase the light-amber ones rather than the darker products, which will quickly overpower the dish. If you have a doubt about the quality of the fish sauce, purchase several brands and do a taste test; use the one that is least salty. *Storage*: Once opened, lasts indefinitely at room temperature. *Substitute*: None. *Best brand*: Squid Brand Fish Sauce or Tiparos Fish Sauce.

FIVE-SPICE POWDER: A powdered blend of various spices including anise, fennel, cinnamon, Sichuan pepper, and cloves, this is a great favorite of the Cantonese for marinades, poultry, and fish. Five-spice powder is sold in one-ounce bags in Asian markets and by some supermarkets in the spice section. *Storage*: Keeps indefinitely at room temperature if tightly sealed in a jar. *Substitute*: None. *Best brand*: Five-spice powder sold by Asian markets is the best.

GALANGAL: Known variously as laos, Thai ginger, and ka, it is botanically part of the ginger family. Galangal is slightly different from ginger, having a smoother and lighter-colored skin, a thicker root, and a wonderfully flowery flavor. Galangal is excellent finely minced and sautéed in a little oil for stir-fried dishes, or thinly sliced and added to simmering soups and stew (in this case the slices are not meant to be eaten). A newcomer to our markets, galangal (the British name for it) may be found in the produce section of Asian markets located in cities with large Southeast Asian populations. *Storage*: Stored at room temperature, galangal will last for at least a month. *Substitute*: While lacking the intense fresh flavor, powdered galangal is sold in one-ounce plastic bags in most Asian markets.

GINGER, CRYSTALLIZED: These are slices of fresh ginger that are candied and coated with sugar. Their sweet, sharp ginger flavor makes them an excellent addition chopped and sprinkled over ice cream, or as a candy served with fresh fruit. *Available*: Available in most supermarkets and all Asian stores. *Storage*: Keeps indefinitely at room temperature sealed in a jar. *Substitute*: None.

GINGER, FRESH: Absolutely indispensable for Asian cooking, these pungent and spicy tasting knobby brown rhizomes are sold by supermarkets in the produce section. Buy firm ginger with smooth skin. To use, never peel ginger. Cut off and discard the exposed end. Cut very thin slices, then finely mince by hand or in an electric minichopper. *Storage*: Store ginger in a dark cupboard where it will stay fresh for up to a month. This is better than placing ginger in the refrigerator, where the moisture quickly causes it to spoil, or freezing ginger, which affects the flavor. When the skin begins to wrinkle and the root softens, discard ginger. *Substitute*: There are no substitutes, since dry powdered ginger has a different taste, while preserved and crystallized ginger is too sweet.

GINGER, RED SWEET: Sold in glass jars at most Chinese markets, these are pieces of bright red ginger packed in a heavy syrup and are not to be confused with Japanese red pickled ginger. *Storage*: Once opened, will keep indefinitely at room temperature provided the syrup covers the ginger pieces. *Substitute*: Preserved ginger, which is amber knobs of ginger preserved in a clear heavy syrup. *Best brands*: Mee Chun Preserved Red Ginger Slices in Syrup, or Koon Chun Red Ginger in Syrup.

HOISIN SAUCE: A thick, sweet, spicy, dark brown-red condiment—hoisin sauce is customarily spread across pancakes for mu shu pork and Peking duck; it flavors many stir-fried dishes, and is the base for delicious Chinese barbecue sauces. Made with soy bean flour, chilies, garlic, ginger, and sugar, it is one of the Chinese condiments most loved by Americans. It is sold by Asian markets in both glass jars and cans. *Storage*: Once opened, keeps indefinitely at room temperature. *Substitute*: None. *Best brand*: No Asian condiment varies so much in quality from brand to brand. Buy only Koon Chun Hoisin Sauce.

JICAMA: This brown-skinned Mexican root vegetable has a sweet white interior with a crunchy texture. It makes a great addition to salads. Ranging in size from a fist to a cantaloupe, jicama is sold by many supermarkets. Peel jicama with a knife before using. *Storage*: Jicama will last for two weeks in the refrigerator if you cover the cut surface with plastic wrap. *Substitute*: Fresh water chestnuts are a good substitute for jicama in salads, but jicama is not a good substitute for fresh water chestnuts in cooked dishes, since jicama does not maintain its crunchy texture during cooking.

LEMONGRASS: This is one of the most important seasonings for Thai and Vietnamese cooking. Available in most Asian markets, lemongrass is a three-foot-long greenish plant having an eight-inch woody stem and long slender leaves. The woody stem, having a faint lemon flavor, is finely minced and added to dishes the same way you would use minced ginger, or it is cut on a sharp diagonal into ½-inch pieces and added to dishes such as stews and soups, which gently simmer on the stove. Added in larger pieces, lemongrass is meant to flavor the dish and not to be eaten. The leafy ends, soaked in hot water, make lemongrass tea to settle an upset stomach. Lemongrass grows very easily in a temperate climate. You can either plant store-bought lemongrass that still has some of the roots attached, or purchase lemongrass in the herb section of some nurseries. *Storage*: Lemongrass just cut from the garden has a subtle flavor that disappears within a week, even with refrigeration. *Substitute*: Powdered lemongrass, available at most Asian markets, has little taste, so you would be better off substituting a little grated lemon peel, although the flavor is not quite the same.

MISO: A naturally fermented soybean paste, miso is used often in Japanese cooking, particularly as a flavoring for soups and as a primary ingredient in dips. Miso is sold in plastic tubs, jars, and plastic bags in the refrigerator section of Japanese (not Chinese) markets and at all health food stores. For the recipes in this book we use the mild-tasting white miso. *Storage*: While miso will last indefinitely refrigerated, it does gradually lose its flavor. *Substitute*: None.

MONOSODIUM GLUTAMATE (MSG): A white crystalline powder sold under various names such as Accent and Ajimoto, it is used by chefs of little skill to rejuvenate food of poor quality. Sold in large plastic bags in Asian markets, sadly M.S.G. has become a staple "seasoning" in many Chinese restaurant dishes and is the cause for throbbing headaches referred to as Chinese restaurant syndrome. Chinese cooks who take pride in their cuisine regard monosodium glutamate as a crutch. It is neither recommended nor used in this book.

MUSHROOMS, DRIED BLACK CHINESE: Chinese markets sell a wide variety of dried mushrooms. When softened in hot water, they add a wonderful meaty flavor to soups, stir-fried dishes, and stews. The thicker the cap, the higher the quality and the more expensive the mushroom. To use, soak mushrooms in a generous amount of hot water. When they soften, cut off and discard the stems. Strain the mushroom-flavored water through a fine-meshed sieve and use it as a substitute for chicken broth. A similar Japanese variety called dried forest mushrooms are sold in many supermarkets. *Storage*: Sealed in jars, they last indefinitely unrefrigerated. *Substitute*: For stir-fried dishes, soups, and stews, substitute fresh mushrooms although the flavor will not be as intense. For spring rolls and dumpling fillings, fresh mushrooms are not a good substitute since they do not have the density of the dried variety.

MUSHROOMS, ENOKI: These are little clumps of mushrooms on long, threadlike stems joined together at the base. Their wonderful sweet smell and delicate look make them a great addition to salads and as a garnish. To use, cut off the base and separate the mushroom threads. Do not wash. *Storage*: Sold in small plastic bags at good supermarkets, they will stay fresh for about four days, refrigerated. *Substitute*: None.

MUSHROOMS, OYSTER: These mushrooms are light gray and have a fairly large trumpet shape with very delicate edges. They are sold in four-ounce boxes in the produce section of good supermarkets. Because of their fragile texture, oyster mushrooms are best used in salads or very briefly cooked in stir-fry and sauté dishes, rather than being added to stews or soups. *Storage*: Transferred to a paper bag, they will last for about five days in the refrigerator. *Substitute*: Substitute other types of fresh mushrooms, but never use the canned oyster mushrooms sold in Asian markets.

MUSHROOMS, FRESH SHIITAKE: Fresh Japanese forest mushrooms, which are never sold at Asian markets because of their expense, are appearing increasingly in fine general food markets. Fresh shiitake mushrooms possess an incredible fragrance and are delicious sautéed in butter as an accompaniment for grilled meats, in stir-fried dishes, simmered in cream sauces, and thinly sliced for salads. They are, however, not good chopped and used in dumpling fillings since they do not have the intense flavor and density of dried mushrooms. Fresh shiitake mushrooms are completely clean and should never be washed. Just discard the tough stem before using the cap. *Storage*: Kept in a paper bag, they will last up to two weeks in the refrigerator. *Substitute*: Dried Chinese mushrooms, although the flavor is not quite the same.

NOODLES, CHINESE DRIED SPAGHETTI STYLE: Thin dried spaghetti-type noodles are sold in one- to five-pound boxes at all Asian markets. They are inexpensive, cook quickly, and have a nice firm texture. *Storage*: Indefinitely at room temperature. *Substitute*: Any dried thin spaghetti-style noodle.

NOODLES, SOBA: These are one of my favorite noodles and I eat them almost everyday for lunch. The size of spaghetti and made from buckwheat flour, they cook very quickly in a large amount of rapidly boiling water. *Storage*: Indefinitely at room temperature. *Substitute*: Any dried thin spaghetti-style noodle.

OYSTER SAUCE: This is also called Oyster Flavored Sauce. You can visit the beaches near Hong Kong and see huge piles of shucked oysters used for making this oyster catsup. Oyster sauce gives dishes a marvelous rich taste without a hint of its seafood origins. A pinch of sugar is usually added in dishes using oyster sauce to counteract the slight salty taste. *Storage*: Keeps indefinitely in the refrigerator. *Substitute*: None. *Best brands*: Lee Kum Kee Oyster Flavored Sauce, Old Brand.

PLUM SAUCE: This chutneylike condiment, a great favorite of Cantonese cooks, is made with fresh plums, apricots, garlic, red chilies, sugar, vinegar, salt, and water. It is different from duck sauce, which is made with plums, apples, and spices. The thick consistency and sweet, spicy flavor of plum sauce makes it an ideal addition to barbecue sauces and as a dip for crisp, deep-fried won tons or chilled shrimp. It is available in cans and glass jars at all Asian markets and in many supermarkets. *Storage*: If canned, once opened, transfer to a glass jar and seal. Keeps indefinitely unrefrigerated. *Substitute*: None. *Best brand*: Koon Chun Plum Sauce.

RADICCHIO: Radicchio is a small, tightly bunched head of red-leaf chicory. Torn or slivered in salads, or sautéed, it's bittersweet flavor and bright color have made this one of the new favorites of chefs at top restaurants. It is available at many supermarkets in the produce section. *Storage*: Stored in a plastic food bag in the refrigerator, it will last for ten days. *Substitute*: While the unusual taste and color of radicchio cannot be duplicated, you can substitute another green such as endive.

RICE, WHITE LONG-GRAIN: The Chinese eat white long-grain rice, while the Japanese prefer the stickier white short-grain variety. Neither of these should be confused with the inferior tasting converted and minute brands, which are precooked and dried at the factory before packaging. White rice is available at all Asian markets and all supermarkets, sold in small clear plastic bags. *Storage*: Keeps indefinitely at room temperature. *Substitute*: None.

RICE STICKS: Rice sticks are long, thin, dried rice-flour vermicelli. Rice sticks put directly from the package into hot oil instantly puff up into a huge white mass many times their original size. They are an essential ingredient in many Chinese salads, and are used as a bed upon which to place stir-fried dishes. For cooking instructions see page 52. Rice sticks are available at all Asian markets and most supermarkets. *Storage*: Keep indefinitely at room temperature. *Substitute*: None. *Best brand*: Sailing Boat Brand Rice Sticks.

RICE VINEGAR: Clear Japanese rice vinegar with its mild flavor is particularly good for pickling, salad dressings, and seafood sauces. Avoid inferior rice vinegars labeled seasoned or gourmet, which indicate that sugar and often monosodium glutamate have been added. Nor should Japanese rice vinegar be confused with Chinese rice vinegar, which has too mild a taste for these recipes. Rice vinegar is available at all Asian markets and most supermarkets. *Storage*: Keeps indefinitely at room temperature. *Substitute*: Possibly Champagne vinegar, although this has a sharper taste. *Best brand*: Marukan Rice Vinegar.

SESAME OIL, ORIENTAL: Sold in small bottles, sesame oil is a nutty golden brown oil made from toasted crushed sesame seeds. It is used to season food and never as a cooking oil, since its low smoking temperature will cause it to ignite. This is an ingredient, like hoisin sauce, that varies greatly in quality. Unfortunately, most Oriental sesame oil sold by supermarkets has a harsh taste, so look for sesame oil in Asian markets. *Storage*: At room temperature, will last for at least a year before turning rancid, and will last indefinitely in the refrigerator. *Substitute*: None. *Best brand*: Sona Sesame Oil. Kadoya Sesame Oil is another good brand, but since it has a very pronounced flavor, use it in smaller quantities. Avoid Dynasty Sesame Oil.

SESAME SEEDS, WHITE: Sold in the spice section of every supermarket, white sesame seeds are far less expensive purchased at Asian markets. They are used in many recipes toasted until light golden in an ungreased skillet. *Storage*: Since white and toasted sesame seeds become stale at room temperature or when refrigerated, keep them in the freezer.

SICHUAN PEPPERCORNS: Labeled Szechuan pepper, wild pepper, fagara, and *fa tsiu*, these are little reddish brown seeds from the prickly ash tree. They have a beautiful aromatic flavor without any of the spiciness of black and white peppercorns. They are available at cookware stores, gourmet shops, and at all Asian markets, sold in two-ounce plastic bags. To use, place Sichuan pepper in an ungreased skillet and toast until the pepper smokes slightly. Transfer to a coffee or spice grinder and pulverize. Tip into a sieve with a medium mesh and shake. The light brown shells remaining in the sieve have no taste and should be discarded. *Storage*: Store ground Sichuan pepper in a small glass spice jar. The aromatic flavor will last for about six months. *Substitute*: None.

SNOW PEAS: These flat, light green pods are sold year-round in many supermarkets. If snow peas are soft when purchased, soaking them in cold water for 30 minutes restores their firm texture. To use, snap off and draw the stem end down the ridge to remove the fiber. Whether stir-fried, blanched for salads, or added to soups, snow peas are done as soon as they turn bright green. *Storage*: Keep for at least a week in a plastic food bag in the refrigerator. *Substitute*: Sugar snap peas, or another quick-cooking vegetable.

SOY SAUCE, DARK: Sold in bottles of varying sizes, dark soy sauce, also called heavy or black soy sauce, is light soy sauce with the addition of molasses or caramel. Chefs use it to add a richer flavor and color to sauces. Never confuse this with thick soy sauce sold in jars, which is a syruplike molasses that will ruin the taste of any recipe in this book. One way to tell the difference between dark and light soy is to shake the bottle. Dark soy sauce will coat the sides of the bottle whereas the more watery light soy will not. *Storage*: Once opened, keeps indefinitely at room temperature. *Substitute*: None. *Best brand*: Mushroom Soy Sauce.

SOY SAUCE, LIGHT: This is the most common soy sauce used in Chinese cooking. Made from soy beans, roasted wheat, yeast, and salt, good light soy sauce is available at all Asian markets and most supermarkets. It is used as a table condiment, in stir-fried dishes, and in soups where a light color and delicate taste are desired. If you are concerned about sodium, it is better to reduce the quantity of light soy sauce in a recipe rather than use the more expensive low-sodium brands, which have little taste. *Storage*: Once opened, keeps indefinitely at room temperature. *Substitute*: None. *Best brands*: Superior Soy Sauce and Kikkoman Soy Sauce. When buying Superior Soy Sauce, look carefully at the label, for the manufacturer bottles another soy called Soy Superior, which is dark soy sauce.

SPRING ROLL SKINS: These are paper-thin skins made from flour and water. Sold 25 to a package in the freezer section of all Asian markets and labeled spring roll skins, Shanghai wrappers, and lumpia skins, they are far thinner and become much more crisp when deep-fried than the thick egg-noodle skins sold in American supermarkets. To use, defrost for an hour, then loosen one corner and peel off one skin at a time. Stack the skins and cover with a towel until ready to assemble the spring rolls. You will find that while the skins appear to be tightly stuck together, the skins are very strong and will not tear as you pull them apart. *Storage*: Kept in the freezer tightly wrapped, they last indefinitely. Spring roll skins can be thawed and refrozen repeatedly without effecting their quality. *Substitute*: None. *Best brands*: Those imported from Hong Kong and Menlo Wrappers.

WATER CHESTNUTS: The size of an English walnut, water chestnuts are botanically no relation to our chestnuts. They are a black-skinned water bulb grown in southern and eastern China. Called horses hooves by the Chinese, they are often covered with a thin layer of mud to prevent them from drying out. Their very sweet taste and crunchy texture are as different from their canned cousins as fresh asparagus is from canned. On the West Coast, fresh water chestnuts come from Hong Kong, while along the East Coast they are grown in Florida. Fresh water chestnuts are available only in a few large Chinatown communities, but are sold throughout the year. When buying fresh water chestnuts, squeeze each one and discard any that are soft; these are rotten in the center. Under cold running water, peel off the skins using a small knife. They can now be used raw in salads, added to soup, or stir-fried dishes, minced for dumpling fillings, and dipped in chocolate. Their wonderful taste and texture remain unchanged despite lengthy cooking. *Storage*: Unpeeled water chestnuts last for two weeks wrapped in a plastic bag and refrigerated. *Substitute*: If you are not fond of canned vegetables, do not use canned water chestnuts! In dumpling fillings, substitute minced carrot. For stir-fried dishes, just substitute another fresh vegetable. In Asian salads, substitute jicama.

WON TON SKINS: Measuring about 3 inches square, won ton skins are thin egg-noodle wrappers. They are sold by every Asian market and in many supermarkets. Purchase the thinnest ones, preferably fresh and not frozen. The latter, which dry out and become brittle in the freezer, tend to tear when folded for dumplings. *Storage*: Keeps for two weeks in the refrigerator if tightly sealed. *Substitute*: None.

CONVERSION CHART

LIQUID MEASURES

Fluid ounces	U.S. measures	Imperial measures	Milliliters	Fluid ounces	U.S. measures	Imperial measures	Milliliters
	1 TSP	1 TSP	5	16	2 CUPS OR 1 PINT		450
¼	2 TSP	1 DESSERTSPOON	7	18	2¼ CUPS		500,
½	1 TBS	1 TBS	15				½ LITER
1	2 TBS	2 TBS	28	20	2½ CUPS	1 PINT	560
2	¼ CUP	4 TBS	56	24	3 CUPS OR 1½ PINTS		675
4	½ CUP		110	25		1¼ PINTS	700
	OR ¼ PINT			27	3½ CUPS		750
5		¼ PINT OR 1 GILL	140	30	3¾ CUPS	1½ PINTS	840
6	¾ CUP		170	32	4 CUPS OR 2 PINTS		900
8	1 CUP OR		225		OR 1 QUART		
	½ PINT			35		1¾ PINTS	980
9			250,	36	4½ CUPS		1000,
			¼ LITER				1 LITER
10	1¼ CUPS	½ PINT	280	40	5 CUPS OR	2 PINTS OR 1 QUART	1120
12	1½ CUPS OR ¾ PINT		240		2½ PINTS		
15		¾ PINT	420	48	6 CUPS OR 3 PINTS		1350

SOLID MEASURES

U.S. and Imperial measures		Metric measures		U.S. and Imperial measures		Metric measures	
OUNCES	POUNDS	GRAMS	KILOS	OUNCES	POUNDS	GRAMS	KILOS
1		28		20	1¼	560	
2		56		24	1½	675	
3½		100		27		750	¾
4	¼	112		28	1¾	780	
5		140		32	2	900	
6		168		36	2¼	1000	1
8	½	225		40	2½	1100	
9		250	¼	48	3	1350	
12	¾	340		54		1500	1½
16	1	450		64	4	1800	
18		500	½				

OVEN TEMPERATURE EQUIVALENTS

Fahrenheit	Gas Mark	Celsius	Heat of oven	Fahrenheit	Gas Mark	Celsius	Heat of oven
225	¼	107	VERY COOL	375	5	190	FAIRLY HOT
250	½	121	VERY COOL	400	6	204	FAIRLY HOT
275	1	135	COOL	425	7	218	HOT
300	2	148	COOL	450	8	232	VERY HOT
325	3	163	MODERATE	475	9	246	VERY HOT
350	4	177	MODERATE				

TERMINOLOGY EQUIVALENTS

U.S.	British	U.S.	British
EGGPLANT	AUBERGINE	BROIL	GRILL
ZUCCHINI	COURGETTE	BROILER	GRILL
HEAVY CREAM	DOUBLE CREAM	SKILLET	FRYING PAN
SUGAR, GRANULATED SUGAR	CASTOR SUGAR		
CONFECTIONERS' SUGAR	ICING SUGAR		

ARTWORK CREDITS

Front jacket: chopsticks by Sue Dorman; plate by Bill Goldsmith/Limoges; background painting by Teri Sandison

page 1: ceramic by Helen Slater and Robin Spear

page 2: tile background by Country Floors

page 5: teapot by Jeff Irwin

page 11: "Bungalow Teapot" by David Gurney

pages 14–15: platter by David Foglia

page 22: platter by Helaine Melvin

page 26: plate by Mesolini Glass

page 31: see front jacket credits

page 33: background by Jeff Stillwell

page 48: plates by Christina Salusti

page 51: plate by George Sowden/Swid Powell; flatware by Sakasi

pages 54–55: plate by Sepanski

page 58: "Pepper and Flowers Teapot" by David Gurney

page 59: background by Jeff Stillwell

page 62: platter by Kerry Feldman; background painting by Teri Sandison

pages 66–67: glassware by John Gilvey; ladle by Nutmeg Pewter

page 70: plate by Barbara Schuppe

page 71: bowl by Barbara Schuppe; background placemat by Judith Klein

page 74: bowls by Barbara Schuppe; background painting by Teri Sandison

page 78: candelabra by Ries Niemi

page 79: background by Jeff Stillwell

pages 82–83: glass by David Foglia

page 87: plate by Kerry Feldman; background placemat by Judith Klein

page 88: teapot by Beverly Saito

page 89: plate by Les Lawrence; background set design by Jeff Stillwell

page 90: tile background by Country Floors

page 95: plate by Sasaki; background drawing by Teri Sandison

page 96: plate by James Gorman; background drawing by Teri Sandison

page 101: platter by Barbara Schuppe; glasses by Magic Sands; background painting by Teri Sandison

page 104: plates by Barbara Schuppe; background drawing by Teri Sandison

pages 108–109: plates by Annie Glass

page 112: platter by Kerry Feldman; silkscreened placemat by Judith Klein

pages 116–117: platter by Nancy Toler; glasses by Fineline Studio; background painting by Teri Sandison

page 121: platters and mugs by Luna Garcia; background painting by Jeff Stillwell

page 124: teapot by Jeff Irwin

page 125: platter by Nancy Toler; background painting by Teri Sandison

pages 128–129: plates by Sugahara

page 132: "Bird and Pepper Vase" by David Gurney

page 133: plate by Lyn Evans; background set design by Jeff Stillwell

page 136: pot by Holly Collins

page 137: platter by Artquake; background painting by Teri Sandison

page 140: platter by James Gorman; glasses by Magic Sands; background painting by Teri Sandison

page 144: ceramic cup by Reed Keller

page 145: platter by Barbara Schuppe

pages 148–149: tile background by Country Floors

pages 152–153: glasses by Rede Guzzini

page 156: plates and teapot by Barbara Schuppe; background placemat by Judith Klein

page 161: plate by Terry Shapiro; silver flatware by Georg Jensen

page 164: plate by Lyn Evans

Back jacket: plate by Mesolini Glass; background by Jeff Stillwell

ACKNOWLEDGMENTS

So many people contributed their special gifts to *Chopstix*. Our publisher, Andy Stewart, sat at the counter at Chopstix on Melrose Avenue and felt the excitement of the first restaurant. We are deeply grateful to Andy and to our editor Leslie Stoker for the opportunity to publish such a beautiful book. We owe a special thanks to the general partners of Chopstix Restaurants, Brant Benun, Bill Milham, Frank Monteleone, Jr., and William O'Connor, who developed the restaurants; to our wonderful staff at Chopstix; and to our thousands of loyal customers.

This book glows because of the efforts of our food stylists. Norman Stewart is a European trained chef who is known for his beautiful food design. After styling *Pacific Flavors*, Norman joined the Chopstix team for this book. He works as a food stylist for top photographers and film companies in Los Angeles and New York. Jean E. Carey, Los Angeles based food stylist, who also styled *Pacific Flavors*, specializes in creative food design for print and film. She has been the production coordinator for 52 half-hour cooking shows for televison and does product conceptualization and design for major food corporations. Stephen Shern is a food stylist for major food publications, top photographers, ad agencies, and production companies in both Los Angeles and New York. His fifteen years experience as a professional chef combined with his eye for design are the foundation for his unique style. Fred Walker received his training as a chef at the Culinary Institute of America. He combines his passion for food and design through his beautifully styled food. Originally based in Philadephia, he now works in Los Angeles for top photographers in film and still photography.

Many friends helped bring this book into print. Our attorney, Susan Grode, helped us refine the book proposal. Many thanks to talented book designer Joseph Rutt, copyeditor Carole Berglie, as well as to Carolyn Petter, Publicity Director, and to Margaret Orto, Director of Sales at Stewart, Tabori & Chang. The following chefs and friends contributed great assistance and ideas: Mary Bempachat, Pat Dall'Armi, Mark Dierkhising, Roger Hayot, Chopstix chefs Dennis and Debbie Lam, Gail McMullen, Grant and Sharon Showley and Osa Sommermeyer. Thank you.

We found rich sources of props and accessories for the photography at several Los Angeles area galleries. We especially want to thank Carol Sauvion at Freehand and Stephen and Diane Reissman of Tesoro Collection for their generosity and support. We were always thrilled by wonderful creations at the Wild Blue and New Stone Age galleries. Thank you also to Lynne Deutch Ltd., By Design, Solo Lo Mejor, and L.A. Hotlites.

After the recipes were tested at home, taught in cooking classes, and served at the restaurants, they were given a final review by the following cooks. This book gained much from your special insights. Thank you Florence Antico, Peggy and David Black, Pamela Blair, Jo Bowen, Yvonne Caan, Bill and Lynda Casper, Karen and Don Cerwin, Jan Debnam, Cary Feibleman, Peter Feit, Diane Ganzell-Brown, Sharie and Ron Goldfarb, Robert Gordon, Blanche Gottlieb, Donna Hodgens, Tim Howe and Ann Janss, Nancy Huntsinger, Diana Kleinman, Joy and John Knox, Jeannie Komsky, Susan Krueger, Patty Lewis, Kris Livos, Betty Mandrow, Bernard Menard, Patricia Niedfelt, Michele Nipper, Joanne Persons, Roy Pingo, Jeannie Riley, Joe Rooks, Kathleen Sands, Michele Sciortino, Jerry Sexton, Mary Jo and Paul Shane, Ellie Shulman, Philip Stafford, Elaine Stein, Suzanne Vadnais, Susan Vollmer, Ruth Walker, Sharon Whelan, and Robert Wills. Thank you all for your help.

INDEX

Page numbers in *italics* refer to illustrations.

Designed by Joseph Rutt

Composed in KABEL and ITC Usherwood
by Trufont Typographers, Inc.,
Hicksville, New York

Printed and bound by
Toppan Printing Company, Ltd.,
Tokyo, Japan